QOS in Wide Area Networks

ISBN 0-13-026497-0

Prentice Hall Series In
Advanced Communications Technologies

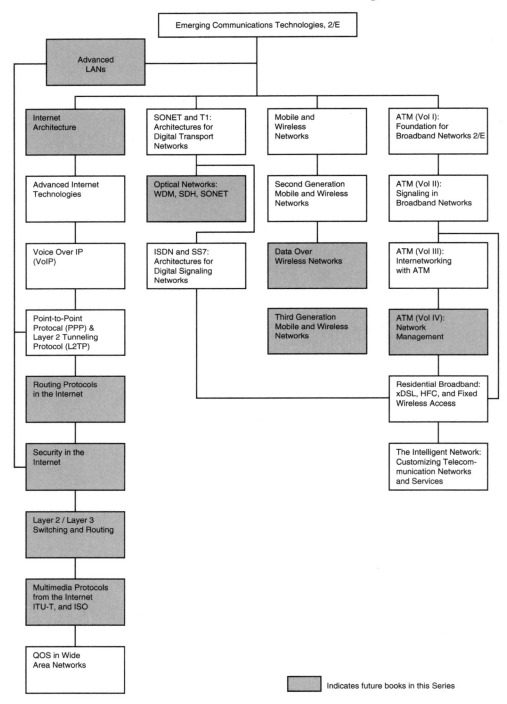

Emerging Communications Technologies, 2/E

Advanced LANs

Internet Architecture

SONET and T1: Architectures for Digital Transport Networks

Mobile and Wireless Networks

ATM (Vol I): Foundation for Broadband Networks 2/E

Advanced Internet Technologies

Optical Networks: WDM, SDH, SONET

Second Generation Mobile and Wireless Networks

ATM (Vol II): Signaling in Broadband Networks

Voice Over IP (VoIP)

ISDN and SS7: Architectures for Digital Signaling Networks

Data Over Wireless Networks

ATM (Vol III): Internetworking with ATM

Point-to-Point Protocol (PPP) & Layer 2 Tunneling Protocol (L2TP)

Third Generation Mobile and Wireless Networks

ATM (Vol IV): Network Management

Routing Protocols in the Internet

Residential Broadband: xDSL, HFC, and Fixed Wireless Access

Security in the Internet

The Intelligent Network: Customizing Telecommunication Networks and Services

Layer 2 / Layer 3 Switching and Routing

Multimedia Protocols from the Internet ITU-T, and ISO

QOS in Wide Area Networks

Indicates future books in this Series

QOS in Wide Area Networks

UYLESS BLACK

Prentice Hall PTR
Upper Saddle River, New Jersey 07458
www.phptr.com

Acquisitions editor: *Mary Franz*
Editorial assistant: *Noreen Regina*
Cover designer: *Talar Agasyan*
Cover design director: *Jerry Votta*
Manufacturing manager: *Maura Goldstaub*
Marketing manager: *Lisa Konzelmann*
Project coordinator: *Anne Trowbridge*
Compositor/Production services: *Pine Tree Composition, Inc.*

© 2000 by Uyless Black
Published by Prentice Hall PTR
Prentice-Hall, Inc.
Upper Saddle River, New Jersey 07458

Prentice Hall books are widely used by corporations and government agencies for training, marketing, and resale.

The publisher offers discounts on this book when ordered in bulk quantities. For more information contact:

Corporate Sales Department
Phone: 800–382–3419
Fax: 201–236–7141
E-mail: corpsales@prenhall.com

Or write:

Prentice Hall PTR
Corp. Sales Dept.
One Lake Street
Upper Saddle River, New Jersey 07458

Printed in the United States of America
10 9 8 7 6 5 4 3 2 1

ISBN: 0-13-026497-0

Prentice-Hall International (UK) Limited, *London*
Prentice-Hall of Australia Pty. Limited, *Sydney*
Prentice-Hall Canada Inc., *Toronto*
Prentice-Hall Hispanoamericana, S.A., *Mexico*
Prentice-Hall of India Private Limited, *New Delhi*
Prentice-Hall of Japan, Inc., *Tokyo*
Pearson Education Asia Pte. Ltd.
Editora Prentice-Hall do Brasil, Ltda., *Rio de Janeiro*

Years of friendship with someone may have little to do with the quality of the relationship. On occasion, we are fortunate enough to come across people who immediately embrace us and call us their friends. On those occasions, if we are even more fortunate, we feel the same way toward these people and are able to reciprocate this love. My "new" friends, Joe and Hilda Mitchell, are a testament to these statements.

This book is dedicated to
Joe and "Hilde"

While I was writing this book, I came across an article on the kangaroo. A picture accompanied the article showing a mother kangaroo with its young nested in the mother's pouch, looking serene and content. And why not? The mother kangaroo's pouch offers a very high quality of service to the new-born infant, about as high as there is in the animal kingdom. Where else can one find a warm ready-made bed, transportation, only one offspring at a time using these accommodations, plenty of food, not to mention complete security?

For the baby kangaroo, or joey as it is called, there is one problem in obtaining these wonderful services: making its way to the mother's pouch after birth. Just after birth, The joey (all 0.03 oz) must crawl up the mother's body to reach the pouch, with little help from the mother. But once there, the effort is worth it, and the joey stays in and around mom's pouch for 7–10 months, almost unlimited QOS at no extra charge.

But alas for the small kangaroo, this good deal ends. After these many months the mother must prepare for another joey, and off the growing kangaroo goes into the big, bad world, never again to experience this level of service.

Contents

CHAPTER 7   **Internet QOS Protocols**   **224**

CHAPTER 8   **Differentiated Services (DiffServ)**   **252**

Preface

This book is one in a series of books called, "Emerging Communications Technologies." As the name of the book implies, the focus is on how wide area networks are being deployed to support different levels of service (quality of service, or QOS) to their curstomers.

The subject matter of this book is vast and my approach is to provide a system view of the topic. In consonance with the intent of this series, this general survey also has considerable detail, but not to the level of detail needed to design a QOS-based network. For that, I leave you to your project team and the various specifications that establish the standards for QOS operations.

This book is considered to be at an intermediate-to-advanced level. As such, it assumes the reader has a background in voice and data communications, Frame Relay, ATM, and the Internet protocol suite.

I hope you find this book a valuable addition to your library.

CREDITS

I have relied on several Internet Request for Comments (RFCs) and Internet Drafts in certain chapters in this book. In some cases, I have summarized the RFCs with a short tutorial, and in other cases, I have extracted key points from the documents. I have so noted these instances in the appropriate part of the book.

Keep in mind that the Internet Drafts are works in progress, and should be viewed as such. You should not use the drafts with the expectation that they will not change. Notwithstanding, if used as general tutorials, the Drafts discussed in this book are "final enough" to warrant their explanations.

For all the internet standards and draft standards the following applies:

In addition to the contributions made by the many Internet working groups, I would also like to thank the ATM Forum and the Frame Relay Forum for their cooperation in providing me the ATM and Frame Relay specifications that I have cited in this book.

1

Introduction

This chapter introduces the concepts of quality of service (QOS) and explains why QOS is important to the user of modern data, voice, and video networks. The QOS components are introduced, including the idea of a "flow." Two models define the operations of QOS—IntServ and DiffServ—and they are described and compared. The chapter also introduces service level agreements (SLAs) and policy-based networking. It concludes with a discussion on how SLA monitoring operations can be performed.

WHY QOS?

In the past few years, it has become evident that network service providers need to differentiate (for some of their customers) between different types of customers' traffic and treat these traffic types differently. Increasingly, some customers are asking for services from the provider that reflect the customer's individual needs.

The basic idea of QOS is that the current arrangement of giving a customer a fixed service that applies to all customers, and restricting each customer to this rigid arrangement, is insufficient to satisfy the "customer universe." This universe reflects a community that is composed of many diverse users, each with their own requirements.

Of course, while users may have their "own" requirements, this idea need not translate into a unique, specific, and tailored service for *each* user. This part of the QOS idea is that a user is known by a "profile" that describes groups of users with similar needs.

But it is fair to say that this customer universe certainly reflects a diversity of needs. Some customers need faster response time to a Web query; others could care less. Still others want a service provider to assure them that their email has not been read by anyone but the intended reader; and others don't care.

The fundamental idea of QOS is to enable customers to ask network providers to establish different levels of service pertaining to the customers' traffic throughput, traffic loss, and response time, and to charge the customer for the actual level of service provided. The basic idea is to realize the well-worn cliché, "You get what you pay for."

But there are skeptics of the QOS concept. Some believe that the market is not large enough to warrant a profit-oriented network service provider investing in the substantial resources needed to implement QOS features. These skeptics say that there aren't enough customers to pay for the QOS service.

Maybe so, but ask yourself these questions: Would you be willing to pay more (say a few dollars a month) for better services from the Internet? As an example, would you be willing to pay more for the assurance that your query to a Web browser will result in a one-second response (in contrast to today's fifteen- to thirty-second response)? Would you be willing to pay for the assurance that your well-spent money will give your browsing activities precedence over others who are not paying those extra dollars?

Certainly, some of the readers of this book will answer no to these questions. Equally certain, others will answer yes. If you answered no, I hope you are still interested in reading this book. Your author thinks the "yes" respondents represent an enormous market. That is the reason I have written this book.

WHAT IS QOS?

We have explained QOS, but only in general terms. This section explains QOS in more detail. The term quality of service (QOS) was used in the Open Systems Interconnection (OSI) Model some twenty years ago, and its meaning refers to the ability of a service provider (a network operator) to support a user's application requirements with regard to at least four service categories: (a) bandwidth,[1] (b) latency (delay), (c) jitter, and (d) traffic loss.

The provision of bandwidth for an application means the network has sufficient capacity to support the application's throughput requirements, measured in packets per second.[2]

The second service category is latency (delay), which describes the time it takes to send a user's packet of information from a sending node to a receiving node. Latency is also measured in round-trip-time (RTT), which is the time it takes to send a packet to a destination node and receive a reply from that node. RTT includes the transmission time in both directions and the processing time at the destination node and any other nodes that process the packet, such as a switch in the network.

Applications, such as voice and video, have stringent latency requirements, and if the packet arrives too late, it is not useful and is ignored. Thus, late-arriving packets result in wasted bandwidth and a reduction in the quality of service to the application.

However, packets that arrive "too early" also present problems at the receiver, since the receiver expects voice and video packets to arrive at a fairly consistent rate. These premature packets may also have to be discarded if the receiver cannot hold them for later use.

The third service category, jitter, is the variation in the delay between the arrival of the packets at the receiver, and usually occurs on an output link where packets are competing for the shared link. In this situation, the packets are held in a buffer until the output link becomes available. Variable delay is onerous to speech and video. It complicates the receiver's job of playing out the audio or visual image to the recipient.

The last service category is traffic (packet) loss. Packet loss is quite important in voice and video applications, since the loss may affect the outcome of the decoding process at the receiver and may also be detected by the end-user's ears or eyes. Certainly, traffic loss is a serious problem in data applications as well, but retransmission procedures mask the effects of traffic loss in data applications. Retransmissions for voice and video traffic are not feasible because the time required to detect the error and resend a packet or packets is too long for their real-time requirements.

---

[1]The term bandwidth is used in this book to describe capacity, measured in bit/s, and not a frequency spectrum.

[2]The term packet is used in this book to describe a unit of traffic sent from a network user to another network user or a node in the network. On occasion, I will use the terms frame, cell, message, datagram, and protocol data unit (PDU) instead of packet, and I will explain why when these terms are used.

There is another aspect of traffic loss; it deals with the complete loss of service in a network. This "hard-down" situation is much more serious than a partial traffic loss, but it is not the subject of this book, and is best left to another text. The assumption for this book is that the network is up and running. The question is how a functioning network can meet the customer's QOS requirements.

Congestion: Death Knell to Effective QOS

The four categories introduced in the previous section have a common theme: congestion. They are influenced by the contention for resources of a service system that has limited resources. Therefore, traffic may become congested while waiting for a resourse to be freed up to service the traffic.

The end result of congestion is the reduction in user-traffic throughput and increased delays in the delivery of the traffic to the receiver. The problems are such an ingrained part of data networks (and especially the Internet), that most of us take them for granted. Indeed, *best effort* (doing one's best, with no guarantees) is the only method of handling users' traffic in most private internets and the public Internet.

But this situation will change. By giving customers the options of purchasing QOS, a "service-level" concept will surely create new network applications. As well, it will create opportunities for the development of new products.

PROVISIONING AND SUPPORTING QOS

The provisioning and support of adequate QOS for a large and diverse user population (running many different applications) is not a simple process. Figure 1–1 illustrates the problems. Because of the complexity of supporting different traffic types, current internets treat all applications' traffic alike, and deliver the traffic on a best-effort basis: That is, the traffic is delivered if the network has the resources to support the delivery. However, if the network becomes congested, the traffic is simply discarded. One could certainly question the use of the phrase "best effort" for these operations; perhaps "mediocre effort" is more descriptive.

Some networks have attempted to establish some method of feedback (flow control) to the user in order to "request" the user to reduce the

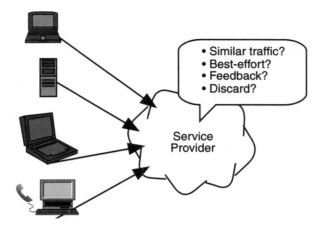

Figure 1–1 Decisions to support QOS

infusion of traffic into the network. This technique may not be very effective, because many traffic flows in data networks are very short, maybe just a few packets in a user-to-user session. So, by the time the user application receives the feedback information, it is finished sending traffic. The feedback packets are worthless and have done nothing but create yet more traffic.

The best-effort concept means traffic is discarded randomly, and no attempt is made to do any kind of intelligent filtering.[3] This approach has the effect of discarding more packets from applications that have high bandwidth requirements and are placing more packets into the network than those that have lesser requirements and are not sending as many packets into the network. So, the biggest "customers," those needing more bandwidth, are the very ones who are the most penalized!

Assuming the customer who is supposedly given a bigger "pipe" is paying more for that pipe, then it is reasonable to assume further that this customer should be given a fair return on the customer's investment in the service.

It is charitable to say that the best-effort approach is not a very good model. What is needed is a way to manage the QOS based on the customer's requirements and investment.

---

[3]Filtering refers to the ability of a node to use fields in the packet header to make decisions whether to delay, discard, or forward the packet.

FLOW LONGEVITY

I spoke briefly about congestion earlier. One of the difficulties in implementing an effective scheme to manage congestion deals with *flow longevity*. This term describes how long a user flow of traffic (say a database transfer, or a Web-site query) persists; that is, how long the flow remains active in the network. Flows for a database transfer may last for minutes or hours. In contrast, a flow for a Web-page retrieval may last only a second or so, or a few seconds (with adequate bandwidth, it should be a very brief time).

Managing short flows is difficult. For example, assume in Figure 1–2(a) that the network service provider decides to apply traffic management operations to a Web-page retrieval flow, and the provider issues a feedback packet to the user application. The packet is a special control

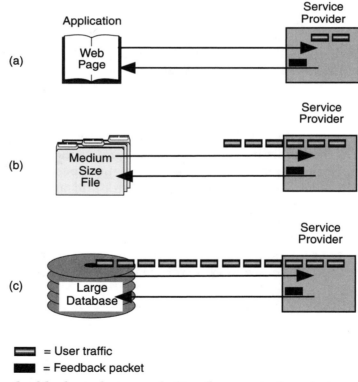

Note: the black packets symbolize flow control packets

Figure 1–2   Flow longevity

packet called "receive not ready," or "explicit congestion notification." It informs the sender to stop sending packets.

A short-lived flow is usually complete by the time the feedback reaches the sending application. Not only did the feedback accomplish nothing, it consumed bandwidth and complicated the system.

One could approach this problem with the decision to issue no feedback to short-lived flows. That might work, but what if most of the users' sessions (the user universe) with the network are short-lived, inquiry-response flows? The network may still become overwhelmed with a multiplicity of short-lived flows.

The flow problem is compounded by the fact that the situation is not a binary matter; that is, a flow is not just short-lived or long-lived. It may fall somewhere in between, as shown in Figure 1–2(b) in which a medium-size file is transferred to the service provider. This flow is also complete before the service provider can react.

The flow problem is compounded if the flow is across high-speed links because the flow is on the channel for a brief time. But that merely exacerbates the problem: Now the network receives the traffic very quickly. It's the same amount of traffic that it would have received on a low-speed link, but the provider must service the traffic in a more timely manner and under tighter time constraints.

The easiest flow to control is shown in Figure 1–2(c), a long flow. The feedback packet arrives at the sender before the sender has completed its transmission to the receiver. Thus, flow is throttled, and the network provider has successfully implemented a congestion management operation.

COOPERATIVE AND NONCOOPERATIVE NETWORKS

Managing a network that supports a mix of traffic (multiapplication or multiservice traffic) is quite different from managing a uniapplication network. See Figure 1–3. Additionally, many of the design concepts for traffic management for voice networks do not pertain to data networks. In effect, a traditional voice network is a cooperative network. This term means that control and routing decisions for a customer are made with the total network in mind, and individual performance objectives for each call is not a major factor (since, within regulatory requirements and the need to satisfy the customer, all connections are treated the same).

Noncooperative networks, such as the Internet, are characterized by the individual user (or a user's agent, such as an Internet Service

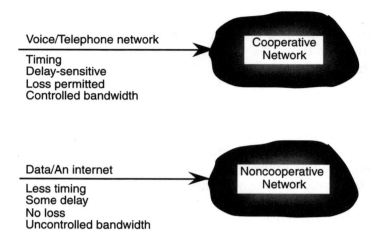

Figure 1–3   Managing a multiservice network

Provider [ISP]) making decisions regarding quality of service objectives. In effect, the user is somewhat independent with regard to using bandwidth; this contrasts with the telephone system, in which the user completely depends on the service provider.

In addition, the traffic load in a data network is more variable than in a voice network. And, of course, individual usage of data networks does not follow the same pattern as on a voice network. For example, the holding pattern for a data service is usually longer than a voice service.

Therefore, the multiservice network must be able to accommodate to diverse requirements, and must take a new approach for its service model to the customer. At a minimum, it requires the separation of different types of traffic, with each type offering different quality-of-service (QOS) features.

THE INTERNET: AN NONCOOPERATIVE NETWORK

It is an understatement to say the Internet is a noncooperative network. First, it has been designed for data applications, therefore it exhibits the behavior of these networks that were just explained. Second, the Internet has evolved as a rather loose amalgamation of disparate networks and service providers who have formed associations in an evolutionary and somewhat fragmented manner. Unlike most telephone networks, the Internet never had a "Ma Bell" or a PTT (Postal, Telephone, and Telegraph Ministry) to define the behavior of the network.

For the reader who is not familiar with the transmission characteristics of the Internet, I refer you to Appendix 1–A, at the back of this chapter.

APPLICATIONS' NATURAL BIT RATE

All applications exhibit natural bit rates,[4] illustrated in Figure 1–4. It is the rate in which the application generates and/or receives a certain number of bits per second (bit/s) based on its "natural requirements." For example, digitized voice using conventional ITU-T standards exhibits a natural bit rate of 64 kbit/s. Large data transfer systems have a fluctuating natural bit rate depending on the nature of the traffic, but it ranges from a few kbit/s to several hundred kbit/s. High-definition television (HDTV) has a natural bit rate of approximately 100–150 kbit/s, depending on the coding schemes employed on the signals.

The challenge of the QOS-based network is to support the natural bit rates of all applications being serviced. Due to variable traffic profiles, it may be imperative to discard traffic from certain users if the network experiences congestion problems. This situation is illustrated in Figure 1–4(a). For a brief period of time, the user exceeds the transfer rate permitted in the network with a burst of traffic. The shadowed portion of the graph is the burstyness of the traffic which exceeds, momentarily, the permitted rate of the network. With some networks, this traffic will be "tagged" (marked by setting a bit in the header in the packet) for possible discard.

An application's natural bit rate (because of its burstyness) may not use the full rate allocated by the network to this application. The possibility of wasted bandwidth occuring is shown in Figure 1–4(b) in the striped area. The network may attempt to allocate this bandwidth to other applications, or the bandwidths may go unused.

With these discussions in mind, the following material examines some approaches to the management of multiapplication traffic.

---

[4]This example is from the writings of Martin DePryker, who is the author of a number of books and papers on ATM. As a member of some of the ATM standards groups, DePryker has many interesting insights into the ATM development process, and his works would be good follow-ups to this book.

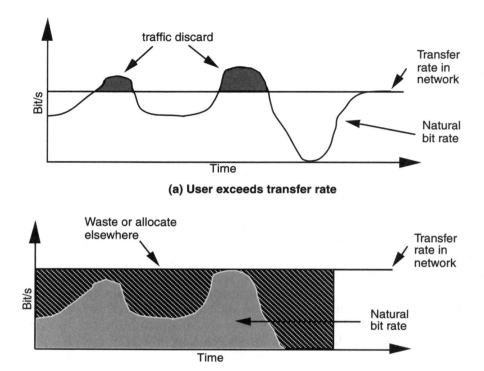

(a) User exceeds transfer rate

(b) Transfer rate greater than user bit rate

Figure 1–4   The natural bit rate

THE QOS MODELS

The Internet Engineering Task Force (IETF) has formed several working groups that are developing QOS standards. Table 1–1 provides a summary of their efforts. The first group deals with Integrated Services (IntServ). The focus is on long-lived unicast and multicast flows, and the Resource Reservation Protocol (RSVP) is used with this approach. This model guarantees each flow's QOS requirements through the complete path, from the sender to the receiver. Each node (router) in the path is aware of each flow's requirements and participates in the QOS support operation.

The second group is working on Differentiated Services (DiffServ). This model does not work with individual flows. Rather, it combines flows with the same service requirements into a single aggregated flow. This aggregated flow then receives levels of service relative to other traffic flows.

Table 1–1   Integrated Services (IntServ) and Differentiated Services (DiffServ)

Internet Working Groups are defining IntServ and DiffServ

IntServ:
   QOS guaranteed for each flow
   All nodes on sender/receiver path set up resources

DiffServ:
   Flows of similar categories are aggregated together
   Service based on relationships to other flows

These two approaches are quite different in how they provide QOS to the user, and we devote much time to them later. For now, it is interesting to note that both IntServ and DiffServ specify QOS at layer 3 in contrast to Frame Relay and ATM, which define QOS at layer 2.[5]

FUNCTIONAL EQUIVALENCE CLASS (FEC)

The term functional equivalence class (FEC) is a new term associated with QOS and switching operations. FEC is a general term and is used to describe an association of discrete packets with a specific destination address, usually the final recipient of the traffic, such as a host machine. FEC implementations may also associate an FEC value with this destination address *and* a class of traffic. The class of traffic is identified with an Internet destination port number, or values in the IP type of service (TOS), or IP protocol ID fields.

Why is FEC used? First, it allows the grouping of packets into classes. From this grouping, the FEC value in a packet can be used to set priorities for the handling of the packets, perhaps giving higher priority to certain FECs over others. FECs can be used to support efficient QOS operations. For example, FECs can be associated with real-time voice traffic, or low-priority newsgroup traffic and so on.

The matching of the FEC with a packet is achieved by using a label to identify a specific FEC. A label value is chosen to identify a specific

---

[5]The supposedly layer 2 operations of Frame Relay and ATM are actually a combination of layer 2 and layer 3 operations. X.25 provides the model: its virtual circuits are managed at its layer 3 in a separate layer 3 header. For Frame Relay and ATM, virtual circuit management has been "pushed down" to layer 2, and the layer 3 header has been eliminated.

packet flow or an aggregate of packet flows of the same type of traffic and destined for the same address.

Another term has emerged in the past few months to describe FEC. It is called layer 4 switching. It means that part of the FEC is based on information contained in the layer 4 header. For the Internet protocols, the TCP/UDP port numbers make up these values. I prefer the term FEC to layer 4 switching. The latter term is not accurate, because the switching decisions are performed on more than layer 4 port numbers.

One last point about the FEC. Recent work in the IETF does not rely on addresses, port numbers, nor the IP protocol ID fields to determine the FEC value. Instead, the IP TOS field has been redefined and is used to identify a class of user traffic. This concept is embedded into DiffServ, covered in Chapter 8.

SCOPE OF QOS SERVICE AND QOS DOMAINS

If QOS is to be provided end-to-end between two end users, the scope of the QOS becomes quite important. The term scope refers to the topological extent over which the customer is given the QOS.[6] See Figure 1–5. The scope may be restricted to one provider, or many. But for meaningful QOS to be obtained, the scope of service should include all providers that are involved in handling the users' traffic.

The concept has become more visible in the past few years as customers have had their traffic transported through more than one service provider. The first major breech of a one-service-provider concept occurred in the United States with the 1984 break-up of the Bell System, leading to the use of local exchange carriers (LECs) and interchange carriers (IXCs). As the Internet matured, it became common practice to use LECs, IXCs, as well as more than one ISP to provide end-to-end service to a customer.

As long as the end-to-end service was "best effort" (no attempt to provide QOS to the customer), the scope of service was not very important. Certainly, the customer needed some level of service end-to-end, but services such as delay, jitter, and throughput were moot points, since they were simply not available. Today, with the increased importance of

---

[6][BERN99] Bernet, Y, et al. "A Framework for Differentiated Services," draft-ietf-difserv-framework-02-.txt., February, 1999.

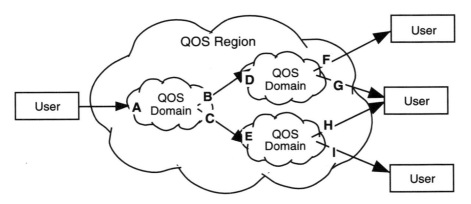

Figure 1–5   Scope of service and QOS domains

QOS, the scope of service becomes a key part of a service level agreement (SLA), discussed later in this chapter.

Figure 1–5 provides a model for the scope of service operations. The scope is defined between an ingress point (where user traffic enters a QOS node or network [a QOS domain]) and an egress point (where user traffic leaves the QOS node or network). Several scopes of service are possible in this figure; as examples:

- Traffic from ingress point A to one egress point
- Traffic from ingress point A to all egress points
- Traffic from ingress point A to a set of egress points

If user traffic spans multiple service providers, it is important that these providers have SLA agreements among themselves in relation to the customer's QOS needs. This idea of a multi-QOS domain is called a QOS region. The agreements for a multidomain service are best met by providing quantitative services, the subject of the next discussion.

QUALITATIVE AND QUANTITATIVE SERVICE LEVELS

A level of service can be provided and measured by qualitative or quantitative means. Figure 1–6 depicts the ideas of these service levels. The qualitative service in Figure 1–6(a) is more subjective than a quantitative service in Figure 1–6(b). It refers to a general description of the service, such as high throughput, low loss, or low latency. The quantita-

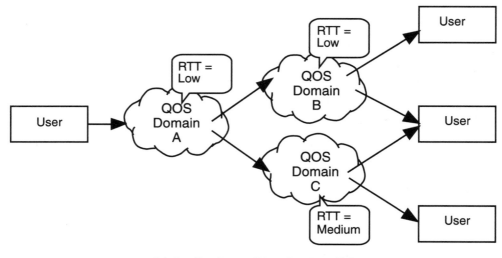

(a) Qualitative at Domains B and C

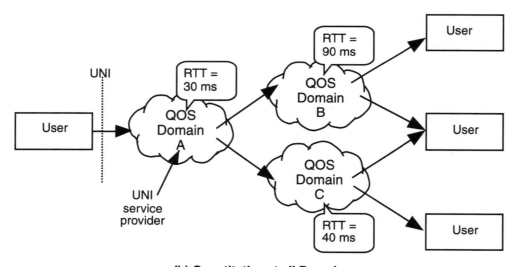

(b) Quantitative at all Domains

Where:
  RTT: Round-trip time

Figure 1–6   Qualitative and quantitative service levels

tive service is described in terms such as throughput at 512 kbit/s; packet loss is no more than .001% of all packets transported; and one-way latency is between 50 ms and 120 ms 99.98% of the time.

Some services may be a combination of qualitative or quantitative descriptions. For example, one specific traffic flow, say flow A, may have a drop precedence ratio of n packets dropped (not delivered) to m packets delivered, certainly a quantitative description. At the same time, a customer may wish to supercede this flow with that of another. For example, flow A will be allowed to have a higher drop precedence than flow B, if the two flows are active at the same time.

As a general note, qualitative service will not work well if a customer is paying quantitative dollars for the service. After all, why pay hard currency for a nebulous service? Perhaps the service provider can say to the customer, "Trust me, I'll give you low delay, low loss, and high throughput." In turn, the customer should be able to say, "Fine, I'll write you a virtual check for this service."

On a more serious note, as the scope of service expands beyond one or a few QOS domains, the need for quantitative services becomes more important, both to the customer, and to the user network interface (UNI) ingress service provider—the first service provider for the customer. This idea is shown in Figure 1–6(b). The customer needs to know if the service is commensurate with its price. The initial service provider (Domain A in the figure) needs protection and explanations if the downstream providers (Domains B and C in the figure) do not meet the customer's QOS requirements. This idea is discussed in more detail in later chapters.

GENESIS OF QOS: X.25

We take a change of pace here, and look at a bit of history. The QOS concept began with X.25. In the late 1960s and early 1970s, various companies, government agencies, and other organizations created many different data communications networks. The design and programming of these networks were performed by each organization to fulfill specific business needs. During this time, an organization had no reason to adhere to any common convention for its data communications protocols since the organization's private network provided services only to itself. Consequently, these networks used specialized protocols that were tailored to satisfy the organization's requirements.

During this period, several companies and telephone administrations in the United States, Canada, and Europe implemented a number of *public data networks;* based on packet switching concepts. These systems were conceived to provide a service for data traffic that paralleled the telephone system's service for voice traffic.

But these packet networks did not nail-up bandwidth like the telephone system. Indeed, X.25 represented a major change in viewing service to a user: Use a best-effort approach but also allow the user to request certain levels of service.

The public network vendors were faced with a major question: How can the network best provide the interface for a user's terminal or computer to the network? The potential magnitude of the problem was formidable because each terminal or computer vendor had developed its own set of data communications protocols. Indeed, some companies, such as IBM, had developed scores of different protocols within their own product line.

X.25 came about largely because these nascent networks recognized that a common network interface protocol was needed, especially from the perspective of the network service providers. Figure 1–7 illustrates this situation. The network interface idea is now called the user-to-network (UNI).

In 1974, the (former) CCITT issued the first draft of X.25 (the "Gray Book"). It was revised in 1976, 1978, 1980, and again in 1984 with the publication of the "Red Book" Recommendation. Until 1988, X.25 was revised and republished every four years. In 1988, the ITU-T announced its intention to publish changes to its recommendations (including X.25) as they were warranted, rather than in the four-year cycle previously utilized.

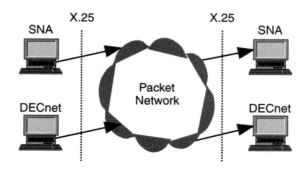

Figure 1–7   Genesis of QOS: X.25

In hindsight, X.25 was (and is) a very sophisticated and forward-looking technology, primarily because it was the first standardized approach in computer-based networks for defining a UNI providing QOS to the end user. These QOS features are implemented with X.25 facilities.

The X.25 operations are explained in more detail later. For this introduction, it is sufficient to note that some commercial offerings did not implement all the X.25 facilities, because the network operators were at a loss on how to translate the facility specifications into service level agreements (SLAs) and billable services.

However, as early as 1980, a number of vendors (for example, Nortel and AT&T) developed useful QOS options in their packet switches. Examples of these early QOS features were the ability to negotiate a throughput rate in a network, and the ability to stipulate a maximum delay end-to-end, or through the network.

Interestingly, many of the X.25 facilities look a lot like telephony features, because many of the X.25 standards group members came from the telephony world. For example, X.25 supports a hunt group facility that allows calls to be dispersed across multiple interfaces, something like the telephony rotary feature. Other examples of telephony-based features found in X.25 are incoming and outgoing calls barred across an interface or on a selected channel basis within the interface.

SERVICE LEVEL AGREEMENTS (SLAs)

Wide area networks (WAN) that offer QOS features are common today. Throughput and delay are examples of these features. Others are traffic loss guarantees. That is the good news. The bad news is that it may be difficult for the customer to know if the network provider is living up to the service level agreement (SLA) contract: the contract between the customer and the service provider.

In a large internet, there may be thousands of connections and services with different network providers. SLA contracts have been signed, and the SLAs are supposedly being supported. Nothing is simple in life, even SLAs. The problem stems from the fact that the SLA for QOS support may be difficult to monitor (but it is not an insurmountable technical problem).

In a public data network (such as a Frame Relay network), a customer enterprise is often billed based on its bandwidth usage on each virtual circuit (VC). It is important for the customer to be able to know how the service provider has billed the customer for the VC and the traffic

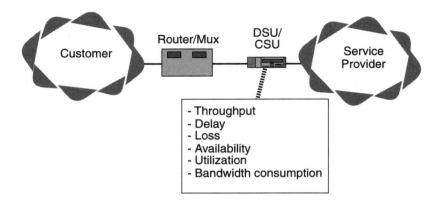

Figure 1–8   Service level agreements and monitoring operations

across the VC. In the past, software was not available to monitor these circuits and provide meaningful information to the customer. This situation is changing, and a number of vendors now have products that enables Frame Relay customers to gather information for monitoring their SLAs.

Figure 1–8 shows the topology for implementing an SLA monitor. The enhanced channel service unit/data service unit (CSU/DSU) collects performance data by monitoring the traffic passing through it. The data are passed to software that generates reports on key QOS operations: (a) availability, (b) delay, (c) throughput by VC or physical port, (d) traffic discards, (e) port utilization over time, and (f) percentage of bandwidth being used by a protocol (SNA, IP, etc.).

The price for these enhanced CSU/DSUs range from $1000 to $4000. They are available from a number of vendors [TAYL98][7] and [JAND99].[8]

At each service customer/provider boundary, the SLS specifies the overall features and performance which can be expected by the customer and the provider [BERN99].[9] Part of the SLA is the traffic conditioning

---

[7][TAYL98] Taylor, Steven and Wexler, Joanie, "Maturing Frame Relay Make New Demands," *Business Communications Review*, July, 1998.

[8][JAND99] Jander, Mary, "SLA Monitoring Tools," *Data Communications*, February, 1999.

[9][BERN99] Benrnt, Yoram, et al., A Framework for Differentiated Services, draft-ietf-difserv-framework-02.txt., February, 1999.

specification (TCS). The TCS specifies detailed service parameters for each service level. Such parameters include:

- Service performance parameters such as expected throughput, drop probability, latency.
- Constraints on the entrance (ingress) and exit (egress) points at which the service is provided.
- Traffic profiles (rules) which must be obeyed if the requested service is to be provided.
- Disposition of traffic submitted in excess of the SLA profile.
- Marking (tagging) services provided (placing special bits in the customer packet for use in meeting the SLA).
- Shaping services provided (delaying the transmittal of the customer's traffic to meet an SLA performance requirement).

The SLS may specify more general service characteristics such as:

- Availability/Reliability, which may include behavior in the event of failures resulting in the rerouting of traffic.
- Authentication and encryption services.
- Mechanisms for monitoring and auditing the service.
- Responsibilities such as location of the equipment and equipment functions.
- Pricing and billing, and clauses for describing SLA nonconformance.

Figure 1–9 shows two examples of reports that are generated from an SLA monitoring system. The first example is a report on the availability and round-trip delay of a Frame Relay permanent virtual circuit (PVC), identified with the Frame Relay data link connection identifier (DLCI) of 321. The committed information rate (CIR) is shown, as well as the physical port speed. (CIR is explained in the Frame Relay material; see Chapter 5). The availability of the DLCI is provided as well as the round-trip delay of the Frame Relay frames through the network from the source to the destination.

The second example is a report on port utilization at various sites in a network. For example, location A might be a company branch office in Seattle, and location B might be a manufacturing plant in Denver. The sample times are shown, as well as the transmit (Tx) and receive (Rx) utilization.

Example One:

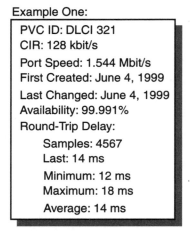

PVC ID: DLCI 321

CIR: 128 kbit/s

Port Speed: 1.544 Mbit/s
First Created: June 4, 1999

Last Changed: June 4, 1999
Availability: 99.991%

Round-Trip Delay:

    Samples: 4567
    Last: 14 ms

    Minimum: 12 ms
    Maximum: 18 ms

    Average: 14 ms

Example Two:

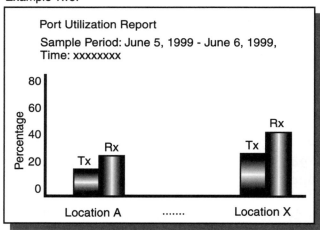

Port Utilization Report

Sample Period: June 5, 1999 - June 6, 1999,
Time: xxxxxxxx

Figure 1–9   Examples of SLA monitoring reports

POLICY-BASED NETWORKING

The QOS SLA monitoring operations are certainly important and
can be an effective tool to help an organization check their service
provider's SLA contract adherence. But the operations that were just discussed are narrow in their scope in that they do not enable the user to actually define the QOS level. Taken further, there is no means for an
organization to establish a policy for QOS and implement that policy

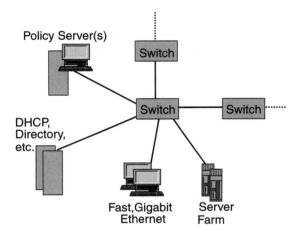

Figure 1–10   Policy-based networking

across the organization's networks. This idea is called policy-based networking, and it is a vital part of the QOS picture.

The idea is simple and illustrated in Figure 1–10. The network administrator uses a console to set up (configure) policies that stipulate the QOS levels that are granted to applications and end users. This information is downloaded to the components in the network that are responsible for the QOS operations.

The implementation is not so simple. The reasons are: (a) there are no standards available for policy-based networking, (b) vendors that offer a product vary in the criteria used to establish and monitor the policy decisions, and (c) the so-called policy-based networking protocols are not always up to the task of true policy-based networking. Even if they were, vendors use different protocols in their products.

Notwithstanding, the policy-based networking "industry" is hard at work developing systems (not standards) and a wide variety of products are available in the marketplace. A good reference for the products is [DATA99].[10] The products are expensive, with an average price of $566 per end user.

Figure 1–10 is a general view of the configuration for policy-based networking. The specific implementation varies between vendors. As mentioned earlier, the policies are entered through either a network-management console for special-designed policy server. The protocol used

---

[10][DATA99] www.data.com/issue/990507/policy_table1.html

to convey this information varies. Some vendors use a new Internet protocol, the Common Open Policy Service (COPS); others use the Simple Network Management Protocol (SNMP); some use the Lightweight Directory Access Protocol (LDAP); others use a proprietary scheme.

Some vendors concentrate their efforts on LANs, some on WANs, and some on both network types. There is more interest in the WAN arena because the user is paying hard dollars for the purchase of WAN bandwidth and other QOS features.

Another interesting aspect to these systems is that some vendors tie-in their product with the Dynamic Host Configuration Protocol (DHCP). When a user logs on to the network, DHCP assigns the user an IP address and an associated mask (prefix). Then, the DHCP assigns a default set of service classes to the user.

Most of the products also support the Internet Remote Monitoring Protocol (RMON), which allows the network manager to monitor the performance of RMON-configured systems.

In summary, the approaches vary widely, as do the prices. But this aspect of the QOS picture is new, and we can expect much progress in policy-based networking in the near future.

SLA MONITORING POINTS

The monitoring operations discussed earlier (see Figure 1–8) can be expanded to include more monitoring points than just a DSU/CSU node and more information for the customer and network provider. Figure 1–11 depicts a model for these operations, based on work by the Frame Relay Forum [FRFO98].[11] The reference points for the monitoring activities are listed below. This model will be used in subsequent chapters.

Source Reference Point (*SrcRP*): Measurement point at source end system

Ingress Reference Point (*IngRP*): Measurement point at the ingress to the ingress node

Traffic Policing Reference Point (*TpRP*): Measurement point after traffic policing functions have processed a packet

---

[11][FRFO98] Frame Relay Forum. Service Level Definitions Implementation Agreement (IA), FRF.13, 1998.

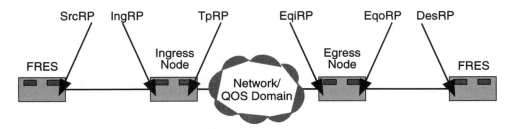

Where: FRES = Frame Relay end system

Figure 1–11   SLA monitoring points

Egress Queue Input Reference Point (*EqiRP*): Measurement point prior to interface transmission queue

Egress Queue Output Reference Point (*EqoRP*): Measurement point after interface transmission queue

Destination Reference Point (*DesRP*): Measurement point at destination end system

SUMMARY

QOS concepts are not new, but they have not seen wide-scale interest or deployment until recently. Now, with the network customer looking for service providers that can offer ranges of services at different pricing levels, QOS features become quite important.

QOS and service level agreements (SLAs) represent pragmatic approaches to the use of network services and paying for them. While they are new now, in a few years, QOS and associated SLAs will be commonplace.

APPENDIX 1A   CHARACTERISTICS OF THE INTERNET

The Internet was developed for the transfer of data traffic with the use of adaptive routing features. By adaptive routing, I mean that the traffic may take different routes through the Internet depending on the conditions at a specific time. In addition, the Internet is designed as a connectionless system which means that there are no "affiliations" established between the machines in the Internet. As a result, the Internet does not maintain an ongoing knowledge of the user's traffic. In effect, the Internet Protocol (IP) is stateless; that is to say, it does not build tables to maintain information about a connection because there is no connection.

The Internet is a "best-effort" delivery network. The term *best effort* means that the Internet will attempt to deliver the traffic, but if problems occur, the traffic is discarded.

ROUND-TRIP TIME (RTT)

Round-trip time (RTT) is a measure of the time it takes to send a packet to a node and receive a reply from that node. RTT includes the transmission time in both directions and the processing time at the far-end node. Most RTTs in the Internet are within the range of 70–160 ms, although large variations to RTT do occur. Because of the asynchronous nature of the Internet, RTT is not consistent.

ITU-T G.114 Recommendation limits RTT to 300 ms or less. This performance factor is based on many studies and observations that longer delays in a telephone-based conversation leaves the impression on the conversationalists that they are using a half-duplex circuit. However, other surveys show some people tolerate large RTTs of up to 800 ms. But this tolerant population is in the minority.

During periods of light-to-moderate activity, the Internet's RTT performance is acceptable to most data applications. Rarely is the RTT short enough to support real-time voice or video. However, during periods of high activity, the Internet provides very poor RTT for even data applications. (I try to avoid large transfers of data during these times.)

TRAFFIC LOSS

Another Internet characteristic that is important to audio and video applications is packet loss. Two factors are involved: (a) how often packet loss occurs and (b) how many successive (contiguous) packets are affected. Packet loss is masked in the data application by using TCP to resend the lost TCP traffic. Certainly, the loss of many user packets and their retransmissions will affect the application's performance. But on the whole, the end-user data application is not concerned (or aware) of packet loss.

Packet loss is quite important in audio and video applications, since the loss may affect the outcome of the decoding process at the receiver and be detected by the end-user's ears or eyes. Notwithstanding, today's voice coders can produce high-quality audio signals in the face of about 10 percent loss of the voice packets (G.723.1 as the example), *if* the packet losses are random and independent. G.723.1 compensates for this loss by using the previous packet to simulate the characteristics of the vocal signal that was in the lost packet.

Traffic loss in the Internet is bursty: Large packet losses occur in a small number of bursts. This characteristic of Internet behavior complicates the support of telephony, because packetized voice works best if the packet loss is random and independent.

The effect of packet loss can be alleviated somewhat by the use of forward error correction (FEC) schemes, and studies have been conducted to test the effectiveness of compensating for loss bursts [BORE97].[12] These schemes add extra delay to the process and may result in the loss of the packet because it is made available to the user in a time domain that is too late to be useful.

The FEC approach borrows from the tried-and-true mobile wireless technology: repeat the signal more than once. With mobile wireless systems, this operation interleaves successive copies of the coded voice image across multiple packets (slots in the mobile wireless terminology). With Internet telephony, experiments are underway to send copies of the packet 1 to n times. If one copy is lost, say copy n, it can be recovered from the other copies. However, this operation is only effective if a copy arrives safely, and therefore implies that one of the copies survives the burst error. If the copies are spaced out too far in time to survive the error, they may arrive too late to be useful.

The subject of the order of the arrival of packets at the receiver is not of keen interest to the data application if it is supported by TCP, because TCP (within limits) can reorder the TCP segments and present the traffic to the application in the correct order. TCP is not used for voice and video, so the order of packet arrival is an important subject to these applications. As of this writing, studies are underway to capture statistics and discover the incidences of misordered packet arrival. The Paxson study[13] shows that out-of-sequence arrival is not unusual.

---

[12][BORE97] Borella, M.S. et al., "Analysis of End-to-End Internet Packet Loss: Dependence and Asymmetry," *IEEE Network*, Preprint, 1997.

[13]This information represents a small part of the study that is available from: [PAXS97] IEEE/ACM Transactions on Communications, "End-to-End Routing Behavior in the Internet," by Vern Paxson, Vol. 5, No. 5, October 1997.

Table 1A-1 Routing persistence [PAXS97]

Time	% of Total	Comments
Seconds	NA	Used in load balancing
Minutes	NA	In tightly coupled routers
Tens of minutes	9	Changes usually through different cities or Autonomous Systems
Hours	4	Usually intranetwork changes
6+ hours	19	Usually intranetwork changes
Days	68	(a) 50% of these routes persist for < 7 days (b) Other 50% persist for > 7 days

Another factor is to note that Internet delays follow a diurnal cycle. During the hours of 8:00 A.M. to 6:00 P.M., delays are greater. For example, in the middle of the business day, delays are about 20 ms greater than in the evenings.

FIXED VS. DYNAMIC ROUTING

Given that fixed routing is a desirable feature for real-time traffic (to reduce delay and jitter), one can ask: Is it needed? That is, does an internet (or more precisely, the Internet) shuffle traffic around frequently, with the routers altering routes often?

Studies conducted on the routing behavior of the Internet reveal that most of the traffic between two or more communicating parties remains on the same physical path during the session. In fact, route alteration is more an exception than the rule. One study on Internet "routing persistence" is summarized in this Table 1A-1 [PAXS97].

Paxson defines routing persistence as how long a route endures before changing. Even though routing changes occur over a wide range of time, most of the routes in the Internet do not change much.

A point should be emphasized in Paxson's study. The not applicable (NA) entries in this Table 1A-1 represent situations in which frequent routing fluctuations do occur in parts of the Internet. While they are not a factor in the "big picture," if your traffic flows through that part of the Internet, it will be affected by these changes.

2

QOS Concepts and Operations

This chapter introduces the QOS concepts and operations. The key topics are congestion management and traffic integrity. We learn how credits, congestion notification, packet acknowledgments, and sliding widows are implemented to reduce or eliminate congestion, and enhance traffic integrity. Buffering and queuing techniques, and the weighted fair queuing operations are also covered.

STATISTICAL MULTIPLEXING

Modern communications networks are digitally-based, and allocate capacity based on time division multiplexing (TDM) or statistical time division multiplexing (STDM)[1] operations. Time division multiplexing (TDM) provides a user the full channel capacity but divides the channel usage into time slots. The idea is shown in Figure 2–1(a). Each user is

---

[1]We will not deal with frequency-division multiplexing (FDM), which divides the channel's bandwidth spectrum into multiple channels, so that each channel occupies a part of the larger frequency spectrum. This technique is also called frequency-division multiple access (FDMA). The assumption in this book is that the FDM channel (if one exists) is a given.

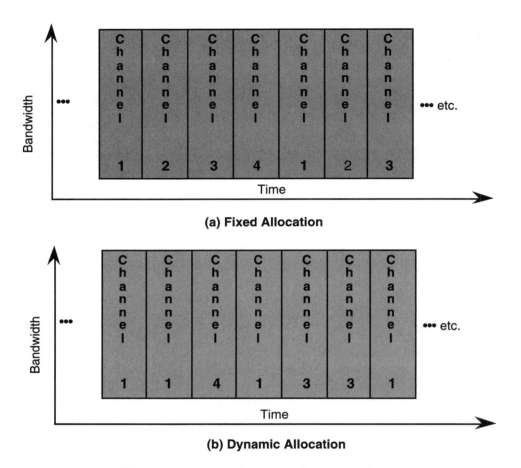

(a) Fixed Allocation

(b) Dynamic Allocation

Figure 2–1 Allocating capacity on the link

given a slot, and the slots are rotated among the users. A pure TDM (such as a T1 system) cyclically scans the input signals (incoming traffic) from the multiple incoming link interfaces. Bits, bytes, or blocks of data are separated and interleaved together into frames for transmission onto a single high-speed communications link.

The conventional TDM wastes the bandwidth of the communications link for certain applications because the time slots are often unused. Vacant slots occur when an idle terminal has nothing to transmit in its slot. Yet the TDM technology has been quite pervasive for over thirty-five years, because TDM was the method developed for digital telephony traffic and the ubiquitous T1 technology. But it is clearly not the technology that we want for today's multiapplication environment.

Statistical TDM multiplexers (STDMs) dynamically allocate the time slots (or traffic bursts) among active terminals. The idea is shown in Figure 2–1(b). Dedicated time slots (TDMs) are not provided for each user application or terminal on a STDM. Consequently, idle terminal time does not waste link capacity. Instead, the capacity is used by another application that is active. It is not unusual for four to seven times as much traffic to be accommodated on lines using STDMs in comparison to TDM.

The STDM multiplexing concept is used with data networks. Routers are essentially STDM machines with forwarding capabilities. Almost all the protocols and networks covered in this book use STDM concepts.

CONGESTION PROBLEMS

Any network that admits traffic and users on a demand basis (statistical multiplexing) must deal with the problem of congestion. The management of all users' traffic to prevent congestion in the QOS domain is a vital aspect of the QOS picture. Congestion translates into reduced throughput and increased delay. Congestion is the death knell of effective QOS.

Most networks provide transmission rules for their users which include agreements on how much traffic can be sent to the network before the traffic flow is regulated (flow-controlled). Flow control is an essential ingredient to prevent congestion in a network. It is easy to understand the concern network managers have about congestion, because it can result in severe degradation of the network operations both in throughput and response time.

As the traffic (offered load) in the network reaches a certain point, mild congestion begins to occur with the resulting drop in throughput. Figure 2–2 depicts the problem. If this proceeded in a linear fashion, it would not be so complex a problem. However, at a time when utilization of the network reaches a certain level, throughput drops precipitously because of serious congestion and the buildup of packets at the servers' queues.

Therefore, networks must (a) provide some mechanism of informing switches *inside* the network when congestion is occurring, and (b) pro-

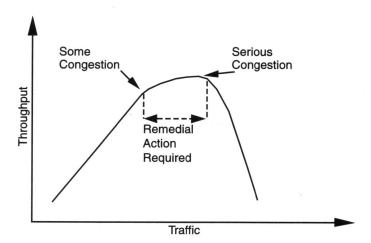

Figure 2–2 Potential congestion problems

vide a flow control mechanism on external user devices *outside* the network.

FLOW CONTROL MECHANISMS

We just learned that traffic management in a QOS domain requires some type of flow control mechanism to prevent the network from becoming congested and discarding packets.

Many techniques are available to provide flow control and can be classified as follows: (a) based on an SLA contract: monitoring traffic, with packet tagging (marking)[2] and possible packet discard actions in the event of problems; (b) using no SLA contract: monitoring traffic, with feedback mechanisms (a control loop) to the sender to direct the sender's rate of packet emission into the network.

Technique (a) is also known as an open loop and technique (b) is known as a closed loop. Table 2–1 summarizes the major features of these two techniques.

---

[2] We now expand the definition of tagging/marking, introduced in Chapter 1. Special bits in the user packet are set to indicate a reduction in the importance of the packet. Therefore, it is now a packet of lower priority than a "nontagged" packet.

Table 2–1 Flow-control mechanisms

Technique (a):

  Network and user have an SLA contract

  Traffic is predictable

  User adheres to the contract

  No feedback loop is necessary

Technique (b):

  No SLA contract between user and network

  Traffic may or may not be predictable

  User and network use a feedback loop mechanism

As a general rule, technique (a) assumes the user traffic is fairly predictable, and that the user will "behave" and not send traffic beyond an agreed amount. Therefore, under normal operations, there should be no need for a feedback mechanism such as congestion notification, or some other flow control signal.

For technique (b), it is assumed the user traffic load is less predictable, and/or the network has no formal arrangement with the user regarding the amount of traffic the user can send. With this arrangement, some method of feedback is needed to protect the network and to prevent the user from resending traffic that the network discarded because of the network's inability to deliver it.

EXPLICIT AND IMPLICIT FLOW CONTROL

An important aspect of communications networks is the nature in which the amount of traffic is controlled in its ebb and flow into and out of the network. The operation in which user traffic is controlled is called, naturally enough, congestion management operations. Figure 2–3 depicts the two methods used for congestion management: explicit flow control and implicit flow control.

As the name suggests, explicit flow control places a specific limitation on how much user traffic can enter the network. See Figure 2–3(a), where SW symbolizes a network switch. If the network issues an explicit flow-control message back to the user, then the user has no choice but to stop sending traffic. In turn, the user may not send any more traffic until

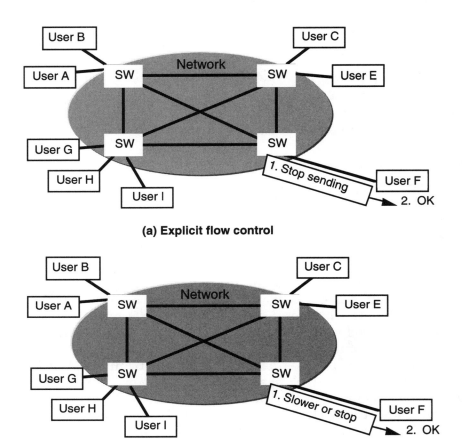

Figure 2–3 Explicit and implicit flow control

the network releases this "throttle." The reader may be familiar with these forms of explicit flow control operations with the familiar terms *receive not ready* (RNR) (establishing flow control) and *receive ready* (RR) (releasing flow control). A more recent term is explicit congestion notification (ECN).

Implicit flow control does not restrict flow completely. See Figure 2–3(b). Rather, it suggests that the user either stop sending traffic or at least reduce the amount of traffic it is sending to the network. Typically, the implicit flow control message is warning that the user (a) is violating its SLA with the network and/or (b) the network is congested. In either case, if the user continues to send traffic, it risks having that traffic tagged and possibly discarded.

A word of caution is needed here about these two terms. They may have different meanings, depending upon the specific protocol. I am using the explicit and implicit flow control definitions in a generic sense. It is possible to use a congestion notification to execute a complete throttle—just like a receive not ready. But in practice, the most common approach is to use congestion notification in concert with another piece of information to control traffic emissions from a node. This other information is called a credit or window value, and is used to inform a node of (a) congestion, and (b) how much traffic this node is allowed to send. Usually, the affected node, upon receiving this information will adjust its transmissions, based on this credit value.

We need to make a few more points about this subject before we move on. Some systems do not associate a congestion notification value with the credit value, and some do. Two cases illustrate this idea. In the first case, the credit value is used by itself to flow control the node and *does not* include the RR or RNR signals (for example, credit = 1000 packets). In the second case, the system uses *only* the RNR and RR techniques with no credit (for example, RNR = stop!). X.25 uses the RNR and RR operations.

Newer protocols no longer use the terms RNR or RR, but use in their place explicit congestion notification (ECN). These protocols use one of two techniques: (a) explicit congestion notification (ECN = stop!), or (b) explicit congestion notification with a credit value (ECN = a credit of 1000 packets). Frame Relay and ATM use these new techniques in several ways, and they are explained further in the Frame Relay and ATM chapters.

Figure 2–4 compares the use versus nonuse of ECN in a data network [WERN92].[3] In this example, it is assumed that the receipt of the congestion notification message forces the node and/or application to obey, and either stop sending completely, or reduce its emission rate, based on the credit value in the message. The example assumes that all end users are reacting to the ECN, if necessary. It also assumes the reaction to the ECN happens quickly.

The ECN reduces the loss of traffic by forcing the users to slow down their transmission rates to the network and their number of retransmis-

---

[3][WERN92] Wernik, Marek et al., "Traffic Management for B-ISDN Services," *IEEE Network*, September, 1992.

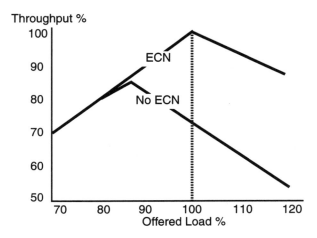

Figure 2–4 Explicit congestion notification [WERN92]

sion attempts. It has been demonstrated the ECN is effective in situations where the congestion periods are at least an order of magnitude longer than the round time (RTT) of the traffic end to end.

Of course, slowing down transmission rates for real-time traffic (voice and video) is usually self-defeating, because it leads to excessive delays in delivering traffic to the destination application. Flow control is focused on data flows, and less on voice and video flows.

Notwithstanding, voice and video flows can be flow-controlled within certain limits, as long as the resulting traffic delays can be dealt with at the receiver. Later discussions in this chapter will explain this idea in more detail.

Problems with Internet Flow Control Services

The previous discussion spoke of the need for the network users to react to the ECN quickly. This important point was introduced in Chapter 1 (see Figure 1-2). In most networks (and especially in the Internet), a quick reaction to an ECN message is difficult to execute, because the Internet protocols have not been so-designed. Figure 2–5 helps explain why. Two end user systems are exchanging traffic (nodes A and F). Four routers (B, C, D, and E) participate in the forwarding of the traffic between users A and F. Typically, one or two methods are used (increasingly, both are used on the same flow . . . more on this later) for the flow control operations, and they are shown in Figure 2–5 as methods A and B. Here are the salient features of these two methods.

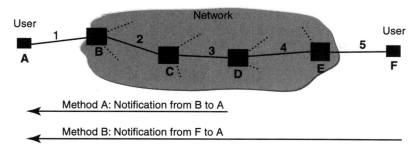

Figure 2–5 Origins of ECN messages

With method A, the flow control message emanates from the network, and the network node that is closest to the user node (router B in this example). With method B, the flow control message emanates from the peer user node (end station F, in this example). Obviously, method A produces better results, because it takes less time for the user to react to the flow control message.

However, the Internet protocols are not designed to execute method A. They are designed to execute method B using the Transmission Control Protocol (TCP). With very few exceptions, TCP is not executed between the network node (node B) and the user node (node A). IP is the major protocol operating between these two machines, so method A is not available.

Solutions to the Problem

How can an internet (or the Internet) handle this critical issue of flow control in a more efficient manner? The answer is to implement another procedure to execute method A. We spend considerable time on this subject in later chapters, but for this discussion we can state that configuring nodes A/B, E/F with additional flow control operations is the answer. As we shall see, X.25, Frame Relay, and ATM have tools to support method A.

CONGESTION, TRAFFIC CONTROL, AND CONNECTION ADMISSION CONTROL

Some of the networks in operation today perform not only flow control operations, but other control operations as well. For example, in a Broadband ISDN (B-ISDN), using ATM as the network transport service), the terms congestion, traffic control, and connection admission control describe different aspects of network operations.

Congestion is defined as a condition that exists in network elements (NEs), such as switches and transmission links, where the network is not able to meet a stated and negotiated performance objective.

In contrast, traffic control defines a set of actions taken by the network to avoid congestion. Therefore, traffic control takes measures to adapt to unpredictable fluctuations in traffic flows and other problems within the network.

Connection admission control is the procedure by which the network makes a decision whether to allow the user's traffic into the network. In ATM networks (as well as X.25 and Frame Relay) the decision is made on the granting or denial of a connection to the network. If the connection is not granted, then the user cannot transfer traffic. The idea is quite similar to the telephone network; if the network is busy, the calling party is not granted a connection.

The objectives of traffic control and connection admission control are to protect the network and at the same time provide the user with its stated SLA objectives (its QOS needs). For B-ISDN, this includes formally stated QOS objectives.

Table 2–2 lists and describes the principal terms and concepts associated with traffic control and admission control. Subsequent discussions will expand upon these definitions.

ARRIVAL RATE AND TRAFFIC LOAD

In any demand-driven network, a (somewhat) unpredictable load can be imposed on the network. Traffic policing and remedial action is required to ensure that the traffic load does not jeopardize the performance of the network. Ideally, one would not like to impose undue restrictions on a user and the user's ability to present payload to the network (after all, payload is so named because it produces revenue).

Table 2–2 Traffic control and admission control operations

- Connection admission control (CAC): Determine if user connection will be accepted or rejected
- Usage parameter control (UPC): Monitor and regulate traffic at the UNI
- Loss priority (LP): Establish priorities for different types of traffic
- Traffic shaping: Establish mechanisms for managing traffic
- Feedback: Provide mechanism to inform user of bandwidth availability

In an ideal world, a network is able to accept all user traffic. Unfortunately, such is not the case in the real world. Due to simple economics, busy signals must be returned to telephone users when the network is busy. It would be impractical for a network to be designed to accommodate all calls, for example one that could handle all Mother's Day traffic. Therefore, any network which has an unpredictable (within limits, of course) load offered to it must be able to monitor this traffic and take remedial action, if required.

Some networks provide these important operations by monitoring the packet arrival rate for each connection across the user-network interface (UNI). Of course, if the network were monitoring only one user and its packet arrival profile at each physical interface, the matter would be relatively simple. With the ability to multiplex (potentially) hundreds of user sessions onto one physical interface, it becomes important to monitor each user's traffic pattern and to make adjustments accordingly, which might mean discarding or flow-controlling a specific user's traffic.

Figure 2–6 shows the problem faced by a QOS-based network. In Figure 2–6(a) the packet arrival rate to the network node is relatively low. The nature of the user's application and the behavior of the application at this instance mean relatively long intervals are occurring between the arrival of successive packets at the network QOS switch. Of course, this simplifies greatly the network's ability to handle the traffic.

On the other hand, in Figure 2–6(b), the packets are arriving at a much faster rate, which results in the concomitant decrease in the interval between the packets. In a commercially oriented network, Figure 2–6(b) is more preferable to Figure 2–6(a), because more packets produce more revenue. However, for the network manager, Figure 2–6(b) presents a more challenging problem in that the network must adjust and accommodate to the higher traffic loads.

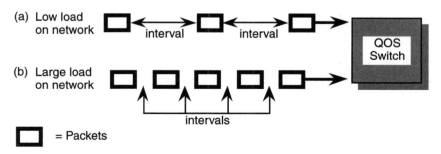

Figure 2–6 Arrival rate patterns

Also, the packets depicted in Figure 2–6 may be carrying traffic from different user applications (such as voice, video, and data) and traffic within these applications may require a different level of QOS support from the network. Consequently, a multiapplication network must deal with issues other than simple packet arrival rates in accommodating to varying traffic loads.

The QOS network must accommodate to the different QOS requirements emanating from each application. Granted, some applications will have the same QOS profile, which simplifies some of the policing and congestion control operations at the UNI. Notwithstanding, the universe of applications' traffic presented across the UNI will vary in their QOS requirements. Therefore, the network must be able to support these diverse traffic profiles and support the packet rate intervals.

With these thoughts in mind, the following sections examine some ideas of how networks accommodate to a diverse environment wherein each application may exhibit different packet intervals and different packet arrival rates. ATM will be used as the model for these discussions, so the term "cell" is used in place of packet.

QUEUE MANAGEMENT OPERATIONS

Figure 2–7 depicts the traffic flows that a node might receive (assuming the machine is truly a multiapplication node, and capable of multiplexing the input streams into the output stream). Regardless of the capacity of the network, the aggregate transfer rates of all the input lines n (ingress) must not exceed the transfer rate of the output line m (egress)—at least not for a prolonged period. Notwithstanding, some buffering of traffic at the node allows n to exceed m for a brief time.

Each queue must be serviced by the multiplexer in a fair and equitable manner. Proper queue service operations should result in appropriate delays and acceptable traffic losses vis-à-vis the application. As examples:

    (a) *Constant bit rate (CBR)* queues should be serviced often enough to keep the queue depth shallow. Examples of CBR traffic are real-time video conferences.

    (b) *Variable bit rate (VBR)* comes in two flavors: (a) variable bit rate–real time (VBR–rt), and (b) variable bit rate–nonreal time (VBR–nrt). Voice queues (VBR–rt) should not allow the loss of

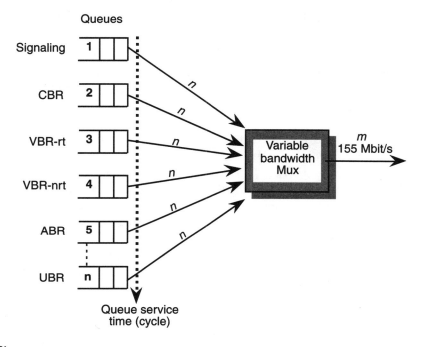

Figure 2–7 Allocating bandwidth using multiple queues

traffic to exceed 1–10% of the samples (the range depends on how traffic is dropped), and the queue depth should be shallow enough to avoid lengthy queue processing. VBR–nrt has less stringent queue depth and timing requirements, for example, bulk video need not have the same timing requirements as real-time video.

(c) *Data queues* also come in two flavors: (a) available bit rate (ABR) and (b) unspecified bit rate (UBR). ABR traffic is given at least a minimum bandwidth to keep the applications running, but this traffic will not preempt CBR, VBR–rt, and VBR–nrt traffic. Additionally, ABR traffic will have a feedback mechanism applied in order to control packet emission into the network. An example of ABR traffic is LAN-to-LAN flows, which are very bursty and volatile. UBR traffic is the lowest priority and receives bandwidth if it is available after the other flows have been serviced.

(d) *Signaling queues* contain control information, such as feedbacks and alarms and should receive the highest consideration of any of the other queues.

As Figure 2–7 shows, the queues may be serviced on a cyclical basis (the queue service cycle). Each queue is examined; payload is extracted and transported through the 155 Mbit/s output link. The next queue is examined, payload is extracted, and so on, until the last queue is examined and the process starts over again on the first queue.

A better approach is to use different service cycles for the high-priority and low-priority traffic in order to service the delay-sensitive traffic more often than the nondelay-sensitive traffic.

The manner in which the queues are set up (how many, how deep, and how often they are serviced) is not defined in the ATM (or any other) specifications. For example, separate queues may be established for each voice and video connection.

The service cycle must assure that delay-sensitive traffic (CBR and VBR–rt) is serviced frequently, let's say within 1–2 ms.[4] Given this requirement, let us assume a cycle time of 1.5 ms, which translates to 666.6 service cycles per second (1 sec/.0015 = 666.6). Further, assume that the 155.52 output link can accept 353,207 cells per second [155,520,000 (less overhead of the 155.52 Mbit/s frame yields a rate of 149.760 Mbit/s)/ 424 bits in a 53 octet cell = 353,207]. Therefore, this configuration can service 529 cells per service cycle (353,207 / 666.6 = 529).

Figure 2–8 shows that all queues are serviced during the service cycle. The multiplexer may adjust to the changes in the number of connections and the resultant queues, and it may vary the service times on the queues accordingly. If the mux reacts in this way, it must be able to add/delete queues (or entries in the queues) and adjust its queue extractions accordingly.

The example is based on the use of a SONET STS-3c 155.52 Mbit/s link. Other links with different bit rates obviously affect the value of the cells per service cycle. For example, if the output link were a 44.736 DS3

---

[4]The 1–2 ms value is chosen as an example. The value will depend on the speed of queue servicing, speed of the processors at the switch, queue depth, and delay at other nodes.

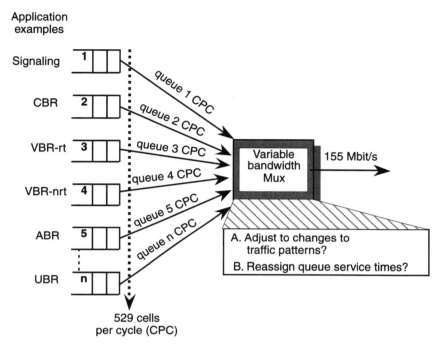

Figure 2–8 Servicing the queues

link, the cells could use 40.704 Mbit/s of this capacity—the other bits are overhead. Therefore, 40,704,000 / 424 = 96,000 for the number of cells that can be transported per second across the DS3 link. This configuration supports 144 cells per service cycle (96,000 / 666.6 = 144).

The task now is to determine which queues are to have their cells withdrawn during the service cycle, and at what rate the cells will be withdrawn from the queues. The general strategy is:

- The signaling queue is given the highest priority and should experience as little delay as possible and experience no loss.
- Delay-sensitive queues are serviced next (CBR and VBT-rt). The cells are in the queues for T_1 ms, or until these queues are empty.
- Next, delay-insensitive queues (VBR–nrt and ABR) are serviced for T_2 ms.
- In the absence of traffic in high-priority queues, the other queues can be serviced more frequently, and the UBR queues are given some bandwidth.

- When the signaling queue is serviced, either T1 or T2 are suspended, and resumed (not restarted) when this queue service is finished.

[SRIR93][5] defines three equations for computing the parameters to be used for servicing the queues.

The first equation assures queue$_i$ that a fraction f_i of the output link bandwidth is available:

$$f_i = \frac{T_i}{\sum\limits_{i=0}^{n} T_i}, \ 0 \le i \le n,$$

The second equation assures that all the bandwidth assigned to all queues cannot exceed a fraction of $(1 - f_o)$ for the output link capacity:

$$\sum_{i=0}^{n} f_i \le 1 - f_0$$

The third equation shows that the cycle time for all queues should be from 1–2 ms, in order to guarantee consistent service to delay-sensitive traffic.

$$\sum_{i=0}^{n} T_i \le D_c ms (D_c \approx 1 \text{ to } 2 \text{ ms}),$$

Where: n is number of queues; f_n is a fraction of the bandwidth of the output link; T_n is the time parameter for servicing the queue n; $D_c = M_c$ is the service cycle time; M_c is the number of cells withdrawn from the queue during the service cycle time.

You may wish to follow up on this general discussion by pursuing the references and sources cited in this section. K. Sriram's ongoing work [SRIR93] is especially recommended.

Figure 2–9 shows a common approach to managing time-sensitive and time-insensitive traffic and builds on the concepts discussed in the previous examples. This specific example is from [MODA97].[6]

Two types of queue service algorithms are used in this example. The exhaustive round robin algorithm (ERR) services the highest-priority queue and clears the cells in the queue before proceeding to the next

---

[5][SRIR93] Sriram, K. "Methodologies for Bandwidth Allocation, Transmission Scheduling, and Congestion Avoidance in Broadband ATM Networks, Computer Networks and ISDN Systems," 26(1), September, 1993.

[6][MODA97] Modarres, Houman, "Here Comes UBR+," *Telephony*, October 6, 1997.

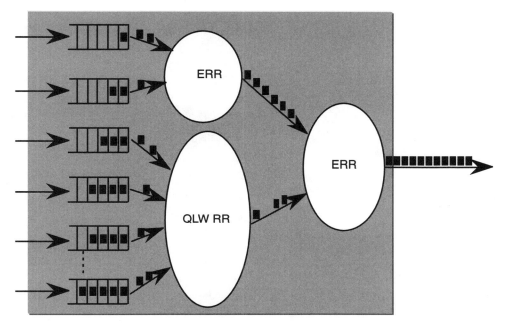

Where:
   ERR   Exhaustive round robin
   QLW RR Queue length-weighted round robin

Figure 2–9 Queue service procedure (weighted fair queuing)

highest priority queue. In addition, it overrides the servicing of any lower-priority queue if cells arrive at a higher-priority queue.

The queue length-weighted round robin algorithm (QLR RR) is used on nonreal-time queues. The servicing of these queues is based on the type of traffic and how many cells are stored in the queue. All traffic then is serviced by another ERR algorithm. Studies show that this approach is quite effective for supporting multiapplication systems (assuming the network machine has adequate CPU horsepower and enough buffer space for the queues).

The concepts shown here vary, and a number of algorithms have been published to support this concept. The important aspect of this idea is that certain time-sensitive traffic is given "more weight" in receiving bandwidth than nontime-sensitive traffic. The specific algorithms are discussed in later chapters.

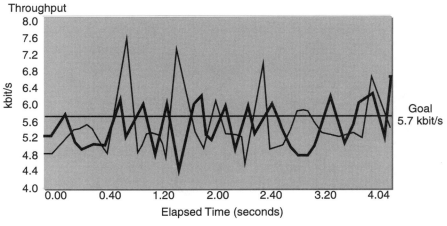

(a) No Weighted Fair Queuing

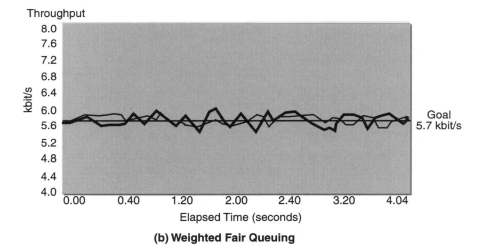

(b) Weighted Fair Queuing

Figure 2–10   Comparison of no weighted fair queuing and weighted fair queuing [McCU99]

Figure 2–10 compares the use (and nonuse) of a weighted fair queuing procedure [McCU99].[7] This study tested two G.723 voice transmissions running across a 64 kbit/s link. In addition, a TCP file transfer application's traffic was also placed on the link, sharing bandwidth with

---

[7][McCU99] McCullough, Daniel J, and Walker, John Q. "Interested in VOIP? How to Proceed," *Business Communications Review*, Voice 2000, April, 1999.

the two voice transmissions. The charts in Figure 2–10 compare the use and nonuse of the procedure.

To make the charts easier to study, they are drawn representing one voice session with a thin line, and the other voice session with a thicker line. The voice sessions ran on UDP in both directions. The figures do not show two other lines representing the flow of the two voice calls in the other direction.

Figure 2–10(a) shows the performance of the two voice sessions (the TCP session is not shown) without the use of weighted fair queuing. The goal was to achieve an average throughput of 5.7 kbit/s. While this goal was met, the variation in throughput varied by large amounts. Over a four-minute period, the authors state that the two conversations experienced almost a 50 percent throughput variation during a four-minute measurement period.

Figure 2–10(b) shows the results of the same traffic mix. There were no changes to the flows, except the enabling of a weighted fair queuing procedure. No other protocols were involved (no RSVP, for example). For this test, the authors report that there was a throughput variation of less than 10 percent.

The test was between two user computers, with two routers in between these user devices. While the test does validate the efficacy of weighted queues, keep in mind that in a larger network, with more router hops (and thus more variable delay), the results will not be this good. There may still be a need for the use of a reservation protocol to guarantee a QOS level.

OPERATIONS AT THE FINAL DESTINATION

Traffic management operations occur not only at the source UNI but at the end-user destination node itself, and possibly, the destination UNI switch. The manner in which traffic management is implemented depends on the type of traffic. Assuming that the traffic has been granted admission at the source UNI into the network, upon its arrival at the destination, further traffic management decisions must be made on how to "play out" the traffic to the user application.

As Figure 2–11 shows, different types of traffic must be handled in different ways. The traffic with high-bandwidth requirements that is delay-sensitive is buffered at the receiver if the traffic arrives sooner than a predetermined time. If it arrives after this time, it is discarded. Delay sensitive, high-bandwidth traffic is handled depending on the spe-

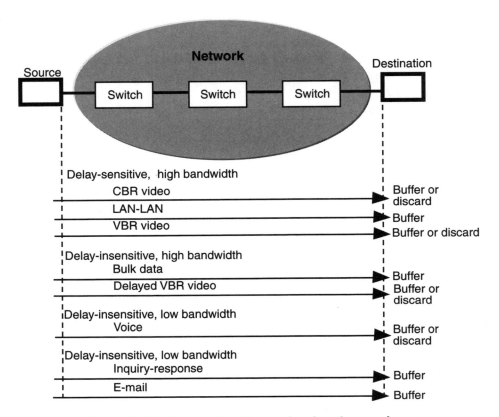

Figure 2–11 Processing the payload at the receiver

cific kind of traffic. For example, LAN-to-LAN traffic would be buffered, whereas variable bit-rate video would be buffered if the traffic arrives early and discarded if the traffic arrives late.

Delay-insensitive, high-bandwidth–type traffic, again is handled differently depending on the specific subtype. Bulk data traffic is buffered and delayed. VBR video traffic (video that must be delivered at a later time) is handled like any type of VBR video traffic which, if it is early it is buffered but if it arrives late it is discarded.

Other traffic is delay insensitive, of high or low bandwidth. This traffic is handled differently for voice than for data. As the reader might now expect, early-arriving voice packets are buffered until a play-out time is reached and then late-arriving packets are discarded.

In essence, any type of traffic involving data is buffered and held in the buffer for quite some time to prevent discarding it. In contrast, video and voice will be discarded if it arrives too late and perhaps buffered (to meet a standard arrival time) if it arrives too early.

Actually, if voice or video packets arrive too early, they can create buffering problems. Therefore, the task is even more complex; the voice or video packet should not arrive too early nor too late.

BUFFER SIZE, PACKET SIZE, AND TRAFFIC LOSS

The QOS administrator in an enterprise must pay attention to buffer sizes, packet sizes, and the packet loss rate. To explain these ideas, we will use a voice application wherein two people are engaged in a conversation over a QOS domain. As Figure 2–12 suggests, the larger the packet loss, the worse the audio quality. Large packet sizes increase the delay in most situations. If the packet size is too long, it will take an excessive amount of time for the traffic to be put on the wire, especially if the link is operating at a low bit rate.

A larger buffer will increase delay, but decrease the loss rate, because the larger buffer allows more flexibility in play-out, and the machine does not have to discard as many packets. Obviously, a larger

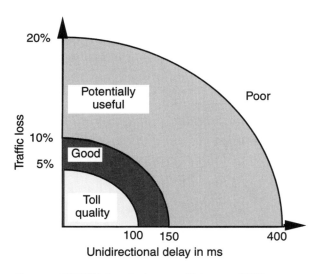

Source: IEEE Network, January/February 1998

Figure 2–12 Delay, traffic loss, buffer, and packet sizes

buffer also translates into a longer and more variable service cycle to service the buffer. Ideally, real-time traffic buffers should be shallow.

But the continued decrease of the buffer size, while decreasing delay, means more packets may be discarded. In effect, as the buffer size approaches 0, the machine operates at wire speed. Obviously, trade-offs are necessary with regard to these factors.

DATA "IN FLIGHT"

Any high-bandwidth network must deal with links that operate at very high transmission rates. Figure 2–13 illustrates the challenge. The one-way propagation delay of a link (with no intervening delay) across the United States is about 20 ms. A T1 network operating at 1.544 Mbit/s

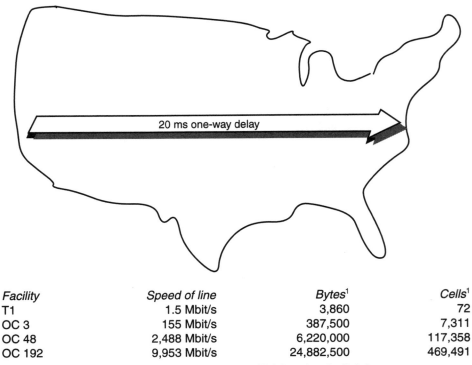

Facility	Speed of line	Bytes[1]	Cells[1]
T1	1.5 Mbit/s	3,860	72
OC 3	155 Mbit/s	387,500	7,311
OC 48	2,488 Mbit/s	6,220,000	117,358
OC 192	9,953 Mbit/s	24,882,500	469,491

[1]Figures assume full bandwidth is available (no T1/OC headers in flight)

Figure 2–13 Data in flight at high speeds

would have 3860 bytes in flight (that is, in the network) during this 20-ms interval, or about 72 cells. This load is not a big problem.[8]

However, with broadband networks operating at higher speeds, the network could have millions of bytes and thousands of cells in flight. For example, in an OC-192 network that carries ATM cell traffic, there could be 24,883,200 bytes and 469,494 cells in flight!

Problems such as link failure or congestion are intensified in these high-speed networks. Consequently, and as we learned earlier, the network must have the ability to perform preventive measures to avoid congestion, and implement mechanisms for rapid dissemination of control information about problems and potential problems. The advanced networks in operation today do just that. They have preventive congestion control mechanisms, and most disseminate control information at link propagation speeds.

ERROR RECOVERY IN HIGH-SPEED NETWORKS

The amount of data in flight in high-speed networks makes it prohibitive to perform retransmissions of corrupted packets. Such a practice would require the sending switch to hold in its buffer copies of all the packets that have not been acknowledged. In the previous example, an OC-48 node would have to have a buffer depth sufficient to hold all the packets until they are acknowledged by the receiving node (the packets, encapsulated into 117,358 cells). Since the acknowledgment that is returned back to the sender also experiences the one-way delay, the sending node has to have a buffer depth twice the one-way delay (234,716 cells): Nice work if you can get it (and sell memory chips). Consequently, modern data communications networks make no attempt to perform retransmissions. These operations are "pushed out of the network" to the user nodes (perhaps a router at a customer site, or more often TCP in the user's computer). Figure 2–14 shows this approach.

In Figure 2–14(a) ACKs are performed at the transport layer (layer 4, with TCP), typically in the user workstation. This ACK is shown in event 6

---

[8]These calculations assume the link has no overhead but the ATM cell header. For the OC n links, about 20 percent of the bandwidth is used for overhead, so the reader can reduce these figures by this amount if SONET is carrying the ATM cells in its envelope.

The figures are based on a simple calculation. Using T1 as the example: 1,544,000 × .02 (sec.)/ 8 (bits per byte) = <u>3860</u> (bytes) / 53 (bytes per cell) = <u>72</u>.8 ATM cells.

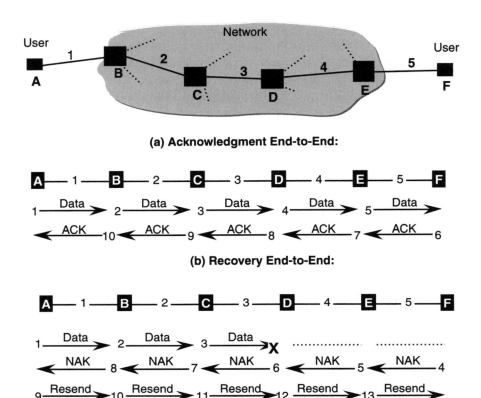

Figure 2–14 End-to-end operations

in Figure 2–14(a). Events 1–5 and 6–10 in Figure 2–14(a) show that the data and the ACK are sent across each link.

In most modern systems, an error check is performed by each data link layer at each node. In Figure 2–14(b), at Switch D, an error is detected in event 3. Switch D takes no other action except to discard the damaged packet, symbolized by the X in event 3. The dotted lines in Figure 2–14(b) symbolize that the traffic is not sent onto the other links and is not received by user F.

It should also be noted that Switch D may not have encountered an actual error. It may have simply discarded traffic because it is experiencing congestion.

Recovery from this error can occur in a number of ways. If other packets are being sent to user F, the transport layer in the user node will note that traffic is arriving out-of-sequence, since the discarded packet is not received by F, and subsequent packets are out of order. Therefore, in event 4, a layer 4 negative acknowledgment (NAK) is sent from user F to user A, which has stored copies of the packets in a transport layer buffer. The transport layer at A will resend the traffic to F, as shown in event 9 in Figure 2–14(b).

Unfortunately, the loss of traffic, whether through a error, or due to traffic discards in the face of congestion often exacerbates the problem. The transport layer keeps trying to recover by resending the erred or missing packets. And the network keeps discarding the packets.

Fortunately, the transport layer is smart enough to back off and reduce its sending rate when these types of problems occur. The drawback to transport layer recovery is that it may take too long. Moreover, if thousands of connections are using the same procedure, the situation can get out-of-hand.

But, we learned another approach is to monitor the traffic at the UNI (in this example, between A and B) and take remedial action more quickly at a lower layer with the ECN procedure. This approach is especially useful for data traffic that has no QOS guarantees with the network. It is also an important tool in high-speed networks where huge quantities of traffic are flowing through the UNIs and the network nodes. Fast reactions to potential congestion problems is essential to maintain acceptable network performance and to meet the users' QOS needs.

MONITORING AND TRAFFIC TAGGING

We now know that one idea behind many QOS operations is to control the customers' traffic before it enters the network. The control procedures are placed at the user-to-network interface, (UNI), which is the interface between the customer's equipment (the user node) and the provider's equipment (the provider's switch). Figure 2–15 shows this arrangement.

The control procedures may require traffic shaping, wherein the packets are delayed in order to prevent congestion in the network, and/or to adhere to the SLA.

The monitoring operations can lead the service provider to actually deny service to the customer, if the customer is violating its SLA, or if the provider's network is experiencing congestion problems. Alternately, the customer's traffic may be "tagged" (marked) to indicate that the traffic is nonconforming to the SLA. In this situation, the packets may be allowed to enter the network, but they are given a lesser QOS level than

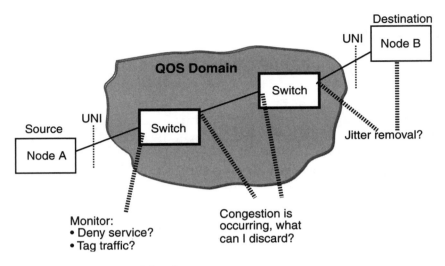

Where: UNI = User-to-network interface

Figure 2–15 Monitoring and traffic tagging

the nontagged packets. Furthermore, in the event that a switch begins to encounter congestion problems, the tagged traffic is the most likely candidate for discarding.

At the egress point in the QOS domain, where the packets are to be presented to the receiving user (Node B), the egress switch may also perform traffic shaping for delay-sensitive traffic. For example, assume the ingress UNI SLA ensures the packets enter the domain with no jitter, but as the packets traverse the network, the ongoing buffering and queuing operations introduce jitter.

It may also be incumbent upon the last switch in the path to perform jitter-removal operations on the packet flow. Also, if the packets are tagged, this final switch is permitted to shed traffic. And as just stated, jitter removal may be performed at the destination end user (node B in this example).

ASSOCIATING LABELS WITH QOS OPERATIONS

The concept of a label is used in many QOS-based systems. The label is also called a tag, a flow label, a codepoint, and a virtual circuit ID (for the latter term, ATM, X.25, and Frame Relay apply). The label is contained in the packet header and is used to identify the packet, to distinguish it from packets associated with other applications and other transmission flows.

Labels are assigned to the packets in a variety of ways. One approach is to place a label value in the packet at the source, and use this label thereafter to identify the packet, and to make decisions about how the packet is treated with regard to providing QOS support. In most implementations, the label value is changed at each node as the packet is transported from the source to the destination. This operation is called label swapping, label mapping, or label marking.

The labels are managed by each node with the use of a label switching (LS) table. Figure 2–16 shows the entries in the LS tables for one path between users XYZ and HIJ. For this discussion, the path is identified with:

- Label 21:   Identifies the path between user XYZ and switch A
  - a: is the output interface at XYZ
  - b: is the input interface at switch A
- Label 30:   Identifies the path between switch A and switch B
  - d: is the output interface at switch A
  - a: is the input interface at switch B

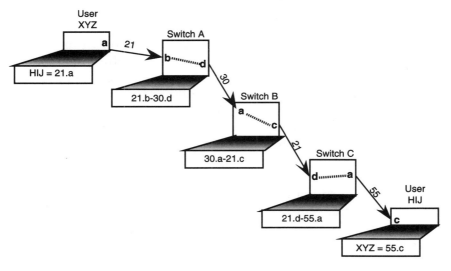

Figure 2–16 Example of label operations

- Label 21: Identifies the path between switch B and switch C
    - c: is the output interface at switch B
    - d: is the input interface at switch C
- Label 55: Identifies the path between switch C and user HIJ
    - a: is the output interface at switch C
    - c: is the input interface at HIJ

Several observations are noteworthy about Figure 2–16. First, there must be some means to associate the labels with the QOS, and the addresses of the switches that participate in the operation. Second, the association must be made at each machine that participates in the end-to-end traffic flow.

Third, in this example, the label is correlated with the sender's outgoing interface and the receiver's incoming interface, and stored in a switching (cross-connect) table, also shown in Figure 2–16. Since the labels associate in this way, they can be reused at each interface on the switches or user machines. In a sense, the interface numbers in the switch act as <u>internal</u> identifiers for the connection.

We have learned that the label is used for forwarding operations—to determine how to relay the packet to a next node. We also learned that it is used to determine the services that will be provided to the packet during its journey through the network. Thus, the label is associated with the packet's QOS support.

Figure 2–17 shows how two packets are processed at a switch. The packets, identifed with labels 30 and 70, are sent to the switch's interface a from an upstream node (say, the user node, not shown in this figure). The labels are then used to access the label switching table. The two table entries for labels 30 and 70 are shown at the bottom of the figure.

Each table entry contains the label number and the associated ingress interface number: 30.a and 70.a for these two packets. This information is associated with the profile conformance entries, which are used to monitor the flow associated with each of these packets. These profile examples are usually relevant to the first switch in the QOS domain; that is, at the user-to-network interface (UNI). They determinine if the packet flow is conforming or nonconforming to the SLA. The profile for flow 30 is a burst tolerance (BT) of 210 packets per second (210 p/s); the profile for flow 70 is a packet delay variation (PDV) of no greater than 1 microsecond.

The service-level entries in the tables also reveal how the packet is to be treated if the traffic for the flow adheres to its SLA. This example

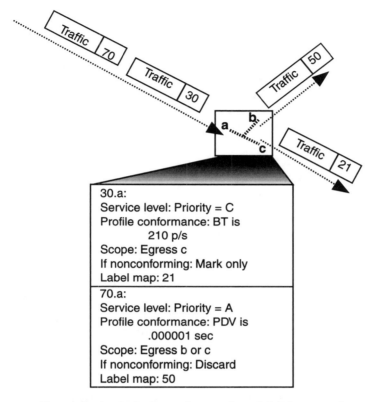

Figure 2–17 Labels and associated QOS operations

uses priorities to differentiate the treatments. Priority = C is for asynchronous traffic of a high priority, and priority = A identifies synchronous, real-time traffic. The priorities in the example are relative; priority C is high, but not as high as A.

Another entry in the table is the scope of service, shown as "Scope" in the figure. The service for these two packets is scoped to the switch's egress interfaces. If the services for these packets are end-to-end, perhaps through multiple QOS domains, the ingress and egress must be provisioned at each node that resides in the QOS region. Therefore, we can assume in this example that these egress ports have been provisioned with an end-to-end path in mind. Notice that packet 70 is scoped to two egress interfaces b and c. This approach enables the packet to be routed to the link that is experiencing better performance.

Another entry in the table reflects the operations that are to be performed on the packet if its flow is nonconforming to the SLA conformance profile. Packet 30 will be marked (tagged) if it is nonconforming. The term "Mark only" means the packet is not to be discarded (unless the switch is in a precipitous situation). The tag will relegate the service on the packet flow to a lesser quality of service. Packet 70 belongs to a synchronous real-time flow, so if it is nonconforming, it is discarded.

The last entry in the tables is the label that is placed in the packet header for transmittal out the egress interface to the next node. Label 30 is mapped to label 21, and label 70 is mapped to label 50.

CONTROLLING DATA TRAFFIC

Many data protocols use the concept of transmit and receive windows to aid in data flow management operations. The concept is a rather involved process and is discussed in some detail in this section. As shown in Figure 2–18, a window (also called a credit in earlier discussions in this chapter) is established for each user session to provide a reservation of resources at both stations for the user traffic. These "windows" are the reservation of buffer space at the receiver for the arriving packets. In most systems, the window defines both buffer space and sequencing rules.

During the initiation of a session handshake, the window is established. For example, if protocols A and B are to communicate with each other, protocol A reserves a receive window for B, and B reserves a receive window for A. The windowing concept is necessary for full-duplex

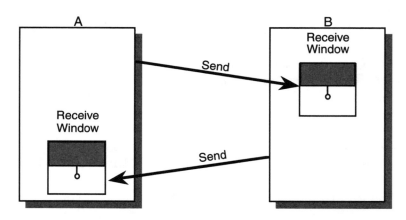

Figure 2–18 Sliding windows for flow control

protocols because they entail a continuous flow of packets to the receiving protocol without any intermittent stop-and-wait acknowledgments. Consequently, the receiver must have a sufficient allocation of memory to handle the continuous incoming traffic.

The windows at the transmitting and receiving protocols are controlled by *state variables and sequence numbers*. Table 2–3 should be used during this discussion. The transmitting protocol maintains a send state variable [V(S)]. It is the sequence number of the next packet to be transmitted.

The receiving protocol maintains a receive state variable [V(R)] which contains the number that is expected to be in the send sequence number N(S) of the next received packet. At the sending protocol, the V(S) is incremented with each packet transmitted and placed in the send sequence field [N(S)] in the packet.

Upon receiving the packet, the receiving protocol checks for a transmission error. It also compares the send sequence number N(S) in the packet with its V(R). If the packet is acceptable and N(S) = V(R), the receiver increments V(R) by one, places it into a receive sequence number field N(R) in an acknowledgment (ACK) packet and sends it to the transmitting protocol.

If an error is detected or if the V(R) does not match the sending sequence number N(S) in the packet, a NAK (negative acknowledgment) with the receiving sequence number N(R) containing the value of V(R) is sent to the transmitter. This N(R) NAK value in the packet informs the transmitter of the next packet that it is expected to send. The transmitter must then reset its V(S) and retransmits the packet whose sequence number matches the value of NAK N(R).

Table 2–3 State Variables and Sequence Numbers

N(S) sequence number:
  Sequence number of transmitted packet
N(R) sequence number:
  Sequence number for acknowledged packets
V(S) variable:
  Value of next packet to be transmitted
  Placed in N(S) field in the next packet
V(R) variable:
  Expected value of N(S) in the next packet received
  Placed in N(R) field in the transmitted packet

Note: These values may be used at the data link, or at the transport layer.

A useful feature of the sliding window scheme is the ability of the receiving protocol to restrict the flow of data from the transmitting protocol by withholding the acknowledgment packets. This action prevents the transmitter from opening its window and reusing its send sequence number values until the same send sequence numbers have been acknowledged. A sender can be completely "throttled" if it receives no ACKs from the receiver.

Many sliding window protocols use the numbers of 0 through 127 for the state variables and the sequence numbers in the packet. Once the state variables are incremented through 127, the numbers are reused, beginning with 0. Because the numbers are reused, the protocols must not be allowed to send a packet with a sequence number that has not yet been acknowledged. For example, the sender must wait for packet number 6 to be acknowledged before it uses a value of 6 again.

Figure 2–19 depicts two packets being transmitted from protocol A to protocol B. This example assumes the transmit window is 7.

The notations in the figure mean the following:

- TLWE: The transmit lower window edge (TLWE) denotes the last packet sent and acknowledged (packet 0) and the smallest numbered packet that has been sent and not acknowledged (packet 1).

- TUWE: The transmit upper window edge (TUWE) denotes the last packet transmitted (packet 2) and the next packet to be sent (packet 3). This latter value of 3 is the value of the V(S).

- RLWE: The receive lower window edge (RLWE) denotes the last packet received and acknowledged (packet 0) and the smallest numbered packet that has been received and not acknowledged (packet 1).

- RUWE: The receive upper window edge (RUWE) denotes the last packet to be received (packet 2) and the next expected packet (packet 3). This latter value of 3 is the value of the V(R).

The bottom part of Figure 2–19 shows these operations with the wraparound counter concept. It is easy to visualize that the TUWE cannot overrun the TLWE because two or more packets with the same N(S) would arrive at the receiver, resulting in the corruption of B's receive window operations.

In Figure 2–20, protocol B has returned an acknowledgment to protocol A with N(R) = 2. This acknowledgment means all packets up to and including N(S) = 1 are acknowledged and packet 2 is expected next.

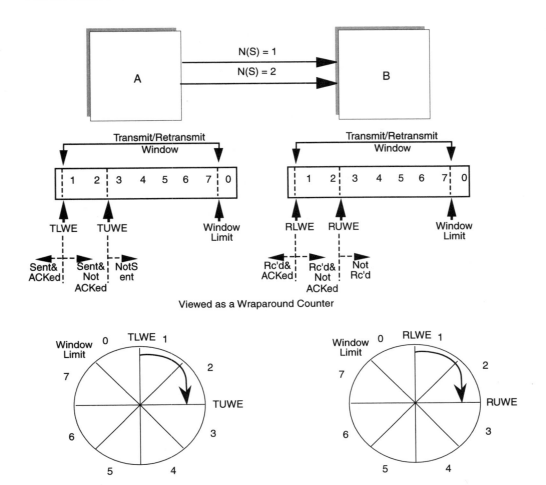

Figure 2–19 Effect of sending two packets

Notice the effect at A of the receipt of this packet. It "slides" its TLWE forward to reflect that packet 1 is acknowledged. Protocol B has also performed the operations on its receive window. Notice also the effect of the wraparound counter at the bottom of the figure.

Now, examine how the window slides at A and B. The window limit (TUWE and RUWE at A and B repsectively) has been increased by 1, due to the ACK enabling the reuse of sequence number 0.

Why did B not acknowledge packet 2 with an N(R) = 3? Typically, in a full duplex environment, B has not had the opportunity to (a) receive

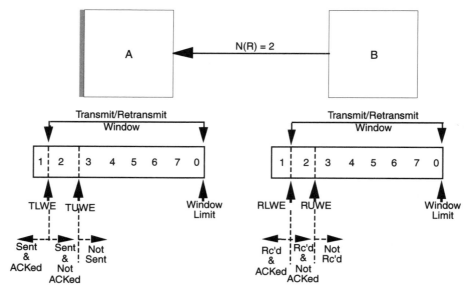

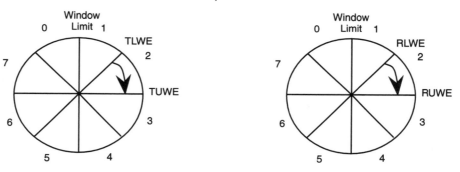

Figure 2–20 Effect of an acknowledgment

N(S) = 2 or (b) has not had the opportunity to process and error-check the packet.

In Figure 2–21, protocol A has sent protocol B four more packets numbered as N(S) = 3, 4, 5, and 6. The transmit and receive windows are updated to indicate that protocol A is permitted to send two more packets (packet 7 and packet 0) before the windows are closed. Remember that packets 2, 3, 4, 5, and 6 are not yet acknowledged. Therefore, with a window limit of 7, two more packets can be sent.

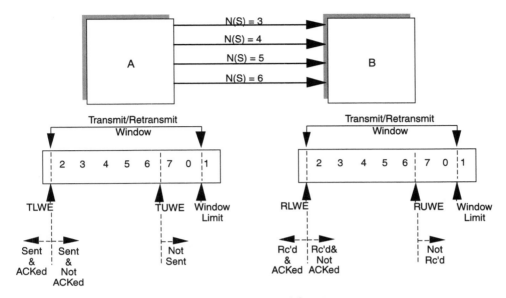

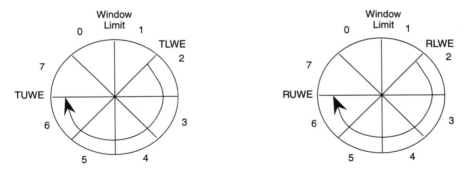

Figure 2–21 Sending more packets

In Figure 2–22, protocol B returns an ACK of 7, which inclusively acknowledges all packets up to and including 6. Since packet 6 was the last packet that was outstanding, protocol A now has a transmit window of 7, and will use the sequence numbers in this order: 7–0–1–2–3–4–5.

One last point should be made about these operations. Some protocols do not use *just* the acknowledgment number for window control. TCP is an example. It has a separate number carried in the TCP packet which increases or decreases the sender's send window. To illustrate, let's sup-

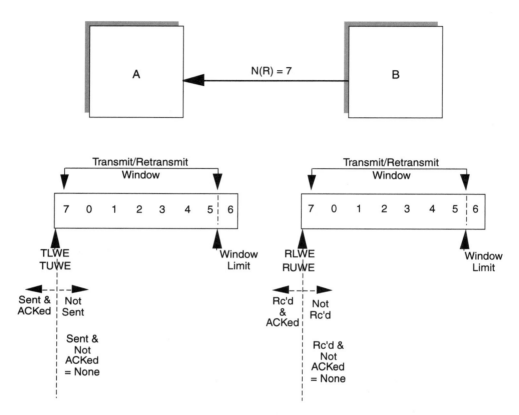

Figure 2–22 ACKing all traffic

pose B returns a packet to A. The packet contains an acknowledgment field = 3 and a send window field = 6. The acknowledgment field simply acknowledges previous traffic. Used alone, it does not increase, decrease, open, nor close A's window. Window management is the job of the send window field. Its value of 6 states that A is allowed to send packets based on this value of 6 *plus* the acknowledgment value. Hereafter, the window limit is 9, because 3 + 6 = 9.

It is possible that the credit for the window could have been reduced by B. Thus, the send window field permits the window to be expanded and contracted as necessary to manage buffer space and processing. This approach is a more flexible one than using the ACK N(R) field for both the acknowledgment of traffic and the window control operations.

SUMMARY

The management of traffic to prevent congestion is a vital aspect of the QOS picture. Congestion translates into reduced throughput and increased delay, and it is the death knell of effective QOS. A number of tools are used to resolve this potential problem, including traffic monitoring and flow control measures. These flow control measures vary, and most implement some form of explicit congestion notification (ECN), often with credits to increase or reduce a transmit window size.

For data traffic, payload integrity services can be invoked to protect the customer's transmissions. This service is implemented with the tried-and-true retransmission scheme and the sliding window procedure.

3

QOS Evolution

T his chapter continues the discussion begun in Chapter 2, and introduces other basic QOS concepts. It also provides an historical perspective of the subject by explaining the origins of QOS. The chapter introduces several new QOS concepts, with emphasis on payload integrity management. The virtual circuit concept is explained as well. The evolution from circuit switching, packet switching, frame switching, and cell switching is also a topic of this chapter.

Previous chapters have used the term "packet" as a generic term to describe a discrete piece of traffic on the network. In this chapter, we use the term in a more concise manner.

NETWORK INTERFACES (REFERENCE POINTS)

Modern communications networks are organized around two or three basic sets of protocols: (a) the protocol that governs the interface between the user and the network, (b) the protocol that governs the interface between networks, and less frequently, (c) the protocol that gov-

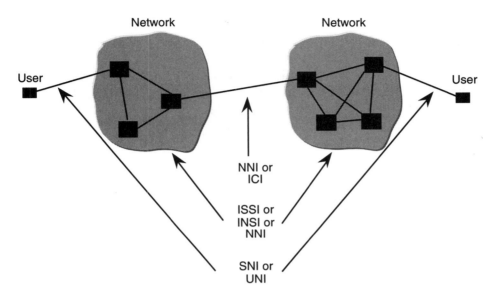

Figure 3–1   Key interfaces (Reference points)

Where:

NNI	= Network to network (or network node) interface
ICI	= Inter-exchange carrier interface
ISSI	= Inter-switching system interface
INSI	= Intra-network switching interface
SNI	= Subscriber network interface
UNI	= User network interface

erns the operations within a network. These interfaces are shown in Figure 3–1, as well as the common terms associated with the interfaces.[1]

The initial thrust of most of the interface definitions during the past 25 years in the industry has been on the interface between the user and the network (the user-to-network/subscriber-network interface [UNI/SNI]). However, the network-to-network interface (NNI) is also quite important, because many organizations that need to communicate with each other are connected through different networks. Therefore, many systems have defined this interface as well. Historically, the operations within a data network have been proprietary and specific to a ven-

---

[1]The reader may also know these interfaces by the term reference point. Some systems use this term. As examples, ISDN and GSM use "reference points" instead of "interfaces."

dor's implementation. This situation is changing, although many internal operations still remain proprietary and are not standardized.

Be aware that the initials NNI can refer to (a) network-to-network interface as well as (b) the network-node interface. Also, the ISSI and INSI terms are not used much; you may encounter them if you are working with the Switched Multi-megabit Data Service (SMDS). Finally be aware that some vendors will use the terms UNI and SNI to mean slightly different interfaces, so check your specifications carefully.

Some protocols do not distinguish their operations with regard to these interfaces. For example, the IP specification does not discuss UNIs or NNIs. Whereas, X.25, Frame Relay, and ATM clearly distinguish these interfaces by defining in considerable detail how traffic is exchanged across these interfaces.

Value of the Interface Concept

The interface (or reference point) idea is a very useful concept, and is employed by many networks in place today. Since it is used to define the protocols and specific types of traffic that are exchanged between two or more machines operating on each side of the interface, it serves as a standardization tool. For example, Frame Relay defines the rules for negotiating several QOS features at a UNI between the user and the network. It also defines the QOS negotiation rules for the NNI between two networks. As a result, guidance is provided to vendors and manufacturers about how to design their products so they will interwork with other products.

Evolution of the Interface/Reference Point Concept

The interface/reference point concept is relatively new, but then so is the computer network industry. I first encountered it in the early 1970s when I began working with X.25. As discussed in Chapter 1, *Genesis of QOS X.25,* this packet-based protocol restricts itself to the description of the UNI, but as X.25-based networks proliferated during the '70s and '80s, the ITU-T also published a network-to-network protocol, and named it X.75.

Frame Relay and ATM have taken similar approaches. They also define the UNI, as well as the network-to-network interface (NNI). However neither X.25 nor Frame Relay define the internal operations "inside the cloud"; that is, the network-node interface (also NNI). ATM does define this third interface.

THE QOS LAYERED MODEL

Whatever the implementation of the user applications at the user machine, the service provider network is not concerned with applications' operations for the ongoing processing of user traffic. Indeed, the network bearer service is "masked" from the application's functions. Figure 3–2 shows this relationship.

The bearer service includes the data link and physical layers of the OSI Model. They are somewhat application independent, and the end-

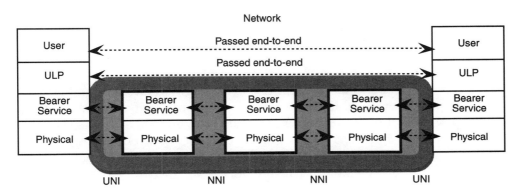

(a) For tranfer of user payload

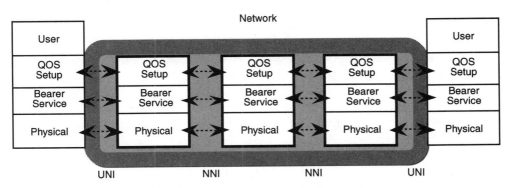

(b) For transfer of QOS provisioning traffic

Where:
  OAM   Operations, maintenance, and administration
  ULP   Upper layer protocols

Figure 3–2   Relationship of user and support layers

user devices are tasked with accommodating the requirements of different applications. Of course, if a network supports QOS features, then the network must have knowledge of the QOS requirements of the application, such as delay and throughput requirements.

However, the network need not interact directly with the application, nor have knowledge of what the application does (browsing, file transfer, etc.). Indeed, it is not a good idea to do so, because it would require the network (and each network switch) to execute the software modules of every application that uses the network.

For the transfer of the user payload, upper layer protocol (ULP) operations are not invoked in the network nodes. The dashed arrows in Figure 3–2(a) indicate that logical operations occur between peer layers at the user nodes and the network nodes. Therefore, the ULP headers and the user payload are passed transparently through the network.

The notation "QOS Setup" in Figure 3–2(b) indicates the operations that are invoked to support the customer's QOS requirements. These operations vary, depending upon the service provider's implementation, and the specific protocol used for QOS. For example, if QOS is to be provided by X.25, Frame Relay, or ATM, the setup entails either (a) the provisioning of the network nodes before the user presents traffic to the network, or (b) provisioning the network nodes when the user sends a connection request packet to the network. Setup (a) is called a permanent virtual circuit (PVC) , and setup (b) is called a switched virtual circuit (SVC), or connection on demand.

As another example, assume an IP-based network. In this situation the Resource Reservation Protocol (RSVP) may be invoked to set up and reserve the QOS resources for the user session.

Whatever the procedure may be, after the QOS is provisioned, ongoing traffic is exchanged as shown in Figure 3–2(a).

CONNECTION-ORIENTED AND CONNECTIONLESS INTERFACES

Most communications networks today are designed to operate as either connectionless or connection-oriented systems. As illustrated in Figure 3–3(a), a connection-oriented network is one in which no connection exists *initially* between the user device and the network (the common term, DTE, for data terminal equipment is used to describe a user device). The connection between the network and network user is in an idle state.

In order for the DTEs to communicate through a connection-oriented network, they must go through a handshake, also called a con-

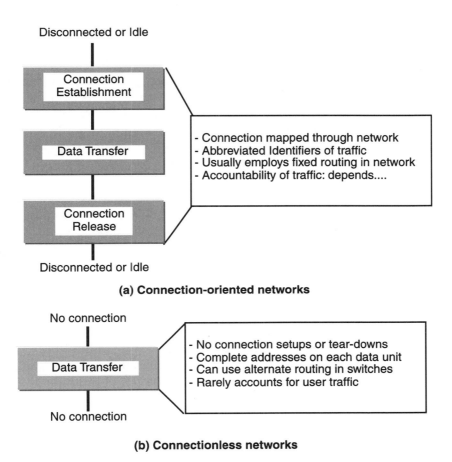

Disconnected or Idle

Connection Establishment

Data Transfer

- Connection mapped through network
- Abbreviated Identifiers of traffic
- Usually employs fixed routing in network
- Accountability of traffic: depends....

Connection Release

Disconnected or Idle

(a) Connection-oriented networks

No connection

Data Transfer

- No connection setups or tear-downs
- Complete addresses on each data unit
- Can use alternate routing in switches
- Rarely accounts for user traffic

No connection

(b) Connectionless networks

Figure 3–3   Connecting networks at the three interfaces

nection establishment. During this process, the users and the network may negotiate the QOS procedures that are to be used during the session. Once the connection is established, data are exchanged in accordance with the negotiations that occurred during the connection-establishment phase. Eventually, the DTEs perform a connection release, after which they return to the idle state.

The connection-oriented network usually provides a substantial amount of care for the signaling traffic. The procedure requires an acknowledgment from the network and the responding user that the connection is established; otherwise, the requesting DTE must be informed as to why the connection request was not successful. The network must also maintain an awareness of the DTE/DTE connection. Flow control (i.e., making certain that all the user packets arrive in order and do not saturate the user DTE) may be required of the network.

In the past, error checking and error recovery were performed by connection-oriented networks. They were designed to recover from lost traffic, misrouted traffic, and out-of-sequence traffic. However, the newer communications networks do not perform these functions. Therefore, if the user wishes to have these operations performed, they must be performed in the user DTE, typically in layer 4 by TCP. Figure 2–14 in Chapter 2 made this point.

The connectionless (also called datagram) network goes directly from an idle condition (the two DTEs are not connected to each other, or to the network) to the data transfer mode, followed later by the idle condition. See Figure 3–3(b). The major difference between this network and the connection-oriented network is the absence of the connection establishment and release phases. There are no state machines governing the behavior of the connectionless network (it is known as a stateless network). Moreover, a connectionless network (in most instances) performs no acknowledgments, flow control, or error recovery of the user's traffic.

One last point to be made here is that connection-oriented networks identify each user's traffic with a value placed in the header of the user's packet. This value is simply a number chosen from a table of numbers. They are managed so that they provide unambiguous identification of the user traffic. These values are known by a number of terms: virtual circuit IDs and labels are examples (introduced in Chapter 2).

For connectionless traffic, the identifiers are not arbitrarily chosen numbers, but specific addresses, that have some type of topological significance, such as a country id, an network id, a DTE id, etc. With these addresses, the connectionless network can easily be one that supports dynamic routing by using topologically significant addresses, in contrast to the connection-oriented network that tends to use static routing because of the nontopologically significant "labels."

QOS in Connection-oriented and Connectionless Networks

QOS features have been more prominent in connection-oriented networks than connectionless networks. Until recently, the design philosophy behind connectionless networks has been to implement a simple, robust, and low-cost service for bulk file transfers, and noninteractive email. In contrast, the connection-oriented approach was part of the public packet networks' architecture, and therefore subject to (potential) pricing, based on levels of service, and QOS facilities.

But the design philosophy of connectionless networks is changing. With the growth of Internet users, and the forthcoming thrust to price Internet services, QOS utilities also become important for connectionless networks.

CONNECTION MANAGEMENT VS. PAYLOAD INTEGRITY MANAGEMENT

Some people confuse connection management (in connection-oriented networks) with that of payload integrity management. They are completely separate from each other in how they operate in networks and at the network interfaces. This confusion exists because in the past, most connection-oriented protocols also provided payload integrity management with features such as ACKs and NAKs, and other features such as explicit and implicit flow control.

Notwithstanding, even though a system may offer a user connection-oriented services, these services do not imply that the network will be responsible for the user payload being delivered correctly through the network.

PAYLOAD INTEGRITY MANAGEMENT

Payload integrity management is one of the most important parts of QOS. The term describes the operations to ensure the user traffic is delivered correctly to its intended destination. The term "correctly" means:

- *Without bit errors:* Using forward error correction (FEC) schemes, correcting damaged bits, and/or resending damaged packets. Due to timing constraints, real-time traffic cannot use the resending operation.
- *In the proper sequence:* Using sequence numbers at the receiver to check for the proper ordering of the arriving packets, and/or forcing the sequencing by using fixed routing, and first-in-first-out queuing.
- *Within a window of time:* Using timestamps for real-time traffic to remove excessive jitter in the packet flow. This operation is not executed for data traffic.

This part of the chapter concentrates on the payload integrity operations for data traffic. This subject was introduced in Chapter 2, and you may wish to review the material pertaining to Figures 2–14, and 2–19 through 2–22.

For data applications, payload integrity management can be executed with three approaches:

- *On a link-by-link basis:* With each link between the communicating parties participating in the operation.
- *At the UNI:* With the user machine and the network node participating in the operation.
- *On an end-to-end basis:* With only the user end stations participating in the operation.

Evolution of Payload Integrity Services

The evolution of payload integrity services in the computer networks industry can be traced as follows:

- *Phase I:* Link-by-link operations
- *Phase II:* Link-by-link operations and UNI operations
- *Phase III:* Use of all three operations at the same time (link-by-link, UNI, and end-to-end)
- *Phase IV:* Elimination of link-by-link operations on high-speed links (see Chapter 2, Figure 2–13)
- *Phase V:* Elimination of UNI operations, resulting only in the use of end-end services.

Link-by-Link Operations

Figure 3–4 shows how payload integrity management is provided at the link level, wherein each node on a link performs operations to ensure the safe delivery of the traffic from node to the other.

In order to account for the user traffic, rather extensive operations may be performed on behalf of the user. For example, error checking can occur at each node where the traffic is received. The sender then is sent either an ACK or NAK by the receiving node. In effect, the system that provides traffic integrity requires that the user payload be sent from the source to the destination with assurance that it will arrive safely and correctly at that destination.

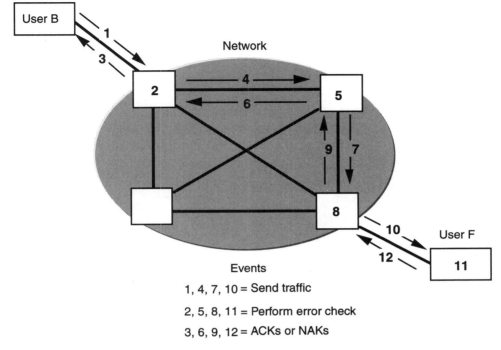

Figure 3–4   Payload integrity management: link level

Link-by-link operations were the first method used in the data communications industry in dealing with errors. They are still used and are quite important if transmissions are occurring on noisy links. For example, many wireless interfaces use link retransmissions. However, they are not used on high-speed links due to their overhead (once again, see Chapter 2, Figure 2–13).

UNI Operations

Some data communications systems provide for payload integrity management at the user-to-network interface (UNI). The prime example of this approach is the X.25 packet interface specification. In Figure 3–5, event 1 depicts the user sending packets to the network where they are checked with a layer 3 protocol. This protocol does not perform bit error checks but implements a routine to check for proper packet sequencing into the network. If the packets are sent to the network in the proper sequential order, the network acknowledges these packets by returning an

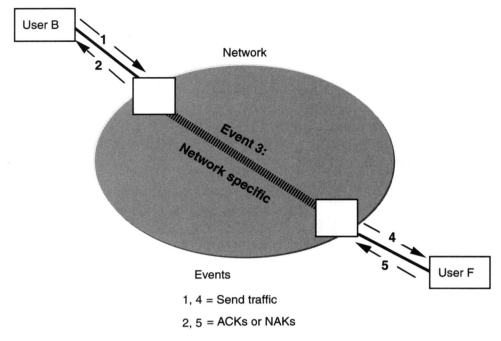

Events

1, 4 = Send traffic

2, 5 = ACKs or NAKs

Figure 3–5   Payload integrity management: network interface

ACK packet to user B as shown in event 2. Otherwise, the virtual circuit is reset (with the loss of packets).

In older UNIs (X.25), the ACK in event 2 also opens user B's transmit window. In newer UNIs (Frame Relay and ATM), transmit windows are managed with provisioned SLAs, congestion notification operations, and (optionally) sending control packets with credit values to open or close the window.

The operations depicted in event 3 in Figure 3–5 have traditionally not been defined in some data communications networks. Consequently, these operations vary depending on the network specific implementations. Some data networks implement event 3 by providing a wide array of network integrity management operations while others provide very few features. Finally, the operations just discussed in events 1 and 2 at the transmitting UNI are mirror images of the events 4 and 5 at the receiving UNI.

End-to-End Operations

Figure 3–6 shows yet another option for taking care of the user payload. It is called end-to-end traffic management because the end users are responsible for the operations. The figure shows two events occurring for this procedure. In event 1, user B sends traffic through the network to user F. In event 2, user F returns an acknowledgment of this traffic to user B. The operations in Figure 3–6 should look familiar to you; they are the same operations as in Figure 2–14, Chapter 2.

In the data communications systems that have evolved in the last 15 years, the operations shown in this figure are performed at layer 4 of the OSI Model, the transport layer. In most systems today, the protocol that provides these services is the Transmission Control Protocol (TCP).

The dashed arrows in this figure depict the traffic flowing through the network. This layer 4 traffic is carried through the network via the invocation of lower layer protocols. Generally speaking, the network and these lower layer protocols are not aware of the layer 4 operations. Their job is to pass the layer 4 traffic safely between users B and F.

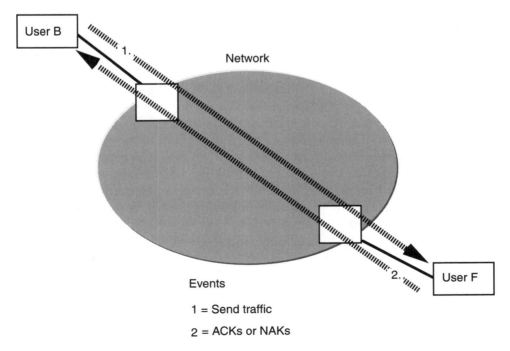

Figure 3–6   Payload integrity management: user end-to-end

By the use of end-to-end payload integrity management procedures, the network implementor may be able to eliminate integrity and management operations at the lower layers, as examples the link-by-link operations at layer 2, and the UNI operations at layer 3. I say "may" because in some situations, the use of layer 3 and/or layer 2 integrity management procedures may still be desirable. For example, if the network is using error-prone links, the use of layer 2 retransmission procedures provides a faster and more efficient way to recover from errors than the use of end-to-end integrity procedures.

EVOLUTION OF SWITCHING AND RELAYING TECHNOLOGIES

We now move to the subject of how traffic is relayed through the network to the receiving user. Several methods are employed and we start this analysis with a description of circuit switching, the principal time-division multiplexing (TDM) technology employed in telephony systems.

Circuit Switching

Circuit switching provides a direct connection between two users or the "illusion" of a direct connection with a switch that provides almost nonvariable delay through the switching fabric, see Figure 3–7. The direct connection of a circuit switch serves as an open "pipeline," permitting the two end users to utilize the facility as they see fit—within bandwidth and tariff limitations.

Many telephone networks use circuit switching systems. The switch uses a technique called time slot interchange (TSI) in which TDM slots are relayed from the input link interface to the output link interface in 125 μsec periods. The switch is provisioned for fixed forwarding. It does not use congestion notification, nor does it dynamically alter the forwarding tables. Thus, it is very fast, but rigid. Indeed, as the industry evolves to QOS-based systems, with dynamic bandwidth management, TDM-based circuit switches will become a thing of the past.

Circuit switching only provides a path for the session users. Error checking, session establishment, traffic flow control, frame formatting, and protocol implementations are the responsibility of the users. Little or no care of data traffic is provided in the circuit switching arrangement. Consequently, the telephone network is often used as the basic transport

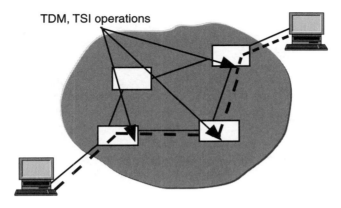

Where: TDM = Time division multiplexing
TSI = Time slot interexchange

Figure 3–7   Circuit switching

(carrier) service for a data communications network, and additional facilities are added by the network service provider, or user organization.

MESSAGE SWITCHING

In the 1960s and 1970s, the pervasive method for switching data communications traffic was message switching. Figure 3–8 shows the topology for this old technology. The technology is still widely used in certain applications, such as electronic mail, but it is not the architecture for a "backbone" network.[2] The switch is typically a specialized computer that operates on the edge of the backbone (not shown in Figure 3–8). It is responsible for accepting traffic from attached terminals and computers. It examines the address in the header of the message and switches (routes) the traffic to the receiving station.

Message switching is a store-and-forward technology: The messages are stored temporarily on disk units at the switches. The traffic is not considered to be interactive or real-time. However, selected traffic can be

_____

[2]An example of the deployment of message switches in modern networks is the airlines' reservation systems. They use message switches at the edge of the backbone network as interfaces to the backbone Frame Relay, ATM, or X.25 network. The message switches readily adapt to variant workloads into/out of the reservation applications (for example, at holidays, etc.) that are attached to the message switches.

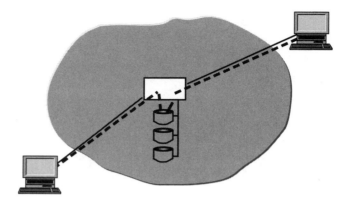

Figure 3–8   Message switching

sent through a message switch at very high speeds by establishing levels of priority for different types of traffic.

The message switches were originally designed with a star topology: Only one switch existed in the network. The reason? The switches were too expensive to warrant the purchase of multiple switches.

PACKET SWITCHING

Because of the problems with message switching and the development of large scale integration (LSI) and cheaper switches, the data communications industry began to move toward a different switching structure in the 1970s: packet switching. Packet switching distributes the workload to more than one switch, reduces vulnerability to network failure and provides better utilization of the communications lines than does message switching. Figure 3–9 shows an example of the packet switching network.

Packet switching is so named because user data (for example, messages) are divided into smaller pieces. These pieces, called packets, have protocol control information (headers) placed around them and are routed through the network as independent entities.

The topology permits the traffic to be routed to alternate switches (a secondary route) in case a particular switch encounters problems, such as congestion or a faulty link. Thus, packet switching provides for a very robust network. In addition, the small packets can be processed more quickly than longer data units, which translates to less delay for the traffic transfer.

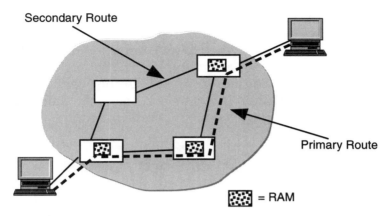

Figure 3–9   **Packet switching (same topology for Frame and Cell Relay)**

FRAME RELAY

The best way to think of the Frame Relay technology is that it is a scaled-down version of the packet-based protocol, X.25. Like X.25, it is a fast relay, hold-and-forward technology. Unlike X.25, it provides fewer value-added features, such as retransmissions. The idea of eliminating features is to reduce delay and increase throughput of the user's traffic. The Frame Relay's topology is similar to a conventional packet switching system in Figure 3–9 in that the architecture allows the distribution of workload and diversion of traffic around problem areas.

Frame Relay is designed specifically for transporting data traffic, although there is increasing interest in the industry for enhancing Frame Relay to support voice traffic. Frame Relay is also distinguished by its use of variable length protocol data units (PDUs) which are called frames.

CELL RELAY

Cell relay represents an evolution from (a) circuit switching and (b) packet/frame switching. In essence, it combines some of the attributes of all the relay/switching technologies we have just discussed. It also uses the topology shown in Figure 3–9.

In relation to these other technologies, cell relay is distinguished by its use of small, fixed-length protocol data units (called cells). In addition, the Asynchronous Transfer Mode (ATM), a cell-relay technology, is designed to support voice, video, and data traffic. Also, the ATM technology provides for extensive quality of service (QOS) features for the user.

The topology of cell relay is distributed, but the routing is fixed. This statement may seem to be contradictory, but the intent of the cell relay network is to provide for alternate paths only in the event of severe problems in the network. But the ATM network keeps the same end-to-end path for each user session unless unusual problems occur.

NETWORK AVAILABILITY: A CRUCIAL QOS FEATURE

For large networks that must support many users, the issue of network robustness is paramount, and the network provider must devise ways to ensure that the customer's traffic is delivered safely. An important QOS operation is network availability. It does little good if the network has been provisioned with wonderful QOS features, such as guaranteed throughput, if the network is down.

One method for providing service availability is called protection switching, which uses alternate links between network nodes to transmit the user packets, in case the primary link fails (in Figure 3–9, the secondary route, or alternate link). Protection switching is a fairly recent innovation and has become an integral part of a service provider's network architecture. This concept is depicted in Figure 3–10(a).

Two links (such as a DS3 or SONET link) connect two network nodes, node A and node B. One link is a working route, and the other link is the protection or backup route.[3] Let us assume traffic is coming into node A through interface a (the traffic on interface b at node A is not germane to our discussion). The packets are switched to the outgoing interface w or x, depending on the conditions of the links attached to node B from node A. In this example, a selector at node B, denoted in the figure by the ➤, determines which link is to be used for the relaying of traffic from interface c onto interfaces y or z.

The operations of protection switching are shown in Figure 3–10(b). The incoming packet on interface a has a label value of 1. The cross-connect table at node A is set up to direct this packet to both output interfaces w and x, with the label of 1 mapped to label 7 across interface w and label 8 across interface x.

---

[3]The terms working copy and protection copy are also used to identify these concepts. These terms are found in SONET and SDH literature.

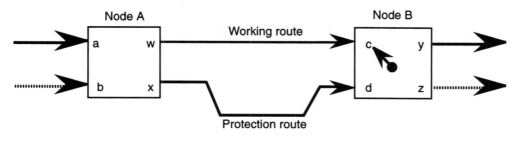

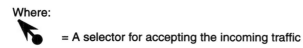

(a) Working and protection routes

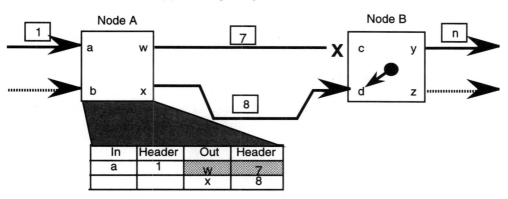

(b) Diverting traffic to protection route

Figure 3–10 Protection switching to enhance availability

In the event of failure of the working link (the link attached to node A's interface w and node B's interface c), another copy of the packet is available on the protection link (the link attached to node A's interface x and node B's interface d). The cross-connect table at node A is configured as shown in the figure to achieve the duplicate transfer of the packet to node B, and the selector at node B selects the packet with label = 8 for further relay. Obviously, the packet with label = 7 did not arrive at node B, and the cross-connect entry of interface out = w, header mapping = 7 is superfluous (depicted in the figure by shading).

There are other forms of protection switching in use. This example is called 1 + 1 protection switching. Both links (routes) are used simultaneously to send the same packets; that is, two copies of each packet are sent to node B. In contrast, the 1 : n operation shares the protection facility with more than one working link.

We must move on. Remember that this book assumes the network nodes and links are up-and-running.

EVOLUTION OF SWITCHING AND ROUTING TECHNOLOGIES

Data communications came along well after the voice communications technology was entrenched in the marketplace. Indeed, compared to telephony, data communications is an infant. Consequently, when data communications systems were first employed in the 1960s and 1970s, they used the circuit-switched telephone infrastructure for the transport of data communications traffic.

However, we learned that the circuit switch was never designed to support variable bit rates and bursty asynchronous traffic. To meet this need, the message switch was developed. The message switch was widely deployed in the late 1960s and early 1970s.

At about this time, a new technology appeared in the data market, the local area network (LAN). This technology uses a broadcast approach on a shared media, so it does not need switches.

As Figure 3–11 shows, the data networks diverged at this point into wide area networks (WANs) and local area networks (LANs). Let us move to the left side of the figure to trace the development of the WANs. As discussed earlier, because of the slow store-and-forward aspect of message switching as well as its star topology, the industry migrated into packet switches in the early 1970s. It was at this time that the concept of L_3 switching was implemented. Packet switches and L_3 switching remain a dominant technology today, but its progeny, the router, has taken over much of the marketplace from the conventional packet switch. The conventional router still employs L_3 relay operations, but it is designed with more data-specific features than can be found in the conventional X.25-based packet switch. In addition, it uses the term routing instead of switching (more on this subject shortly).

The packet switches that dominated the marketplace in the 1970s and early 1980s were designed principally to support wide area networks (WANs). Almost all of them were built to support the X.25 UNI packet protocol, a WAN protocol published in 1974 by the former CCITT (now the ITU-T).

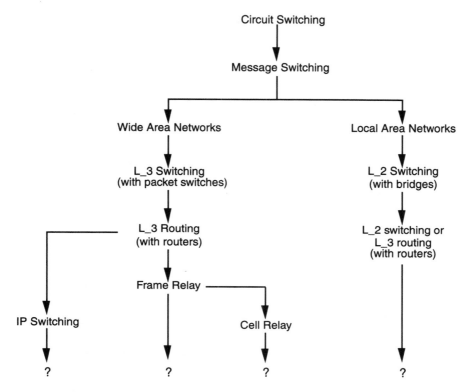

Figure 3–11   Evolution of communications networks

X.25 was not designed to support local area networks (LANs). Although some vendors modified their X.25 packet switches to interface with Ethernet LANs, the implementations were awkward and expensive to use. Thus, the router was born. It is a much more flexible machine and is designed to operate with WANs, LANs, as well as protocols other than X.25. Until recently, the router performed all its relaying operations at L_3, by using a L_3 header of the incoming packet, such as a L_3 IP address, a L_3 AppleTalk address, etc. The operation is known as L_3 routing.

Figure 3–11 shows a divergence at L_3 routing to IP switching, Frame Relay, and cell relay. It should be emphasized that high-end routers can be configured to support all these functions. The point of this figure is to emphasize that conventional L_3 routing is different from IP switching, Frame Relay, and cell relay. These three newer technologies are designed to increase the throughput and decrease the delay at the router. Subsequent chapters explain these ideas in more detail.

Let us take a look at the taxonomy in the figure dealing with local area networks. LANs became prominent in the data communications industry in the early 1980s with the development and implementation of Ethernet. The LAN networks were distinguished from wide area packet switches through the use of a special machine called a bridge. The bridge connects LANs together and performs the same functions as a layer 3 switch except that its operations occur at layer 2. This concept is known in the industry as L_2 switching.

Routers are also placed in local area networks, as suggested in this figure. These routers are quite versatile and are capable of either L_2 switching or L_3 routing.

So, what is the difference between the terms switching and routing? As a general definition, routing has meant executing the relaying decisions in software, whereas switching has meant executing the relay decisions in hardware. Be aware that vendors have different definitions of the terms switching and routing. In fact, the old X.25-based packet *switches* performed their operations in software.

To conclude this brief analysis, the bottom part of the picture shows the evolution to question marks. This depiction is meant to covey that the future of how communications networks are constructed has not been decided. The components of cell relay hold that cell relay is the best answer. The proponents of IP switching back their technology, and so on. In all likelihood, the future communications networks will be hybrids of IP switching, Frame Relay, cell relay, and bridging.

TECHNOLOGY COMPARISONS

Frame Relay and cell relay (also called cell switching) evolved from packet switching. The three technologies are similar in some of their characteristics, but do have differences. Table 3–1 provides a summary of their similarities and differences, as well as the Internet Protocol (IP). For packet switching, the X.25 specification is used. For cell relay, the ATM specification is used. Frame Relay assumes the use of the Frame Relay specification.

Table 3–1 Technology Comparisons

Attribute	IP	Packet Switching (X.25)	Frame Relay	Cell Relay (ATM)
QOS support?	Very little in IPv4; for IPv6, more extensive	Defined, but not used much	Yes, more extensive than X.25, and less than ATM	Yes, extensive
Application support?	Asynchronous data (not designed for voice)	Asynchronous data (not designed for voice)	Asynchronous data (voice use is emerging)	Asynchronous, synchronous voice, video, data
Connection mode?	Connectionless	Connection-oriented	Connection-oriented	Connection-oriented
Congestion management?	None	A receive not ready packet (RNR)	Congestion notification, traffic tagging , and possibly traffic discard	Congestion notification, traffic tagging, and possibly traffic discard
Identifying traffic? (Note 1)	IP address	Virtual circuit id: The LCN and an X.121 or an OSI address	Virtual circuit id: The DLCI and an E.164 address	Virtual circuit id: The VPI/VCI and an OSI address
Congestion notification?	None	A receive not ready packet (RNR)	The BECN and FECN bits in the header	The CN bits in the PTI field
Traffic tagging?	None	None	The discard eligibility bit (DE)	The cell loss priority (CLP) bit

(continued)

Table 3–1 *Continued*

Attribute	IP	Packet Switching (X.25)	Frame Relay	Cell Relay (ATM)
PDU size?	Variable (a datagram)	Variable (a packet)	Variable (a frame)	Fixed at 48 bytes (a cell)
Sequence numbers on payload?	No	Yes	No	Cell header, no; for payload, depends on payload type
ACKs/NAKs/ Resends?	No	Yes, at layer 2	Only for signaling traffic (SVCs)	Only for signaling traffic (SVCs)
Protection SW	Not defined	Not defined	Not defined	Proprietary
Marketplace?	Quite prevalent	Quite prevalent	Quite prevalent	Growing in use

Note 1: For X.25, Frame Relay, and ATM, addresses are used initially for the virtual circuit provisioning. Thereafter, virtual circuit ids are used.

Where:

BECN	Backward explicit congestion notification	FECN	Forward explicit congestion notification
CN	Congestion notification	SW	Switching

LABELS: THE KEY TO FORWARDING

We now take a look at labels, a topic that we have touched on in earlier discussions. Remember that these labels are also called connection identifiers, virtual circuit IDs, and codepoints. The latter term is usually associated with connectionless networks. In this discussion, we will use ATM as the example.

The ITU-T Recommendation requires that an ATM connection be identified with connection identifiers, which are assigned for each connection in the ATM network. The connection (at the UNI) is identified by two values in the cell header: (a) the virtual path identifier (VPI) and

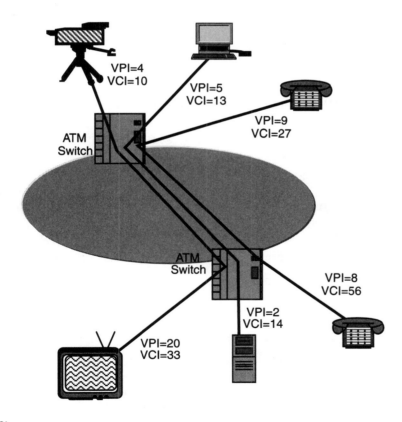

Where:
   VCI   Virtual channel identifier
   VPI   Virtual path identifier

Figure 3–12   Examples of label operations

(b) the virtual channel identifier (VCI). The VPI and VCI fields constitute a virtual circuit identifier. Users are assigned these values when (a) the user enters into a session with a network as a connection-on-demand or (b) when a user is provisioned to the network as a PVC.

Figure 3–12 shows examples of how the VPI/VCI values can be used. Three applications are connected to each other through the network (a) a video conference, (b) a data session between a workstation and a host computer, and (c) a telephone call. Each connection is associated with a VPI/VCI value on each side of the network. For example, the video session's connection is associated with VPI 4 and VCI 10 at one UNI and VPI 20 and VCI 33 at the other UNI. The manner in which VPI/VCI values are established and managed is left to the network administrator. In this example, VPI/VCI numbers have local significance at each UNI. Of course, the network must assure that these local VPI/VCI values at each UNI are "mapped together" through the network. The mapping operation is explained in Chapter 2 (see Figure 2–16).

LABELS FOR CONNECTION-ORIENTED NETWORKS

X.25, Frame Relay, and ATM employ statistical time-division multiplexing (STDM) techniques to transfer the users' traffic into and out of the network. I will use X.25 as the example for this discussion. The user machine and the packet switch are jointly responsible for combining (multiplexing) multiple user sessions onto a single communications line. In other words, instead of dedicating one line to each user, X.25 interleaves the multiple users' bursty traffic across an X.25 UNI. The user perceives that a line is dedicated to the user application, but the user is actually sharing it with other users.

The multiplexing of more than one user onto the physical communications line is called the *virtual circuit*. In this context, virtual means that a user perceives the availability of a dedicated, physical resource when, in practice, the resource is being shared. X.25 uses the term "logical channel" to describe one aspect of this concept. The terms "virtual" and "logical" are often used erroneously to convey the same meaning. It is preferable to define more concisely these two terms, as well as the term "physical circuit." Figure 3–13 should be examined during this next discussion.

- *Physical channel (or link)*. The communications link between two devices. Telephone lines often form the physical channel.

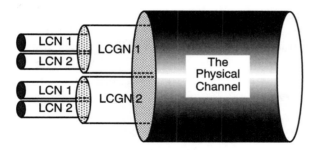

(a) The X.25 Approach

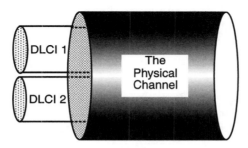

(b) The Frame Relay Approach

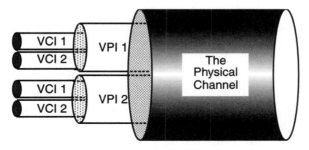

(c) The ATM Approach

Where:
LCN	Logical channel number	LGCN	Logical channel group number
DLCI	Data link connection identifier		
VPI	Virtual path identifier	VCI	Virtual channel identifier

Figure 3–13   X.25, Frame Relay, and ATM labels (virtual circuit Ids)

- *Virtual circuit*. The *end-to-end* connection-relationship (through a network) between two user devices. Since intermediate packet switches are used to route the data through the network, the virtual circuit usually consists of multiple physical circuits. It is the responsibility of the network to maintain the end-to-end connection of the users.
- *Logical channel*. Used only with X.25, it is the *local* connection-relationship between the user node and the network at the UNI. The logical channel has significance only at the UNI on *each* side of the network. Therefore, a logical channel exists on each side of the network cloud. It is the task of the network to *map* the two logical channels to a virtual circuit.

ATM and Frame Relay use very similar concepts, with some minor differences. For Frame Relay, the logical channel is called a data link connection identifier (DLCI), as shown in Figure 3–13 (b). It performs the same functions as the X.25 logical channel number. One difference between X.25 and Frame Relay is that X.25 (as an option) can use two virtual circuit IDs. One is called the logical channel number (LCN), and the other is called the logical channel group number (LCGN). ATM has borrowed this two-identifier idea from X.25, but Frame Relay does not use it; Frame Relay uses only one value to identify a virtual channel. Since X.25 and ATM use the same concept of two virtual circuit IDs, I will defer discussing X.25's implementation, and use ATM for the example.

ATM has two multiplexing hierarchies: the virtual channel and the virtual path. The virtual path (VP) is a bundle of virtual channels. Each bundle typically has the same endpoints. The purpose of the VPI is to identify a group of virtual channel (VC) connections. This approach allows VPIs to be "nailed-up" end-to-end to provide semipermanent connections for the support of a large number of user VCI sessions. Both VPIs and VCIs can also be established on demand.

Two different VCs that belong to different VPs at a particular interface are allowed to have the same VCI value. Consequently, the concatenation of VCI and VPI is necessary to uniquely identify a virtual connection.

THE PROTOCOL STACKS

Figure 3–14 shows four widely-used protocol stacks that are based on the OSI Model. Figure 3–14(a) is the IP stack, and Figure 3–14(b) is the X.25 stack. Figure 3–14(c) is the Frame Relay stack, and Figure 3–14(d) is the ATM stack.

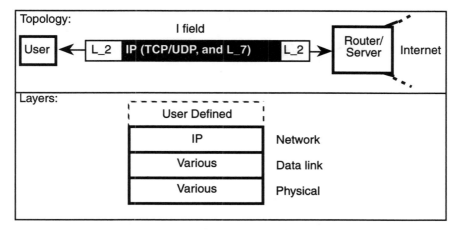

(a) The Internet Protocol (IP)

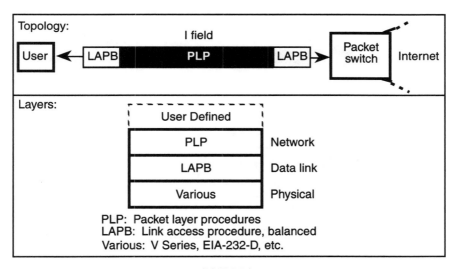

(b) X.25

Figure 3–14   The topologies and protocol stacks

All technologies use the lower layers of OSI. But (with some exceptions) the Internet standards groups do not define the operations at the physical and data link layers. IP runs on top of layers 1 (physical layer) and 2 (data link layer). The job of IP is simple: It is a forwarding protocol. It uses the destination address in the IP header to access a forwarding table to determine how to forward the IP traffic. IP is a best-effort, connectionless layer 3 protocol.

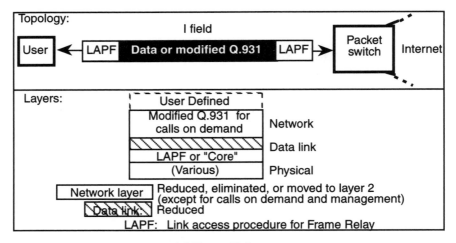

(c) Frame Relay

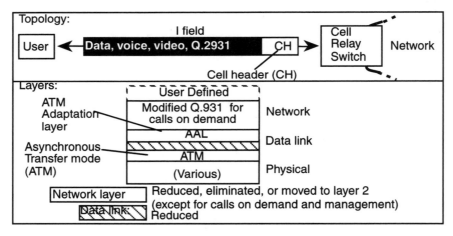

(d) ATM

Figure 3–14 *Continued*

Layer 3 of X.25 is called packet layer procedures (PLP), and is used to set up connections, which are called virtual circuits. These circuits support only data. Since X.25 is based on statistical time-division multiplexing (STDM), voice and video are not supported. As we learned earlier, X.25 is an old packet-based technology that serves as a legacy to the Frame Relay and ATM technologies. X.25's layer 2, is called link access procedure, balanced (LAPB). It is used to ensure the safe delivery of the X.25 layer 3 packets across the UNI.

Some of the newer technologies have not implemented a "full" network and data link layer. Two of the more prominent examples are Frame Relay and ATM. Figures 3–14(c) and 3–14(d) show the protocol stacks for both of these technologies. We have explained several pertinent aspects of Frame Relay and ATM, but a few more comments are warranted.

Frame Relay and ATM are designed to operate at the UNI and NNI. The design philosophy of both Frame Relay and ATM are similar: Eliminate functions in layers 2 and 3 in order to make the network perform more efficiently, exhibiting more predictable performance, as well as higher throughput and less delay. The idea is to push functions out of the network to the edge of the network, which is in keeping with many QOS concepts, such as traffic monitoring and shaping of the customer's traffic at the UNI.

Frame Relay is not a new technology. In fact, as mentioned earlier, it is a scaled-down version of X.25 (it is connection-oriented, using virtual circuit concepts), and the link access procedure for the D channel (LAPD) at layer 2.

ATM is a relatively new technology, although it has been under study for quite some time. Its main features are the use of very small (53 octets) protocol data units, called cells, and its support of multimedia applications (voice, video, and data). The ATM adaptation layer (AAL) plays a key role in supporting QOS in an ATM node, and is tailored for different kinds of traffic; AAL is explained in Chapter 6.

THE X.25 LEGACY

I have made several comments about the legacy of X.25, and how it has served as an efficacious model for Frame Relay and ATM. This part of the chapter explains how and why Frame Relay and ATM: (a) use some X.25 features and (b) eliminate others.

To make certain you understand the relationships (and differences) between the X.25 frame level (L_2) and the packet level (L_3), please examine Figure 3–15. We assume users A, B, and C are involved in sessions with remote users. User A is assigned to LCN 26, user B is assigned to LCN 33, and user C is assigned LCN 45. The LAPB frames are sequenced with the N(S) field in the frame header, and *each* logical channel is sequenced with the packet level P(S) field in the packet header. This feature allows users A, B, and C to flow control and sequence their traffic into and out of the network at the layer 3 layer. For example, if the network issues a packet level (L_3) Receive Not Ready (RNR) on logical channel 33, it does not affect the other two users on the X.25 interface (the UNI).

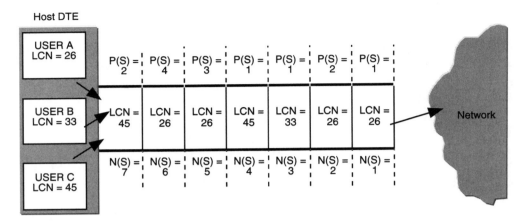

Note: The N(S) values represent the sequencing at the link level and the P(S) values are the sequence numbers at the packet level.

Figure 3–15   Relationship of the X.25 packet and frame levels

The packet level activity at layer 3 is taking place without LAPB's "awareness" and vice versa. Of course, LAPB's actions can affect all users on the interface. For example, if LAPB issues a data link layer (L_2) Receive Not Ready (RNR), then all logical channels (and all users on the interface) are in a flow control state.

From a quick study of the figure, it can be seen that the LAPB sequencing and flow control is performed for all users on the link, and the packet level sequencing and flow control pertains only to a specific logical channel. The relationship is as follows:

Frame Number	LCN	Packet Number
1	26	1
2	26	2
3	33	1
4	45	1
5	26	3
6	26	4
7	45	2

Now we can examine how Frame Relay and ATM have adopted the X.25 architecture. Figure 3–16 shows another way of viewing the Frame

Relay and ATM operations. On the left is a depiction of a typical data communications protocol X.25 stack which encompasses the physical, data link, and network layers.

These layers perform conventional operations. For example, the physical layer is responsible for terminating traffic, providing connectors, as well as physical signaling. The data link layer is responsible for error checking and retransmission of erred traffic that may occur on the UNI communications link. The network layer is responsible for managing the traffic within the network, establishing virtual connections and negotiating quality of services between the network and the users.

In contrast, the Frame Relay and ATM stack virtually eliminate the data link layer and many aspects of the network layer. The major L_3 operations, performed with the L_3 header, are either eliminated or pushed down to layer 2. Therefore, the header of Frame Relay and ATM are combinations of the X.25 L_2 and L_3 headers. The figure shows two major conventional L_3 operations that now reside in L_2 of Frame Relay and ATM: (a) the labels, and (b) flow control (using these labels).

What is eliminated and what is retained from the X.25 architecture? Table 3–2 lists the L_2 and L_3 operations. I have also added IP to the tables, even though IP is quite different from these other three connection-oriented technologies.

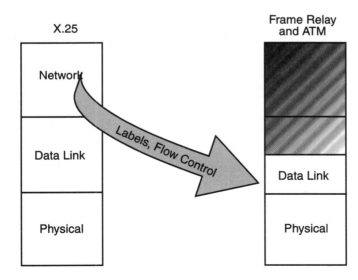

Figure 3–16   Comparison of X.25 with Frame Relay and ATM stacks

Table 3–2   How the stacks stack up

Operations at Layer 2

Service	X.25	Frame Relay	ATM	IP
Flow control?	Yes	Not used	Not used	Not used
Sequence numbers?	Yes	Not used	Not used	Not used
Retransmissions of user payload?	Yes	Not used	Not used	Not used
OAM?	Yes	Not used	Not used	Not used

Operations at Layer 3

Service	X.25	Frame Relay	ATM	IP
Flow control?	Yes	Move X.25-type L_3 operations to L_2	Move X.25-type L_3 operations to L_2	Not used
Sequence numbers?	Yes	Not used	Not used	Not used
Retransmissions?	Defined, but rarely used	Not used	Not used	Not used
OAM?	Yes	Yes	Yes	Not used
Labels?	Yes	Move X.25-type L_3 operations to L_2	Move X.25-type L_3 operations to L_2	Not used

SUMMARY

Connection-oriented and connectionless networks have evolved since the inception of voice and data networks, and switching technologies have migrated to packet-based operations, using IP, X.25, Frame Relay, and ATM protocols. Bridges and routers are recent additions to the "packet" switching family.

IP, X.25, Frame Relay, and ATM are the principal protocols for traffic transport and QOS features in WANs, and IP is being "enhanced" with several QOS protocols that are currently under development.

4

X.25

This chapter examines the X.25 packet network protocol. First, the X.25 connection options are explained, with thoughts on how QOS features can be negotiated during a connection setup. The X.25 packets are analyzed in the next part of the chapter. The last part of the chapter explains how the X.25 facilities are used to implement X.25's QOS operations.

The term "port" is used in this chapter to define the physical communications interface at a user node or a packet switch. Previous chapters have used the term "interface," but this chapter is an exception, because of X.25's use of the term.

MAJOR FEATURES OF X.25

Table 4–1 lists some of the major features of X.25. As we go through this chapter and the Frame Relay and ATM chapters, it will become obvious that X.25 that has many similarities with these newer systems. Indeed, X.25, Frame Relay, and ATM are more similar than they are different.

Part of the reason for these technologies being closely aligned is that they were designed by telephony engineers, who were imbued with

Table 4–1   X.25 Features

Connection-oriented with virtual circuits

Connection multiplexing

Switching operations: not defined

Packet-based

Segmentation/reassembly of user traffic into packets

Asynchronous: Packets filled based on demand

Data only

Switching speed maximized with
   short headers and small packets

connection-oriented design philosophies. The other reason is that Frame Relay was intended to be a scaled-down implementation of X.25, thus retaining many of the X.25 characteristics, and ATM was intended to be the successor to Frame Relay.

X.25 was the first worldwide standard for data networks (it preceded Ethernet by almost ten years). It was (and is) a valuable protocol in the communications industry because it led the way for the unregulated data industry to begin adapting standardized procedures for the exchange of data packets between different vendors' equipment.

It also led the way to the idea of using short units of traffic (packets) for transmission to reduce delay at the packet switches—an idea that has found its way into the ATM cell concept. Equally important, it demonstrated that switches did not have to be built around TDM, fixed slot operations, and this idea was a revolutionary concept in the early 1970s.

X.25 VIRTUAL CIRCUIT AND CONNECTION OPTIONS

X.25 uses the term DTE (data terminal equipment) to identify a user node (a host, a router, etc.). It uses the term DCE (data circuit terminating equipment) to identify the network node.

X.25 stipulates that any two communicating DTEs must have a virtual circuit association between them before they can exchange data. X.25 provides a variety of interface options for these virtual circuits. The standard provides three mechanisms to establish and maintain communications:

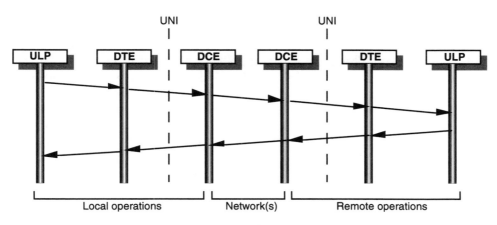

Where:
ULP   Upper layer protocol

Figure 4–1   Template for subsequent illustrations

- Permanent virtual circuit (PVC)
- Switched virtual call (SVC)
- Fast select call

Subsequent figures that depict these operations are labeled with the notations shown in Figure 4–1. The notations of ULP, DTE, and DCE in the boxes on the left side of Figure 4–1 represent the local X.25 operations. The ULP, DTE, and DCE notations on the right side of Figure 4–1 represent the remote X.25 operations. The upper layer protocol (ULP) resides in the DTE. It invokes the network layer (layer 3) of X.25 through the use of primitives.[1] The primitives for X.25 are described in X.213 and X.223.

The notations between the DTE and DCE (the X.25 UNI) will be abbreviated notations for the X.25 packet. The notations between the DCEs will represent the transfer of packets within the network; therefore, little will be said about those operations, because X.25 does not define the operations within the network.

---

[1]Primitives guide programmers about how to code calls to invoke a software function. In X.25, these primitives form the basis for application programming interfaces (APIs).

Permanent Virtual Circuit (PVC) Operations

A permanent virtual circuit (PVC) is analogous to a leased line in a telephone network. The transmitting DTE is assured of obtaining a session (connection) with the receiving DTE through the packet network. X.25 requires that a PVC be established before the session begins. Consequently, an agreement must be reached by the two users and the service provider before a PVC will be allocated. Among other things, this includes reserving a logical channel number (LCN, see Chapter 2) for the PVC user, and the provisioning of QOS features.

Thereafter, when a transmitting DTE sends a packet into the packet network, the identifying LCN in the packet indicates that the requesting DTE has a permanent virtual circuit connection to the receiving DTE. See Figure 4–2. Consequently, predefined QOS facilities will be provided by the network and the receiving DTE without further session negotiation. PVC requires no call setup or clearing procedures, and the logical channel is continually in a data transfer state.

The ULP issues the N-Data primitives to invoke the PVC packet operations. The two arguments required in this function call are the preallocated LCN value and the data parameter.

During the transfer of data across a PVC, the network may occasionally experience problems. X.25 provides two methods for handling these problems. First, if a momentary failure occurs within the network, the DCE must perform a "reset" of the PVC and notify the DTE with a special control packet stating that the network is experiencing "network congestion." The DCE will then continue to handle the DTE's data packets. Second, if a temporary failure occurs within the network, the DCE must reset the PVC and notify the DTE with a control packet stating that the network is "out-of-order." When the network is again ready to accept

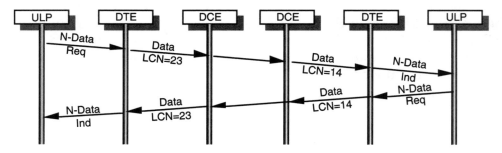

Figure 4–2   Permanent virtual circuit

data, it sends a control packet to the DTE stating "network operational." During all this activity, the DTE need only wait for the proper control packet and simply resume sending packets. It is an attractive way to handle short down periods.

Switched Virtual Call (SVC) Operations

A switched virtual call (SVC) resembles some of the procedures associated with telephone dial-up lines because call setup and breakdown procedures are employed. Figure 4–3 shows the packet flow for the SVC.

This "connection-on-demand" is instigated by the ULP invoking the N-Conn.req primitive. The required parameter in this primitive is the called party address. Optional parameters are: (b) calling party address, and (c) a list of facility services (QOS features) that are requested for this connection.

The *calling* DTE issues a Call Request packet that contains a LCN and the address of the *called* DTE. The network uses the address to route the Call Request packet to the DCE that is to support the call at the remote end. This DCE then sends an Incoming Call packet to the proper DTE.

Logical channel numbering is performed on each side of the network, and the LCN at the local DTE/DCE is most likely a different value

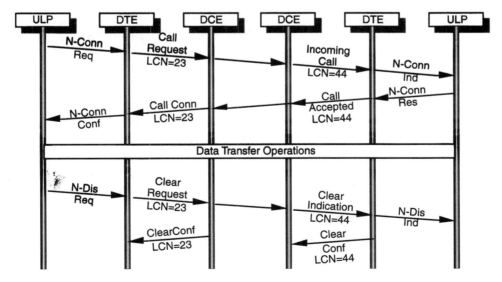

Figure 4–3   Switched virtual call

than the LCN at the remote DTE/DCE. The critical requirement is to keep the specific DTE-to-DTE session identified at all times with the same pair of LCNs.

If the receiving DTE (the ULP) chooses to acknowledge and accept the call request, the DTE transmits a Call Accepted packet to the network. The network then transports this packet to the requesting DTE in the form of a Call Connected packet. This action has created an end-to-end virtual circuit.

During this exchange of packets, QOS features are set up for the user, both by the network, and if appropriate, by the remote DTE.

To terminate the session, a Clear Request packet is sent by either the DTE or DCE. It is received as a Clear Indication packet and confirmed with the Clear Confirm packet. After the call is cleared, the LCNs and network resources are made available for another session. If the DTEs establish another virtual call session with each other, they must repeat the procedures just discussed.

To summarize the VC connection establishment procedure and associated LCN management operations, this list depicts how LCNs are selected:

Packet	LCN Selected By
Call Request	Originating DTE
Incoming Call	Destination packet network node (DCE)
Call Accepted	Same LCN as an Incoming Call
Call Connected	Same LCN as in Call Request

Fast Select Operations

The idea of eliminating the overhead and time delay of the VC establishment and disestablishment packets makes good sense for certain applications, such as those with very few transactions or short sessions. Consequently, the fast select facility was incorporated into X.25 in 1984.

Fast select provides for two options. The first option is *fast select call*. A DTE can request this facility on a per-call basis to the network node (DCE) by means of an appropriate request in the header of a packet. The fast select facility allows the Call Request packet to contain user data of up to 128 octets. The called DTE is allowed to respond with a Call Accepted packet, which can also contain user data.

The Call Request/Incoming Call packet indicates whether the remote DTE is to respond with Clear Request or Call Accepted packet. If a

Call Accepted packet is transmitted, the X.25 session continues with the normal data transferring and clearing procedures of a switched virtual call. Therefore, this procedure is the same as the switched virtual call, except that the fast select procedure allows the call management packets to contain a user data field as large as 128 octets.

Fast select also provides another fast select feature for the X.25 interface, the *fast select with immediate clear* (see Figure 4–4). As with the other fast select option, a Call Request contains user data. This packet is transmitted through the network to the receiving DTE, which, upon acceptance, transmits a Clear Request (which also contains user data). The Clear Request is received at the origination site as a Clear Indication packet. This site returns a Clear Confirmation packet. The Clear Confirmation packet cannot contain user data. Thus, the forward packet sets up the network connection and the reverse packet brings the connection down.

Call Refusal

A connection request can be refused by either the network or the called DTE. A network may refuse a call connection request if it does not have the resources to support the call at that moment. The analogy to a telephone network is receiving a busy signal if all the circuits are tied up. Additionally, the network may refuse a call if the requesting user does not provide adequate passwords, login IDs, etc. It may also refuse a call if it has capacity, but cannot fulfill the requesting user's specific QOS requirements, such as requested throughput, delay, etc. In this situation, it is also allowed to reduce the facility parameters in the Call Request packet, and pass the packet to the called DTE.

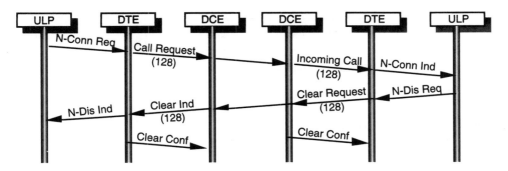

Figure 4–4   Fast select with immediate clear

A connection request can be refused by the called DTE for the same kind of reasons cited for the network, such as the lack of resources, nonacceptance of a password, and so on. The refusal may emanate from the DTE operating system, a communications package or even an end-user application.

X.25 PACKETS

This section introduces the packet structure and the fields within the packet. Using Figure 4–5 as a reference, the standard convention in X.25 is to show the octets (bytes) in the packet on a vertical plane, with the first octet stacked on top of the second octet, etc. The eight bits of each octet are aligned on a horizontal plane with the low-order bits placed to the right side of the page.

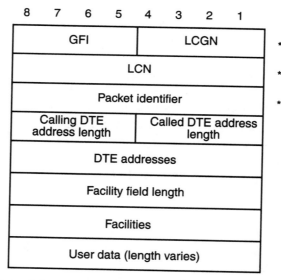

Note: * One octet each, other fields of variable length

Where:
GFI   General format identifier
LCFN   Logical channel group number
LCN   Logical channel number

Figure 4–5   The X.25 packet format (for connection management packets)

Every X.25 packet must contain a three octet header. The header consists of:

General format identifier (GFI)
Logical channel fields (LCGN, LCN)
Packet identifier

The address fields are used only during the connection management operations. During this time, they are mapped to the LCNs that will be used thereafter to identify the packet session. The Facilities field is used to request and negotiate facilities between the two users and the network.

The General Format Identifier (GFI) Field

The general format identifier (GFI) field is shown in Figure 4–6. It is coded in bits 5 to 8 of the first octet. Bits 5 and 6 are used to indicate the sequencing for the packet sessions. Two sequencing options are allowed in X.25. The first option is modulo 8, which permits packet sequence numbers from 0 through 7. Modulo 128 is also available. This option permits sequence numbers ranging from 0 through 127. Coding for these two bits can assume four possible combinations are also shown in the figure.

The seventh bit, or D (delivery confirmation) bit, of the GFI is used with call setup and data packets. It is used to provide for one of two capabilities. First, when the bit is set to 0, acknowledgment of receipt of the data packets is performed by the local DCE. The second alternative is used when D is set to 1. This option provides an end-to-end acknowledgment of the packet (i.e., from one DTE to the other DTE). Since the D bit is set during the call setup, it applies to all data packets associated with the virtual call.

The eighth bit of the GFI is the Q bit (or qualifier bit). It is relevant for data packets (Figure 4–6[a]), but not call management packets (Figure 4–6[b]). It is used by X.25 to distinguish between two types of information in the user data field, but it is left to the implementor as to how it is used. As an example of its use, a companion protocol to X.25, X.29, uses the Q bit to differentiate between user and control data.

The A-bit feature was added to the 1988 X.25 release, see Figure 4–6(b). The A bit is the same bit as the Q bit, but it is only relevant for call setup and clearing packets (the Q bit is relevant only for data packets). It is used to identify two possible formats for the address fields:

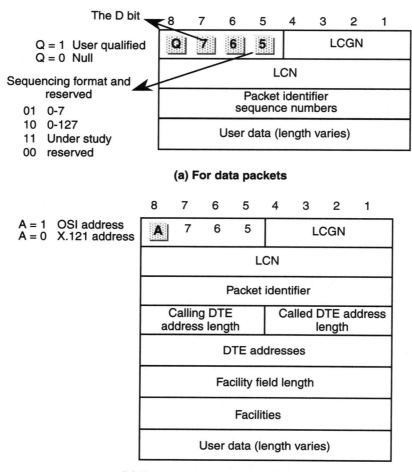

Figure 4–6   The general format identifier (GFI) field

A = 0 is used for the non-OSI address format and A = 1 is used for the OSI address format.

The Packet Identifier

The third octet of the packet header is the packet identifier field. It is used to identify the type of packet and provide other control functions for a data packet. The field is coded in accordance with the scheme shown in Table 4–2. Some of the packets also contain other fields. They are also briefly summarized in Table 4–2 and described in more detail later.

Table 4–2 Packet Identifiers, Third Octet (Modulo 8 format is shown)

Packet Type		Octet 3 Bits
From DCE to DTE	*From DTE to DCE*	8 7 6 5 4 3 2 1
Incoming Call	Call Request	0 0 0 0 1 0 1 1
Call Connected	Call Accepted	0 0 0 0 1 1 1 1
Clear Indication	Clear Request	0 0 0 1 0 0 1 1
Clear Confirmation	Clear Confirmation	0 0 0 1 0 1 1 1
Data	Data	P(R) M P(S) 0
Interrupt	Interrupt	0 0 1 0 0 0 1 1
Interrupt Confirmation	Interrupt Confirmation	0 0 1 0 0 1 1 1
Receive Ready (RR)	Receive Ready (RR)	P(R) 0 0 0 0 1
Receive Not Ready (RNR)	Receive Not Ready (RNR)	P(R) 0 0 1 0 1
	Reject (REJ)	P(R) 0 1 0 0 1
Reset Indication	Reset Request	0 0 0 0 1 1 0 1
Reset Confirmation	Reset Confirmation	0 0 0 1 1 1 1 1
Restart Indication	Restart Request	1 1 1 1 1 0 1 1
Restart Confirmation	Restart Confirmation	1 1 1 1 1 1 1 1
Diagnostic		1 1 1 1 0 0 0 1
	Registration Request	1 1 1 1 0 0 1 1
Registration Confirmation		1 1 1 1 0 1 1 1

Other Fields

- *Cause and diagnostic codes fields.* Several of the control packets contain fields to describe the reason the DTE, DCE, or the network invoked certain actions, such as resets and restarts.
- *Facility fields.* The call setup and clearing packets must contain the facility fields.

Data Packets

The format for the data packet is shown in Figure 4–7. Two formats are permitted, one for sequence numbering from 1–7 (see Figure 4–7[a]) and one for sequence numbering from 1–127 (see Figure 4–7[b]). Remember that the Q and D bits can be used with data packets to obtain special services from the network. The M (more data) bit is used if a full user message must be segmented into two or more packets. It is set to 1 for all these packets, except in the last packet the sequence, when it is set to 0. The M bit is used to assist the reassembly process at the receiver.

Each packet is sequenced with a packet send sequence number, noted as P(S), and a receive sequence number, noted as P(R). If you do

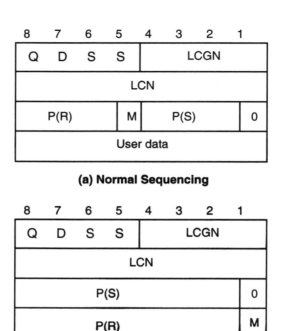

(a) Normal Sequencing

(b) Extended Sequencing

Figure 4–7   Data packets

not remember the functions of these fields, please review Figures 3–5 and 3–15 in Chapter 3.

Flow Control and Reject Packets

The Receive Ready (RR) and Receive Not Ready (RNR) packets serve the important function of flow control. They are depicted in Figures 4–8(a) and 4–8(b) for normal and extended sequencing, respectively. Both of these packets provide a receive sequence number P(R) in the packet header to indicate the next packet sequence number expected from the transmitter. The RR packet is used to tell the transmitter to begin sending data packets, and it also uses the receive sequence number P(R) to acknowledge any packets that have been previously transmitted. The RR packet can be used to acknowledge packets received when there are no data packets to convey to the other node.

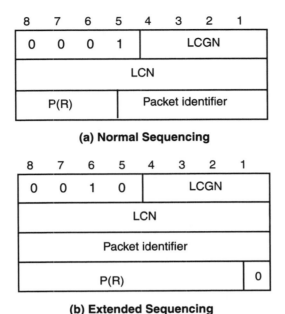

(a) Normal Sequencing

(b) Extended Sequencing

Figure 4–8   Flow control, congestion control, and reject packets

The RNR packet is used to direct the transmitting site to stop sending packets, and it also uses the receive sequence field P(R) to acknowledge any packets that have been previously received. The RNR is often issued when a node experiences a temporary inability to receive traffic. Thus, both packet types provide flow control.

The Reject (REJ) packet specifically rejects the received packet. The DTE requests retransmission of packets beginning with the count in the receive sequence field P(R). The DCE is not allowed to use the Reject packet. Most implementations of X.25 do not use this packet but rely on LAPB at the data link layer to resolve errors.

Diagnostic Packet

The Diagnostic packet is shown in Figure 4–9. It is used by X.25 networks to indicate certain error conditions that are not covered by other methods such as reset and restart. The Diagnostic packet with LCN = 0 is issued only once (and only by the network) for a particular problem. No confirmation is required for the packet.

8	7	6	5	4	3	2	1
GFI *				0	0	0	0
0	0	0	0	0	0	0	0
Packet identifier							
Diagnostic code							
Diagnostic explanation							

*: Coded 0001 for modulo 8 and 0010 for modulo 28

Figure 4–9   Diagnostic packet

X.25 defines over sixty diagnostic codes to aid in determining network or DTE problems. These codes can also be used with other packets (Clear, Reset, Restart).

Interrupt Packet

The interrupt procedure is shown in Figure 4–10. It allows a DTE to transmit one nonsequenced Interrupt packet without following the normal flow control procedures established in X.25. The interrupt procedure is useful for situations where an application requires the transmittal of data for unusual conditions. For example, a high-priority user message could be transmitted as an Interrupt packet to ensure that the receiving DTE accepts the data. User data (1 to 32 octets) is permitted in an Interrupt packet. The use of interrupts has no effect on the regular data packets within the virtual circuit.

The Interrupt packet requires an Interrupt Confirmation packet before another Interrupt packet can be sent on the logical channel. The confirmation must be returned by the remote DTE.

Figure 4–10 also shows an example of the Interrupt packet operations. Figure 4–10(a) shows the packet format and Figure 4–10(b) shows the packet flow. As stated, Interrupt packets are not restricted to window control. Therefore, each logical channel is allowed to send one Interrupt packet, regardless of the status of its send window. An Interrupt Confirm packet (not shown in this figure) must be returned to the DTE from the local DCE before another Interrupt packet can be issued by the logical channel. Also, be aware that Interrupt packets are often treated as high-priority packets by the network. They may arrive before previously trans-

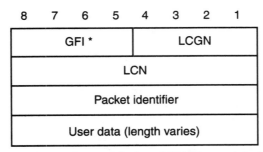

* Coded 0001 for modulo 8 and 0010 for modulo 128

(a) Interrupt packet

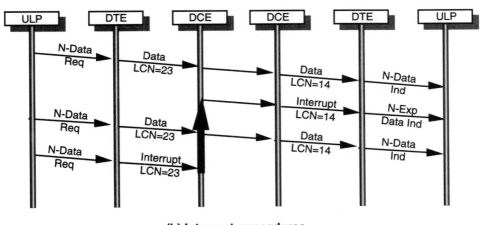

(b) Interrupt procedures

Figure 4–10   Interrupt packet and interrupt procedures

mitted packets. Since they have no sequence numbers, they should not be used for conveying regular traffic that is part of the ongoing packet flow.

Registration Packet

The Registration packet, shown in Figure 4–11, is used to invoke or confirm the X.25 facilities. This feature allows the end user to request changes to facilities in an on-line mode without the manual intervention of the network provider. Its intent is to provide a means to dynamically assign or modify certain X.25 facility attributes. It was one of the first attempts in the industry to standardize a means of obtaining dynamic QOS. But its use has been limited, and the registration procedures for dynamic QOS operations have not been implemented extensively.

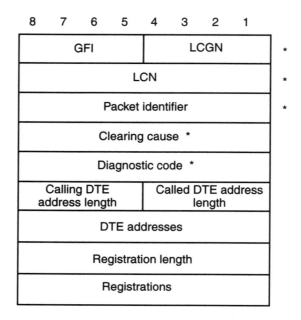

* Contained in confirmation packet, but not in request packet

Figure 4–11   Registration packet

The user asks the network for a change in a facility profile by sending a Registration Request packet. A Registration Confirmation packet is returned to provide a status of the request.

Example of an X.25 Data Transfer

Figure 4–12 shows the relationship of the DTE/DCE layers, and layer 2 frames and the layer 3 packets. Starting from the bottom of the figure, we assume user data is to be sent from a user node (DTE) through a packet network to a remote destination. The user data is passed from the upper layer protocol (ULP) to the X.25 network layer. Here, the packet header is created, and several of the operations described thus far in this chapter are performed. The packet and the user data are passed to the data link layer, which encapsulates the packet into the frame.[2] It

---

[2]The notations of F, A, C, and FCS are control and error-checking fields in the LAPB protocol. If you are not familiar with layer 2 operations, see my book on *Data Link Protocols,* published by Prentice Hall, 1993.

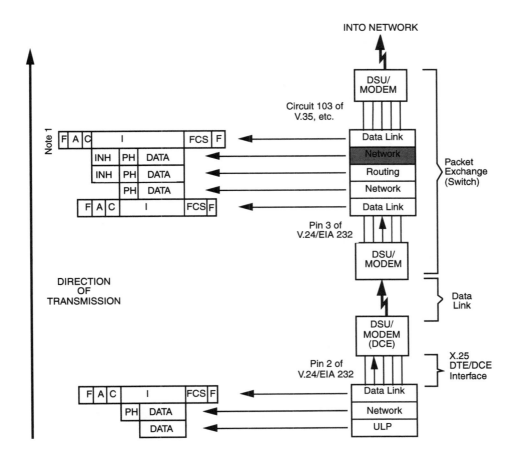

Figure 4–12   X.25 layers and protocol data units

is then passed to the physical layer across an interface, to the modem or data service unit (DSU) and then onto the communications link.

The frame is received at the packet switch. It passes through the physical, data link, and network layers of X.25. The switch performs its requisite X.25 functions and passes the packet to the vendor's proprietary network software. This software contains the forwarding protocol to relay the packet to the next node in the network (for example, IP).

Typically, the network adds its own internal network header (INH) to the packet. Notice that the X.25 packet header is not disturbed, but it is encapsulated with the user data into the internal network protocol data unit.

For example, the INH could be an IP header, so the X.25 packet is encapsulated inside the IP datagram for delivery through the network.

Also notice the shaded X.25 network layer on the out-bound side of the switch. This layer may not be invoked if the internal network does not use X.25. In fact, most networks do not use X.25 internally.

Figure 4–13 is another view of the process just discussed. The internal network has been drawn around the layers and protocol data units

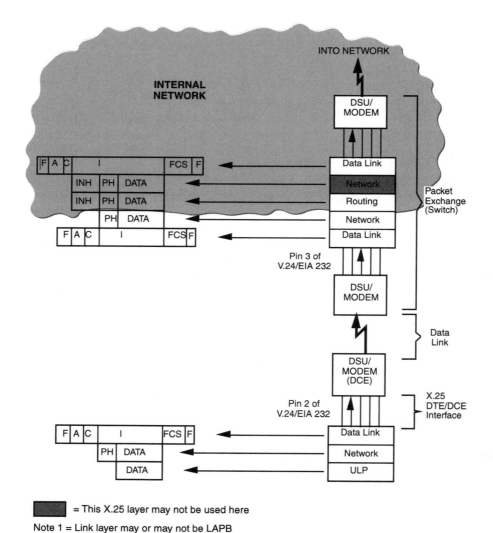

Figure 4–13   Relationship of the network "cloud" to X.25

that are not part of the X.25 specification. Even though the figure shows the X.25 network and data link layers inside the network cloud on the out-bound side of the packet switch, they need not reside there. For example, the LAPB frame need not be used inside the network. Some vendors place the X.25 packet and the international network header (INH) inside other link protocols, such as the synchronous data link control (SDLC). Several offerings are available that multiplex the packets into a T1 carrier frame. Offerings are now available that carry the X.25 packet on a SONET link.

Also, note the annotation of "X.25 DTE/DCE interface." From the perspective of the ITU-T, this point marks the X.25 interface with the user DTE, although the network's X.25 layers 2 and 3 operations are actually performed by the switch. Some countries require that user access lines, modems, DSUs, etc. be furnished by the national Postal, Telephone, and Telegraph Ministry (PTT). Therefore, the network "boundary" is considered to extend to the user DTE/DCE interface.

This concept of the network cloud also found its way into the Frame Relay and ATM technologies. Frame Relay does not define the operations "inside the cloud." However, ATM does, because full interface definitions make it much easier to interwork different vendors' switches.

This summary concludes the discussion on X.25's basic architecture. The remainder of the chapter is devoted to the X.25 QOS operations, known as facilities.

THE X.2 RECOMMENDATION

The ITU-T Recommendation X.2 describes the use of facilities (QOS features) for a variety of networks such as ISDN, circuit-switched networks, and packet-switched networks. The recommendation indicates whether a facility is essential (should be used with the network), or an additional facility (which is optional), and whether it is applicable to a switched virtual call (SVC) or permanent virtual circuit (PVC). Table 4–3 defines the X.25 packet switched facilities as: E = Essential, A = Additional, FS = for Further Study, VC = Virtual Call, PVC = Permanent Virtual Circuit.

The User Class of Service values of 8–13 and 20–22 are used to identify if the operation is with asynchronous protocols (8–13) or synchronous protocols (20–22).

Table 4–3 Facilities for packet-switched service

Facility		8–13 SVC	8–13 PVC	20–22 SVC	20–22 PVC
1.	**Optional user facilities assigned for an agreed contractual period**				
1.1	Extended frame sequence numbering	A	A	–	–
1.2	Multilink procedure	A	A	–	–
1.3	On-line facility registration	A	–	FS	–
1.4	Extended packet sequence numbering (Modulo 128)	A	A	–	–
1.5	D-bit modification	A	A	FS	–
1.6	Packet retransmission	A	A	–	–
1.7	Incoming calls barred	E	–	A	–
1.8	Outgoing calls barred	E	–	A	–
1.9	One-way logical channel outgoing	E	–	–	–
1.10	One-way logical channel incoming	A	–	–	–
1.11	Non-standard default packet sizes 16, 32, 64, 256, 512, 1024, 2048, 4096	A A	A A	FS FS	FS FS
1.12	Nonstandard default window sizes	A	A	–	–
1.13	Default throughput classes assignment	A	A	FS	FS
1.14	Flow Control parameter negotiation	E	–	FS	–
1.15	Throughput class negotiation	E	–	FS	–
1.16	Closed user group	E	–	E	–
1.17	Closed user group with outgoing access	A	–	A	–
1.18	Closed user group with incoming access	A	–	A	–
1.19	Incoming calls barred within a CUG	A	–	A	–
1.20	Outgoing calls barred within a CUG	A	–	A	–
1.21	Bilateral closed user group	A	–	A	–
1.22	Bilateral CUG with outgoing access	A	–	A	–
1.23	Fast select acceptance	E	–	FS	–
1.24	Reverse charging acceptance	A	–	A	–
1.25	Local charging prevention	A	–	FS	–
1.26	Network user identification subscription	A	–	A	–
1.27	NUI override	A	–	–	–
1.28	Charging information	A	–	A	–
1.29	RPOA subscription	A	–	A	–
1.30	Hunt group	A	–	A	–
1.31	Call redirection	A	–	FS	–
1.33	A bit (TOA/NPI)	A	A	FS	–
1.34	Direct call	FS	–	A	–

Table 4–3 *Continued*

	Facility	User Class of Service			
		8–13		**20–22**	
		SVC	PVC	SVC	PVC
2.	**Optional user facilities on a per–call basis**				
2.1	Flow control parameter negotiation	E	–	–	–
2.2	Throughput class negotiation	E	–	–	–
2.3	Closed user group selection	E	–	E	–
2.4	Closed user group with outgoing access selection	A	–	FS	–
2.5	Bilateral closed user group selection	A	–	FS	–
2.6	Reverse charging	A	–	A	–
2.7	Fast select	E	–	FS	–
2.8	Network user identification selection	A	–	A	–
2.9	Charging information	A	–	A	–
2.10	RPOA selection	A	–	A	–
2.11	Call deflection selection	A	–	–	–
2.12	Call redirection or deflection notification	A	–	FS	–
2.13	Called line address modified notification	A	–	FS	–
2.14	Transit delay selection and indication	E	–	–	–
2.15	Abbreviated address calling	FS	–	A	–

THE X.25 QOS OPERATIONS: FACILITIES

As noted in Table 4–3, all X.25 facilities are not required for a vendor to pass a conformance test, yet they provide some very useful functions to end users and some are considered essential to networks. The facilities allow a user to "tailor" somewhat how the network supports the user session. They also provide some useful services for the packet network user and supplier.

Calls Barred Facilities

The incoming calls barred and outgoing calls barred facilities (a) prevent incoming calls from being presented to the DTE, and (b) prevent the DCE from accepting outgoing calls from the DTE. These operations are shown in Figure 4–14(a). Both facilities apply to all logical channels at the DTE/DCE interface and cannot be changed on a per-call basis. A DTE subscribing to incoming calls barred can initiate calls but cannot accept them. A DTE subscribing to outgoing calls barred can receive calls

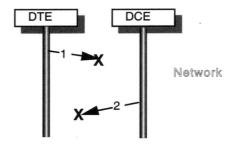

1 = Outgoing calls barred
2 = Incoming call barred
Note: All logical channels on an interface are affected

(a) Incoming/outgoing calls barred

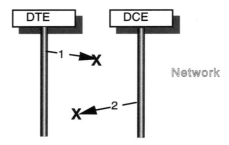

1= Logical channel outgoing
2= Logical channel incoming

Note: Channels can be selected on the interface

(b) Logical channel incoming/outgoing

Figure 4–14   Calls barred and channel screening

but cannot initiate them. Once the call is established, the session operates at full-duplex.

Some network administrations use the calls barred facility to restrict DTE access to the network on the basis of the permitted protocol-
to-protocol agreement between DTEs. This technique, called *protocol
screening*, is enforced by the DCE. If the permitted protocols for either
user do not include the protocol of the other, the call is cleared by using
the calls barred facility.

The logical channel incoming and logical channel outgoing facilities
are useful in reserving a group of logical channels at the DTE/DCE inter-

face, see Figure 4–14(b). It helps place a limit on the number of X.25 calls that can be made. For example, a server might keep some channels designated as incoming only for the customers that call in to use the server. The idea is similar to a telephone-based PBX (private branch exchange) that restricts certain telephone lines to incoming or outgoing calls only. Note the following relationships:

- All virtual calls are one-way outgoing = the incoming calls barred facility
- All virtual calls are one-way incoming = the outgoing calls barred facility

Closed User Group (CUG) Facilities

The closed user group (CUG) facilities allow users to form groups of DTEs from which access is restricted. The CUG facilities provide a level of security/privacy in an "open" network. Some people call this feature a virtual private network (VPN), a term that has been in use for many years and has been dusted-off and reapplied to secure networks. The CUG facilities are established for a period of time, although a DTE that has subscribed to the facility can call other CUGs on a per-call basis. A DTE can belong to a variable number of CUGs; the limitation depends upon the network implementation. This QOS service set consists of several facilities which are summarized in Table 4–5.

As Figure 4–15 suggests, a user can belong to more than one CUG. In so doing, the network administrator must be careful not to build an overly complex CUG membership structure. Some CUGs are outgoing only, some are incoming only, and some are two-way. Therefore, CUG configurations must be consistent, and they should not be redundant.

Reverse Charging Facilities

The reverse charging and reverse charging acceptance facilities allow the packet network charges to accrue to a receiving DTE. They can be used with virtual calls and fast selects. The facility is like "calling collect" on a telephone. Although the two facilities have a close association, they need not be used together.

The reverse charging facility asks the remote DTE to pay for the call. It is requested by the calling DTE on a per-call basis. The reverse charging acceptance facility authorizes the remote DCE to pass to the DTE the Incoming Call packet which request the reverse charging. Oth-

Table 4–5 Closed User Group Facilities

- *Closed user group (CUG).* Allows a DTE to belong to one or more CUGs. It is established for a period of time. When a DTE belongs to more than one CUG, a preferential CUG must be specified.

- *Incoming calls barred within a CUG.* A DTE may initiate calls to other members of the CUG but cannot receive calls from them. This facility is equivalent to establishing all logical channels as one-way outgoing (originate only).

- *Outgoing calls barred within a CUG.* A DTE may receive calls from other members of the CUG, but cannot initiate calls to them. This facility is equivalent to establishing all logical channels as one-way incoming (terminate only).

- *CUG with incoming access.* A DTE will receive calls from DTEs belonging to the open part of the network (open means a non-CUG) and from DTEs which are members of other CUGs with outgoing access.

- *CUG with outgoing access.* A DTE may initiate calls to all DTEs belonging to the open part of the network and to DTEs which are members of other CUGs with incoming access. If the DTE has a preferential CUG, then only the CUG selection facility can be used at the DTE/DCE interface.

- *CUG selection.* May be used by the DTE in a Call Request packet to specify the CUG for the call. It can be used if the DTE has subscribed previously to the CUG with outgoing access facility or the CUG with incoming access facility. It cannot be requested in a call setup, unless one of these facilities has been assigned for a contractual period.

- *CUG with outgoing access selection.* Allows the DTE to specify in the Call Request packet the CUG for the virtual call. It also indicates that outgoing access is desired. The called DTE receives the Incoming Call packet with the identification of the CUG. The packet also indicates that outgoing access is applied at the calling DTE.

erwise, the DCE will not pass the calls, and the originating DTE will receive a Clear Indication packet.

Some networks keep records in their accounting/customer database on attempts to use the user data field in an unsuccessful reverse charge call. The network then charges the user for this call to discourage the use of the free one-way transmission of data (in the small user field of the Call Request packet).

Network User Identification (NUI) Facilities

The network user identification (NUI) facilities enable the DTE to provide billing, security, and/or management information on a per-call basis to the DCE. They can also be used to invoke subscribed facilities or a different set of subscribed facilities with each call. They allow the user

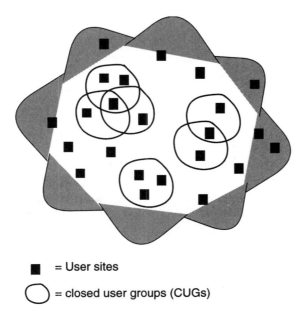

■ = User sites

◯ = closed user groups (CUGs)

Figure 4–15   Possible CUG memberships

to tailor the X.25 facilities to the specific call. Three facilities are grouped under NUI and are described in this section.

The NUI facilities employ network user identifiers to associate a set of facilities with an identifier. Each NUI can be associated with a different set of facilities. The identifier is transmitted to the DCE by the DTE.

The *NUI Subscription* facility allows the DTE to furnish the network information on billing, security, or management matters. The information is contained in either the Call Request packet or the Call Accepted packet by using the *NUI Selection* facility.

The *NUI Override* facility is used on a per-call basis by the NUI Selection facility to override the subscription-time facilities. The override only pertains to the specific call. X.25 places restrictions on which subscription-time facilities may be associated with the NUI and the NUI override facility.

The *NUI Selection* facility is requested by the DTE for a given call, if it has subscribed to one or both of the other NUI facilities. The facility permits the DTE to identify which NUI is to be used with the other two NUI facilities.

Networks have a variety of methods for using the NUI facilities. For example, the NUI can identify a network user independent of the port being used. It allows a dial-up port to be used without requiring a reverse charge call. Some vendors' products use NUI to prevent calls into specific ports. For example, a particular port may not be made available unless the DTE furnishes a valid NUI. Some networks also use the NUI to check against its accounting/customer database to determine the billing address for the call.

Charging Facility

The charging facility requires the DCE to provide the "charged" DTE information about the packet session relating to the charges. The facility can be invoked on a per-call basis or as a subscription for a period of time. If the latter option is in effect, the DTE to be charged does not have to ask for the charging information in the Call Request or Call Accepted packet.

Non-Standard Packet Sizes

The selection of the non-standard packet sizes facility can be different for each direction of data flow. Some networks that allow different levels of priorities will also allow different packet sizes for different priority calls. Be aware that some vendors use different packet size options for (a) the DTE/DCE, (b) the DTE/PAD,[3] and (c) the STE/STE[4] interfaces (X.75 gateway interfaces). The default sizes for each of these interfaces should be checked against the charges for a transmitted packet.

Non-Standard Window Size Facility

The non-standard default window size facility allows the packet window sizes to be expanded beyond the default size of 2, for all calls on the interface, and for an agreed period of time. It is possible for the window sizes to be different at each end of the connection, and some networks constrain the default window size to be the same for each direction of transmission across the DTE/DCE interface.

The DCE may change the DTE/DCE packet window size based on the negotiated packet size and throughput class (discussed shortly). Such an action allows the network to control the buffer requirements for the network.

---

[3]The PAD is a packet assembler/disassembler. It is used to interface non-X.25 equipment into the X.25-based network.

[4]The STE is the signaling terminal equipment, which is a DCE that is configured to run the X.75 NNI.

Example of Facility Negotiations

Figure 4–16 shows one example of how an X.25 negotiation takes place. The local DTE has requested a window size of 6 and a packet size of 512 octets. The packet is transported to the remote DCE and an Incoming Call packet is sent to the DTE with 256 in the size field. This DTE chooses to attempt to negotiate the window size to 3 and the packet size to 128 octets. It places these values in the Call Accepted packet, which is relayed through the network to the local DTE that originated the call request. The local DCE sends a Call Connected packet to the DTE.

In this example, the network did not alter the values that were negotiated between the two DTEs. However, it does have this option during the exchange of the Call Request packet to the remote DTE. Also, X.25 requires that the negotiation move toward the standard default values of 2 for window size and 128 for packet size.

The negotiation features of X.25 represented the first time this operation had been attempted on any scale. The lessons learned have been applied to many protocols and systems that are in place today, such as Frame Relay, the Point-to-Point Protocol (PPP), and ATM.

Throughput Facility

The default throughput classes assignment facility provides for the selection of one of the following throughput rates (in bit/s): 75, 150, 300, 600, 1200, 2400, 4800, 9600, 19200, 48000, and 64000 (other values are

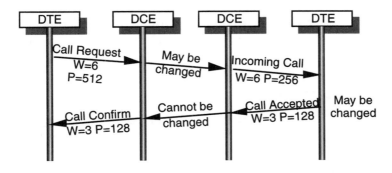

Where:
P   Packet size
W   Window size

Figure 4–16   Negotiating facilities

supported by some networks, but X.25 stipulates these rates). Throughput describes the maximum amount of data that can be sent through the network when the network is operating at full capacity. Factors that influence throughput are line speeds, window sizes, and the number of active sessions in the network.

Other values can be negotiated with the throughput class negotiation facility. Also, throughput class indicates the desired bit transfer rate between the DTE and DCE. Default values are specified at subscription time.

In the event that a throughput class is not accepted, the call need not be cleared or blocked. The DCE can lower the requested throughput to the subscribed value.

Transit Delay and Indication Facility

The transit delay selection and indication facility permits a DTE to select a transit delay time through the packet network. This feature can be quite valuable in giving the user some control over response time in the network. It is established on a per-call basis. The network must inform both DTEs as to the transit delay applicable to the call by using the Incoming Call packet for the called DTE, and the Call Connected packet for the calling DTE. This time may be equal to, greater than, or smaller than the value in the Call Request packet.

Packet Retransmission Facility

The packet retransmission (reject) facility was introduced earlier. It applies to all logical channels at the DTE/DCE interface. The reject facility is not implemented by many networks, because the link level is tasked with the error-detection and retransmission of data. Moreover, X.25 has other conventions for rejecting packets, such as restarts and resets.

Extended Packet Sequencing

The extended packet sequence numbering facility provides packet sequence numbering using modulo 128 (sequence numbers 0 to 127) for all channels at the DTE/DCE interface. In its absence, sequencing is done with modulo 8 (sequence numbers 0 to 7). Bits 5 and 6 in the general format identifier (GFI) field are used to request this service.

This 1984 addition was deemed important in order to contend with the long propagation time of signals on satellite channels and on other media that have a very high bit transfer rate, such as optical fiber. In these situations, the sequence numbers P(S) of 0 through 7 are exhausted by the transmitting station before the receiving station has an opportunity to acknowledge the packets.

X.25 does not allow a sequence number to be reused until the first number is acknowledged. In other words, a DTE cannot send a packet with P(S) = 3 if a preceding packet has used this value and is not yet acknowledged. A limited range of sequence numbers might require the DTE or DCE to "shut down" the sending of packets on the channel. As a consequence, the virtual circuit is forced into an idle condition. This facility simply extends the range of sequence numbers available, which allows the channel to be more fully utilized. This facility is used by networks as a flow control mechanism; it limits the number of packets that can be presented to the network.

Hunt Group Facility

The call destination management facility (the hunt group) distributes incoming calls across a designated grouping of DTE/DCE interfaces. It gives users the ability to allocate multiple ports on a front-end processor or computer. It allows the selection of different front-ends or computers at a user site for the X.25 traffic. These multiple ports are managed by the DCE, which is responsible for distributing the calls across them. The manner in which they are distributed is not within the purview of X.25.

Figure 4–17 illustrates how a hunt group feature operates. DTE 2 and DTE 3 transmit packets to DTE 1. Instead of using addresses A, B, or C in the packet address field, the sending DTEs use the hunt group address Z. The DCE that is servicing DTE 1 receives the packets and determines that address Z is actually a hunt group address for ports A, B, and C. It then passes the packets to DTE 1 across one of these links.

People should ascertain how their networks administer a hunt group. Some networks restrict their use in relation to geographic boundaries served by the hunt group. Others require naming conventions for the hunt group addresses. Also, be aware that the hunt group is sometimes related to a group of subscription time facilities.

Call Redirection and Deflection Facilities

The call redirection and call deflection facilities are used to redirect or deflect packet calls when the destined DTE is out of order, busy, or has requested a call redirection. The destination DTE is called the "originally

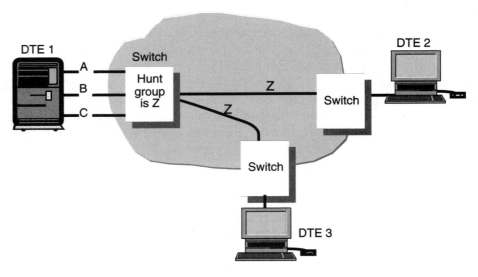

Figure 4–17   Hunt group

called DTE." The DTE receiving the call is called the "alternative DTE." These facilities allow a call to be rerouted to a backup DTE, which keeps problems and failures isolated from the end user. The call redirection could also permit calls to be redirected to different ports of a country due to time-zone considerations. These facilities are limited to the network of the originally called DTE. Figure 4–18 shows the basic differences between the call redirection and call deflection services.

- *Call redirection*: The originally called DTE (remote) does not receive an Incoming Call packet when the redirection is performed.
- *Call deflection*: The originally called DTE (remote) receives an Incoming Call packet and then deflects the call.

Online Facility Registration Facility

The online facility registration permits the local DTE (with a Registration Request packet) to request facilities or to obtain the parameters (values) of the facilities at any time. The local DCE returns a Registration Confirmation packet containing the current value of all the facilities applicable to the DTE/DCE interface. Figure 4–19 shows the dialogue between the DTE and the DCE.

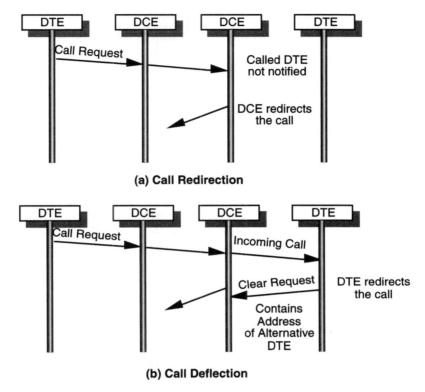

(a) Call Redirection

(b) Call Deflection

Figure 4–18   Call redirection and call deflection

Some networks do not offer all the X.25 facilities; other networks offer their own proprietary facilities. To avoid requesting facilities that are not available or not allowed, the DTE can transmit a Registration Request packet to the DCE containing no facilities values. In turn, the DCE sends back the Registration Confirmation packet containing any facilities that can be negotiated. The DTE can then modify these values in a subsequent Registration Request packet. When the DCE returns the Registration Confirmation packet, the facilities are in effect for any subsequent virtual calls.

It is certainly possible that a facility requested by the DTE is not available or not allowed. It may be allowed, but it could be beyond the bounds of a permissible value. If so, the DCE reports in the Registration Confirmation packet the values allowed and a cause code.

If the DCE cannot accommodate the DTE requests, it will not alter the values of the affected facilities. As examples, the request may conflict

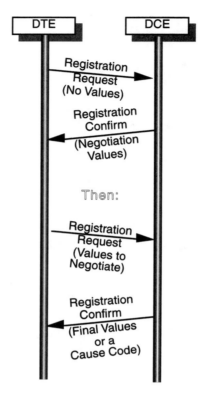

Figure 4–19   On-line facility registration

with the use of other facilities at the DTE/DCE interface, or the request packet may have been issued when a virtual circuit was active at the interface (which would cause a great deal of confusion to the ongoing DTE/DCE dialogue).

Recognized Private Operating Agencies (RPOA) Facility

The RPOA facility allows a calling DTE to specify one or more recognized private operating agencies (RPOA, or service provider) to handle the packet session. The RPOA is a packet network carrier (a value-added carrier), and it acts as a transit network within one country or between countries. See Figure 4–20 for an example of this facility.

The *RPOA subscription* facility is used with all virtual calls involving more than one RPOA and one or more gateways. The *RPOA selection* facility is used for an individual virtual call, and it is not necessary to

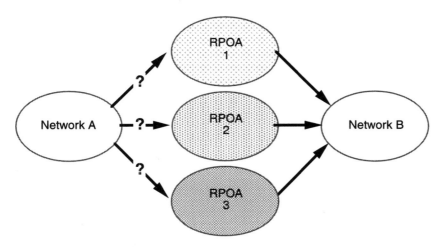

Figure 4–20   RPOA selection

subscribe to the RPOA selection facility to use this facility. With these facilities, the Call Request packet contains a sequence of RPOA transit networks to handle the call. The call is set up, and the packets are routed
based on this information. The selection facility overrides the subscription facility, if both are used.

SUMMARY

While X.25 is an old technology, it is still prevalent in many data
communications networks. Many of its features have found their way
into Frame Relay and ATM. X.25 was the first data communications
technology to include QOS features as part of its services to a user. Its
use is now diminishing, as the industry migrates to Frame Relay, ATM,
and IP-based networks.

5

Frame Relay

This chapter describes how Frame Relay networks can be configured to support several QOS features for the network user. We begin with an analysis of the Frame Relay frame, highlighting the bits in the frame that are used for congestion management and traffic discards. Next, the committed information rate (CIR) is examined in relation to the committed burst rate (Bc) and the excess burst rate (Be). The other QOS parameters are then introduced, as well as the rules on emission and discard priorities. The chapter also includes some recent additions to Frame Relay, including voice over Frame Relay (VoFR). It concludes with a summary of the Frame Relay Forum's Service Level Definitions Implementation Agreement.

FRAME RELAY FEATURES

Frame Relay is the relay technology for many data networks deployed in North America and Europe. This technology provides for demand access to a network by multiplexing user information into frames similar to the High Level Data Link Control (HDLC) frames. The traffic is identified and managed through virtual connection ids, called Data Link Connection Identifiers (DLCIs).

Table 5–1   Frame Relay Features

Connection-oriented with virtual circuits

Connection multiplexing

Switching

Frame (packet)-based

Asynchronous: Cells filled based on demand

Designed for data applications

Switching speed maximized with:

  (a) short headers

  (b) no link-to-link error recovery

Frame Relay has been a very successful technology, especially in the United States, because it is simple to use and is priced attractively. Many companies have opted for Frame Relay in lieu of leased lines because of the attractive price/performance attributes of Frame Relay.

Table 5–1 lists some of the major features of Frame Relay. As we progress through this chapter, and as you read the ATM chapter, it will be evident that Frame Relay and ATM have much in common.

THE FRAME RELAY FRAME

The term "frame" is used by Frame Relay to identify the protocol data unit on the communications link. The Frame Relay frame resembles many other protocols that use the HDLC frame format. It is illustrated in Figure 5–1. It contains the beginning flag used to delimit and recognize the frame on the communications link. The ending flag signals the beginning of the next frame. Frame Relay does not contain a separate address field; the "address" field is contained in the control field which together is designated as the Frame Relay header. The information field contains user data, such as TCP/IP traffic. The frame check sequence (FCS) field, as in other link layer protocols, is used to determine if the frame has been damaged during transmission over the communications link.

The Frame Relay header consists of six fields. They are listed and briefly described here and explained in more detail in subsequent discussions:

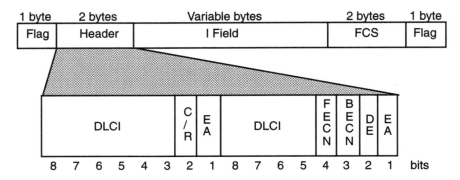

Figure 5–1   The Frame Relay PDU (Frame)

Where:

BECN   Backward explicit congestion notification
C/R   Command/response
DE   Discard eligibility
DLCI   Data link connection identifier
EA   Address extension
FECN   Forward explicit congestion notification
PDU   Protocol data unit

- *DLCI:* The data link connection identifier identifies the virtual circuit user (which is typically a router attached to a Frame Relay network, but can be any machine with a Frame Relay interface). This field is contained in the 10 bits shown in Figure 5–1.
- *C/R:* The command response bit (not used by Frame Relay)
- *EA:* The address extension bits, shown in bit positions 1 in the two octets of the header in Figure 5–1.
- *FECN:* The forward explicit congestion notification bit
- *BECN:* The backward explicit congestion notification bit
- *DE:* The discard eligibility indicator bit

CONGESTION NOTIFICATION

Two mechanisms are employed to (a) alert the user nodes and Frame Relay switches about congestion, and (b) take corrective action. Both capabilities are achieved by the backward explicit congestion notification (BECN) bit and the forward explicit congestion notification (FECN) bit. The use of these bits is depicted in Figure 5–2.

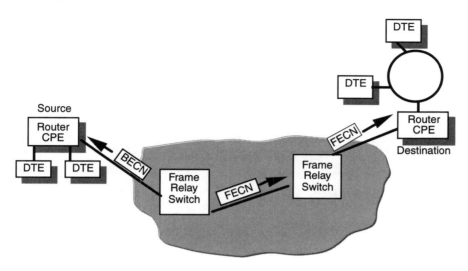

Figure 5–2   The congestion notification bits

Assume that a Frame Relay switch is starting to experience congestion problems. It may inform both the upstream (source) node and the downstream (destination) node of the problem by the use of these bits. The BECN bit is set to 1 in the frame and is sent upstream to notify the source of the traffic that congestion exists at a switch. This action permits the source to reduce or cease its traffic flow transmissions until the congestion problem is solved.

In addition, the FECN bit can be sent to the downstream node to inform it that congestion is occurring upstream. One might question why the FECN bit is used to notify the downstream device that congestion is occurring. After all, the upstream device is the one creating the traffic problem. The answer is that it varies, depending on remedial action that the destination machine might wish to take. For example, the FECN bit could be passed to an upper layer protocol which will allow it to slow down its acknowledgments (which in some protocols would flow-control the upstream traffic flow).

DISCARD ELIGIBILITY

Since congestion can be a problem in a demand-driven network, Frame Relay may discard traffic or reduce its QOS level to avoid congestion problems. In some instances, it is desirable to discern among the

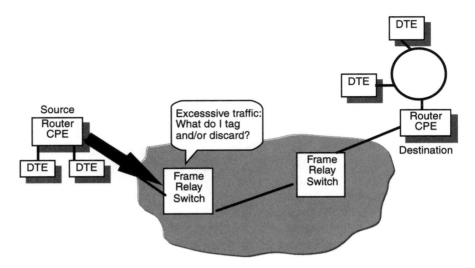

Figure 5–3   The discard eligibility (DE) bit

user's traffic as to which frames should be discarded or have the QOS level reduced. Figure 5–3 shows how discard eligibility is executed.

The approach is to implement the discard eligibility (DE) bit. How the DE bit is acted upon is an implementation specific decision. However, in most instances the DE bit is turned to 1 to indicate to the network that in the event of problems the frame with this bit set to 1 is "more eligible" for being discarded than others in which the bit is set to 0.

Of course, the DE bit need not be implemented. When congestion occurs, a node simply may throw away traffic at random. Not only is this approach not fair, it may entail discarding critical data.

THE CIR

While an end user might be allowed to manipulate the DE bit, a better approach is for the network to use this bit to aid in determining what to do with the traffic. One approach is the technique called the *committed information rate (CIR)*. An end user estimates the amount of traffic that it will be sending during a normal period of time. In turn, the network measures this traffic during the same time interval and if it is less than the CIR value, the network will not alter the DE bit. If the rate exceeds the CIR value during the specified period of time, the network may allow the traffic to go through unless it is congested. If the network is congested, this traffic will be "tagged" by setting DE = 1, and perhaps discarded, or treated with a reduced QOS level.

FLOW CONTROL AND CONGESTION MANAGEMENT

ITU-T Recommendation I.370 provides guidance for flow control and congestion management. It explains the operations at both the user and network interfaces for channel access rates of 2.048 bit/s or less.

The goal of congestion management is to maintain a very high QOS for each user. Congestion management includes (a) congestion control, (b) congestion avoidance, and (c) congestion recovery. Congestion control provides for recovery from congestion during periods of high traffic activity and/or traffic overloads. It includes both congestion avoidance and congestion recovery.

Congestion avoidance seeks to detect congestion and to take remedial actions to prevent or recover from congestion. It attempts to provide high throughput and low delay for each DLCI. As shown in Figure 5–4, congestion management attempts to avoid congestion by taking actions before or at points A and B, and to prevent the situation from deteriorating to point C. Of course, at point C, congestion avoidance cannot be performed, and congestion recovery operations must be executed. These

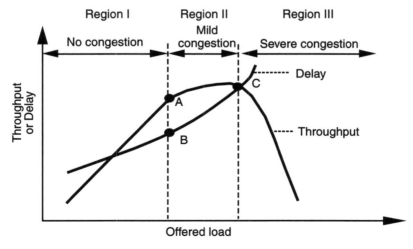

Figure 5–4   Congestion avoidance and throughput

operations attempt to "minimize the damage" to user traffic and network operations. Nonetheless, any operations within Region II many mean a deterioration of QOS to the network subscriber. At point C, frames may be discarded to prevent further congestion.

THE CIR REVISITED

One attraction of the Frame Relay approach is that a user is not constrained to a specific fixed rate at which traffic is sent to the network. This capability is quite attractive for data applications that are bursty in nature.

The majority of Frame Relay networks provide the user with a guaranteed service (relating to throughput) if the user's input rate is below a specified CIR. If the user exceeds the CIR for some period of time, the network may discard traffic. The clause "may discard" means that the network will most likely not discard traffic if it has sufficient resources to transport the user traffic during the time the CIR is exceeded. After all, discarding traffic is tantamount to discarding revenue.

Figure 5–5 illustrates a CIR gauge that is used to show the relationship of CIR and network pricing. The vector moves to the right as traffic

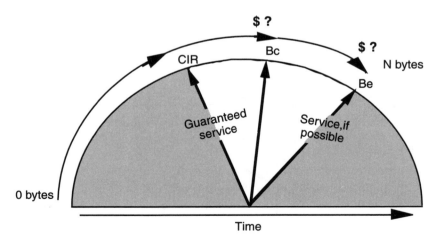

Where:
  Bc   Committed burst rate
  Be   Excess burst rate

Figure 5–5   The committed information rate (CIR) gauge

increases and to the left as traffic decreases. This figure is useful because it permits us to visualize the possible services of a Frame Relay network in relation to possible discard requirements. As we have learned, a Frame Relay network attempts to guarantee service as long as the user traffic falls within the CIR value, and as long as it falls within a committed burst rate (Bc) (and perhaps even an excess burst rate [Be]). Beyond the CIR, service is provided, if possible.

If the network cannot support the traffic load, it will first discard traffic tagged with DE = 1. In addition, it is certainly conceivable that a network would charge more when the vector of the gauge moves past CIR. We could then hypothesize that some maximum rate (typically traffic beyond both burst and excess rate) would allow the network to discard more traffic.

The Bellcore Model

The public Frame Relay networks provide a wide variety of prices and services in relation to CIR, Bc, and Be. Bellcore defines a traffic policing mechanism at the UNI, depicted in Figure 5–6. The approach entails using two credit pools: one for Bc traffic and one for Be traffic. The two credit pools are maintained for every active DLCI.

When the DLCI is provisioned (as either a PVC or a SVC), the CIR parameters are established, and the following values are initialized:

- Bc_credits = Bc
- Be_credits = Be
- Tc = Bc/CIR
- Credit accrual timer = measurement interval (ΔT)

When a frame arrives across the UNI at the network switch, it is processed in accordance with the operations shown in Figure 5–6. Note that arriving frames with DE = 0 and DE = 1 are handled differently. When the accrual ΔT expires, Bc_credits and Be_credits are recomputed based on:

(a) Bc_credits = Min[Bc_credits + (Bc * (ΔT/Tc)), Bc]
(b) Be_credits = Min[Be_credits + (Be * (ΔT/Tc)), Be]

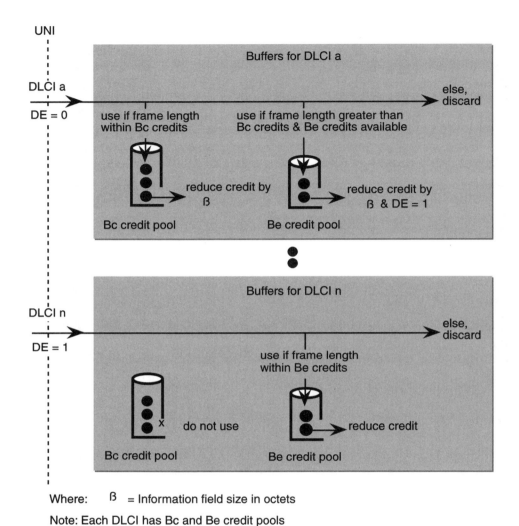

Figure 5–6   Bellcore DLCI traffic policing

COMMITTED AND BURST RATE MANAGEMENT

Let's take another look at the committed and excess burst concepts. Figure 5–7 will be of use during this discussion. The committed burst rate (Bc) describes the maximum amount of data that a user is allowed to offer to the network during the time interval Tc. The Bc is established (perhaps negotiated) during a call setup or pre-provisioned with a PVC.

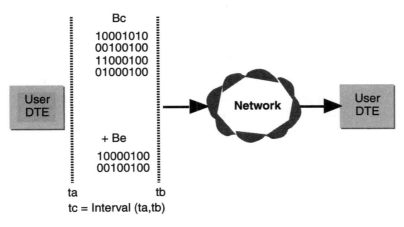

Figure 5–7   Burst rates and time interval

Tc is sometimes called a bandwidth interval, in that it can be used to govern the interval for a burst (or bursts) of traffic to enter the network.

The excess burst rate (Be) describes the maximum amount of data that a user *may send*, which exceeds Bc during the time interval Tc. The value Be can also identify the maximum number of bits that the network *will attempt to deliver* in excess of Bc during an interval Tc. Be is also negotiated during the call setup or pre-provisioned with a PVC. The idea is for Be traffic to be subject to a lower probability of delivery or a lesser QOS level than Bc traffic.

Measurement at Intervals

One issue that must be addressed is how the network and user determine a measurement interval (and agree on it). I.370 also provides guidance for the setting of Tc. The I.370 recommendation defines the measurement interval as shown in Table 5–1.

Table 5–1   Measurement Intervals

CIR	Bc	Be	Tc
>0	>0	>0	Tc = (Bc/CIR)
>0	>0	=0	Tc = (Bc/CIR)
=0	=0	>0	Tc = (Be/access rate)

Example:
1) Bc = 72 kbit/s and CIR = 64 kbit/s sec, then Tc = 1.125 sec.

EXAMPLES OF BC AND CIR OPERATIONS

Figure 5–8 provides two examples of Frame Relay resource allocations at the UNI between the user and the service provider. In both examples, the users inform the network of a data rate (a CIR) that they intend to pass to the network for their applications. In turn, the network is expected to support this data rate.

A key concept here is the fact that each user is allowed to use the physical media at the raw access rate of the media. For example, suppose the link from the user to the network is a DS3 link operating at 45 Mbit/s. While the users in this example are not given the entire 45 Mbit/s capacity on a permanent basis (they don't need it), each is given the full DS3 pipe when transmitting. Therefore, each user's frame is sent across the interface at the DS3 rate and not at the CIR.

Figure 5–9 expands the discussion from Figure 5–8, and concentrates on the traffic from user B. The bottom of the figure shows a profile of user B's bursts to the network during interval Tc. The 256 kbits CIR requirement over Tc of 1.125 sec is consumed by four separate bursts from the user. The example assumes the user's frames are 16 kbits in

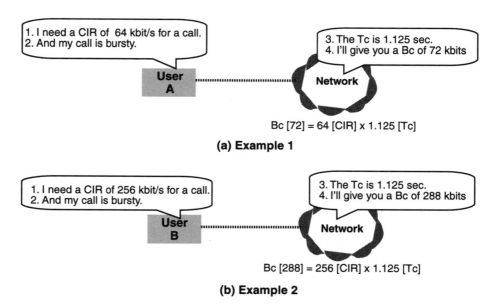

Bc [72] = 64 [CIR] x 1.125 [Tc]

(a) Example 1

Bc [288] = 256 [CIR] x 1.125 [Tc]

(b) Example 2

Figure 5–8   Examples of CIR Bc Assignments

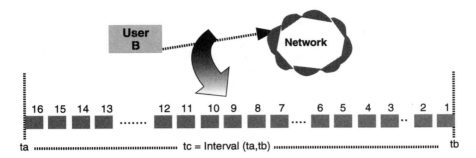

Figure 5–9   Example of a burst profile

length (a big frame to be sure). Sending 16 frames of 16 kbits over Tc = 256 kbit/s. The bursts are:

- Burst 1: Frames 1 and 2
- Burst 2: Frames 3–6
- Burst 3: Frames 7–12
- Burst 4: Frames 13–16

RELATIONSHIP OF CIR, FRAME SIZE, AND LINK SPEED

The implementation of the Frame Relay CIR requires considerable study of how the frames from different users on the interface are queued at the provider's switch and how the queue is serviced. It also entails additional study for traffic arriving from different input interfaces that are destined to the same output interface. For the latter situation, different CIRs and different link speeds will translate into different users' frames (likely) being interleaved (multiplexed) through the outgoing interface, because these frames are arriving at different times on the input interfaces.

Table 5–2 shows the relationships for the CIR, the frame size, and the link speed in relation to the delay factor and the arrival time of the frame [SMIT93].[1] The table entries show that the input order of the frames coming into the switch are not the same as the order in which

---

[1][SMIT93].   Smith, Philip, *Frame Relay: Principles and Applications,* Addison-Wesley, 1993.

Table 5–2   Queuing as a result of CIR [SMIT93]

Frame	CIR (kbit/s)	Frame Size	Arrival Time (sec)	Arrival Order	Delay Factor (sec)	Output Order
A1	64	1000	.00049	1	.01563	2
A2	64	1500	.00122	2	.03906	4
A3	64	600	.00151	4	.04844	7
B1	128	5000	.00244	5	.03906	5
B2	128	8000	.00635	8	.10156	8
B3	128	6000	.00928	9	.14844	9
C1	256	3000	.00146	3	.01172	1
C2	256	5000	.00391	6	.03125	3
C3	256	4000	.00586	7	.04688	6

they are output to the egress interface. These operations take into account the arrival time of the previous frame if more than one frame arrives at the switch from the users. A delay factor must take into account the delay of the previous frame because two frames cannot be output onto the same link at the same time. The calculations suggested by [SMIT93] are (link speed is an E1 2.048 Mbit/s link):

> Arrival time = Frame size/Link speed + arrival time of previous frame
>
> Delay factor = Frame size/CIR + delay factor of previous frame

The important point about this discussion is that a higher CIR will likely lead to faster service through the switch. In this table, frame C1 was the third to arrive, but the first to be sent, because its CIR was higher than the other two users.

CIR AND Tc

The ITU-T recommends that end-user terminals should have the ability to receive explicit congestion notifications and react to them. Remember that the end-user terminal is not a workstation but a router, a multiplexer, etc.

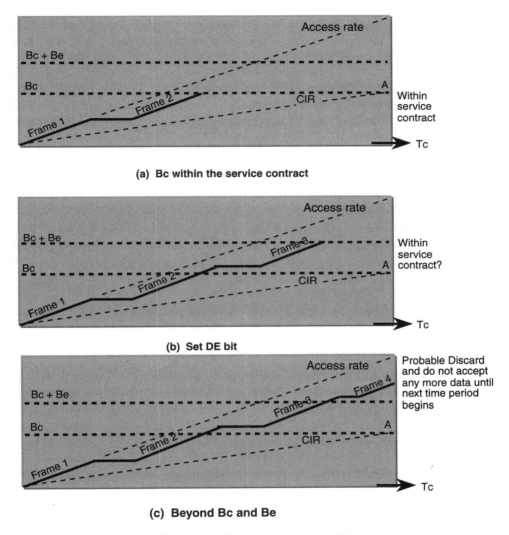

(a) Bc within the service contract

(b) Set DE bit

(c) Beyond Bc and Be

Figure 5–10   Relationships of the Frame Relay parameters

I.370 provides a useful diagram and explanation of the relationships of Bc, Be, and the CIR over measurement period Tc. Figure 5–10 shows these relationships. In Figure 5–10(a), frames 1 and 2 should be delivered through the Frame Relay network with the guaranteed QOS. These frames are sent at the raw access rate within the Bc agreement. Notice that the line representing CIR represents the slope determined by Bc/Tc.

Indeed, both CIR and Bc (and Be) are slopes (gradients). However, the frames' gradient is the same as the access rate, and not the CIR, since CIR is less than Bc (and Be).

In Figure 5–10(b), frame 3 (with frames 1 and 2) are greater than Bc but do not exceed Bc plus Be. The user's QOS may be met, and frame 3 would most likely be delivered—although it could be marked as a possible discard if unusual conditions exist in the network.

In Figure 5–10(c), frame 4 (and the accumulation of frames 1, 2, and 3) violates the Bc plus Be provision and could be marked for probable discard or could be discarded at the entrance to the network.

In the ideal world, the last bit of the last frame of a user's burst would be sent to the network during interval Tc exactly at point A. This means that the user would send CIR $\times$ Tc bits, which is not likely to happen. For example, for a time interval of T_C = 1.125 sec., and a CIR of 64 kbit/s the total burst would be exactly 72 kbit/s (64 kbit/s $\times$ 1.125).

GUIDELINES ON USE OF FECN AND BECN

The Frame Relay specifications provide guidelines and rules on how the user and network can react to the receipt of FECN = 1, the receipt of BECN = 1, or loss of traffic, and Table 5–3 summarizes these guidelines. Before we examine this subject, a few comments about congestion should prove helpful.

The Frame Relay switch at the ingress UNI must exercise prudence in the amount of traffic that it allows to enter into the network. For example, due to the effect of queuing and its potentially severe consequences on network throughput, flow control measures must be undertaken at the UNI before congestion becomes severe. In other words, the network UNI switch must have the capability to know when to flow-control the user traffic. Since traffic in a data network is bursty, the soft-

Table 5–3   FECN and BECN implementations

FECN Usage	*Windows*
User	FECN with no traffic loss
Network	FECN when traffic loss is detected
BECN Usage	BECN with no traffic loss
User	BECN when traffic loss is detected
Network	

ware at the switch must be somewhat "smart," in that it must be able to predict the time at which the traffic load will become a problem. Certainly, the software must not be so unintelligent that it waits too long before taking remedial action. The consequences of serious network congestion and the precipitous drop in throughput only result in unhappy users.

The buildup of excess queues and the resultant severe effect on network throughput also holds true for its effect on response time and delay. One might think that there is a one-to-one relationship between degraded throughput and degraded response time. While congestion degrades the QOS of both of these features, overall network throughput may actually benefit from longer queues because the network can build these queues and use them to smooth traffic conditions over a period of time.

However, achieving superior performance relating to delay-and-response time requires the network to keep the queues small. Indeed, the smaller the queues, the better the response time. However, in the final analysis, congestion eventually degrades QOS for both throughput and delay.

ANSI T1.618, Annex A provides guidelines for the use of the BECN and FECN bits by both the user and the network. I will first discuss some ideas for FECN usage, and follow that with some ideas for BECN usage. Next, I include in these discussions how window-based mechanisms can be employed, and how the detection of lost traffic can affect flow control. Again, see Table 5–3 for this discussion.

FECN Usage

User. The user device compares the number of frames it receives from the network in which the FECN bit is set to 1 to the number of frames in which the FECN bit is set to 0 over a measurement period. During this period, if the number of FECN bits set to 1 are equal to or exceed the number of FECN bits set to 0 the user device should reduce its throughput to .875 of its previous throughput value. Conversely, if the number of FECN bits set to 0 exceed the number of FECN bits set to 1, the user device is allowed to increase transmissions by $\frac{1}{16}$ (0.0625) of its throughput (a slow start operation). The measurement interval is to be equal to approximately four times the end-to-end transit delay.

Network. For the network use of the FECN bit, the Frame Relay node continuously monitors the size of each queue, based on what is known as a regeneration cycle. This cycle begins when a queue on an out-going channel goes from idle (the queue is empty) to busy (the queue has traffic). During a measurement period, which is defined by the start of the previous regeneration cycle and the present time within the current measuring cycle, the average size of the queue is computed. When this average size exceeds a predetermined threshold value, this circuit is considered to be in a state of "incipient congestion." At this time, the FECN bit is set to 1 and remains set to 1 until the average queue size falls below this preestablished threshold.

ANSI T1.618 defines an algorithm to compute the average queue length. The algorithm consists of computing a queue length update, a queue area update, and an average queue length update, making use of the following variables:

t = Current time
t_i = Time of the ith arrival or departure event
q_i = Number of frames in the system after the event
T_0 = Time at the beginning of the previous cycle
T_1 = Time at the beginning of the current cycle

The algorithm consists of three components:

• Queue length update:

Beginning with q0 = 0,

If the ith event is an arrival event, $q_i = q_i + 1$

If the ith event is a departure event, $q_i = q_i - 1$

• Queue area (integral) update:

Area of the previous cycle = $\sum_{t\ell\epsilon T1,t} q_i - 1 (t_i - t_i - 1)$

Area of the current cycle = $\sum_{t\ell\epsilon T1,t} q_i - 1 (t_i - t_i - 1)$

• Average queue length update:

Average queue length over the two cycles =

$$\frac{\text{Area of the two cycles}}{\text{Time of the two cycles}} = \frac{\text{Area of the two cycles}}{t - T_0}$$

BECN Usage

If a user receives n consecutive frames with BECN = 1, the traffic should be reduced from the user by a step below the current offered rate. The step count (S) is defined in this order:

0.675 times throughput

0.5 times throughput

0.25 times throughput

Likewise traffic can be built up after receiving n/2 consecutive frames with BECN = 0. The rate is increased by a factor of 0.125 times the throughput.

The value of S is computed as follows:

$$IR_f = \frac{TH_f}{8} + \left(\frac{Be_f}{Be_f + Bc_f}\right)\frac{Ar_f}{8}$$

$$IR_b = \frac{Th_b}{8} + \left(\frac{Be_b}{Be_b + Bc_b}\right)\frac{Ar_b}{8}$$

$$S = \frac{F_b}{F_f}\left(IR_f\frac{EETD}{N202_f} + IR_b\frac{EETD}{N202_b}\right)$$

where

IR_f	=	information rate in the forward direction
IR_b	=	information rate in the backward direction
S	=	step function count
TH_f	=	throughput in the forward direction agreed during call establishment
TH_b	=	throughput in the backward direction agreed during call establishment
EETD	=	end-to-end transit delay
$N202_f$	=	maximum information field length in the forward direction
$N202_b$	=	maximum information field length in the backward direction
Ar_f	=	access rate forward
Ar_b	=	access rate backward
Be_f	=	excess burst size forward
Be_b	=	excess burst size backward
Bc_f	=	committed burst size forward
Bc_b	=	committed burst size backward
F_b/F_f	=	ratio (either expected or measured over some implementation-dependent period of time) of frames received to frames sent.

Network. For network use of the BECN bit, it is recommended that the network begin setting the BECN to 1 prior to encountering serious congestion and having to discard frames. However, it is clear that if congestion reaches a point of creating severe throughput and delay problems, the network should start to discard frames, preferably frames with the DE bit set to 1.

Use of Windows

FECN with no traffic loss. If the user device employs a protocol that uses windows for flow control, it compares the number of frames received with FECN = 1 and FECN = 0 during a measurement interval equal to two window turns (the maximum number of frames that can be sent before an acknowledgment is required represents one window turn). If the number of frames with FECN = 1 are greater than or equal to the number of frames with FECN = 0, the user reduces the window size to 0.875 of its current value. If, on the other hand, the number of FECN = 1 frames is less than the number of FECN = 0 frames, the user increases the window size by one frame (not to exceed the maximum window size for the virtual circuit). With each adjustment, the process begins anew.

FECN when traffic loss is detected. Assuming the user device can detect the loss of traffic, upon the detection of nonreceipt of a frame, the user reduces the window size to 0.25 of its current value. However, if it is known that the network is providing congestion notification and no FECN = 1 frames were received during the measurement interval, it is likely that congestion is not the problem. After all, the network would normally send FECN = 1 frames if problems were occurring. Therefore, it is assumed that frame loss is due to errors (noise on the line, etc.) and not congestion. In this situation, the working window size is reduced by a factor of 0.625 instead of 0.25.

BECN with no traffic loss. In this situation, the step count S (discussed earlier) is used to govern the user's traffic flow. For this discussion, S is defined as one window turn. If a frame with BECN = 1 is received, the user reduces the window size by 0.625, and continues to reduce the window size if S consecutive frames of BECN = 1 are received. The window cannot be reduced to less than one frame. As soon as BECN = 0 frames are received, the user increases the window by one frame after receiving a total of S/2 FECN frames.

BECN when traffic loss is detected. Assuming the user device can detect the loss of traffic, upon detection of the nonreceipt of a frame the user reduces its sending rate to 0.25 of the current rate if either the rate is being reduced due to congestion notification, or the network does not provide BECN = 1 operations.

OTHER QOS OPERATIONS AND MEASUREMENTS

Throughput

Throughput is defined as the number of bits [in the frame's information (I) field] that have been successfully transferred in one direction per unit time over a virtual connection. Figure 5–11 illustrates the throughput concept. The virtual connection can include any number of intermediate components between two user devices (data terminal equipment, or DTEs). The term "successful transfer" means that the frame check sequence (FCS) check indicates that the frame transfer has been completed successfully.

Transit Delay

Transit delay is the time taken to send a frame across a link between two machines, and Figure 5–12 shows the ideas behind transit delay. Transit delay is a function of the access rate of the link, the link distance, and the size of the frame. Link distance is usually ignored since it is a small value. Thus, transit delay is calculated as frame size (in bits)/link access rate (in bits/s).

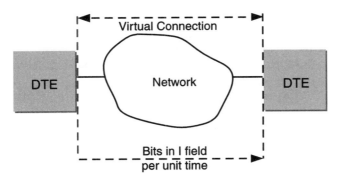

Figure 5–11   Throughput

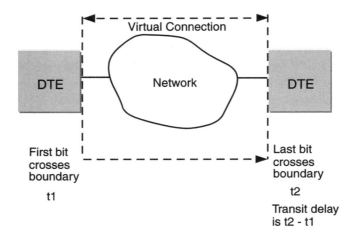

Figure 5–12   Transit delay

Transit delay is measured between pairs of boundaries. The boundaries can be defined in a number of ways, although ITU-T X.13 uses the following definition: A boundary separates a network section for the adjacent circuit section or it separates an access circuit section from the adjacent DTE.

Transit delay can define a boundary between two DTEs, or between two international networks, or between national networks, etc. Whatever the boundary is, transit delay starts at the time T_1, when the first bit of the PDU crosses the first boundary. It ends at time T_2, when the last bit of the PDU crosses the second boundary. That is to say, transit delay = $T_2 - T_1$. Transit delay through each boundary is summed to equal the total transit delay across a virtual connection.

Virtual Circuit Transit Delay

The virtual circuit transit delay is the sum of all the section delays. The decision to sum all delays (and each section delay) depends upon the agreements between network administrations. Figure 5–13 illustrates the virtual circuit transit delay concept.

Residual Error Rate (RER)

The residual error rate is measured through the exchange of the Frame Relay service data units (FSDUs)[2] during a specified period and

---

[2]The SDU is an OSI term that is used in Frame Relay (and ATM) to describe the unit of traffic submitted to a lower layer from an upper layer.

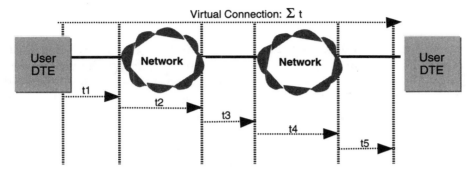

Figure 5–13   Virtual circuit transit delay

across a specified boundary—typically, between the core functions of Q.922 and the protocol implemented above Q.922. Figure 5–14 illustrates the operations of RER. The RER is defined as

R = 1 – (total correct SDUs delivered)/(total offered SDUs).

Without question, parameters such as throughput and delay are important in obtaining bandwidth on demand. Therefore, a user should pay close attention to these parameters when examining network offerings. The RER is equally important. After all, it is important for the user to

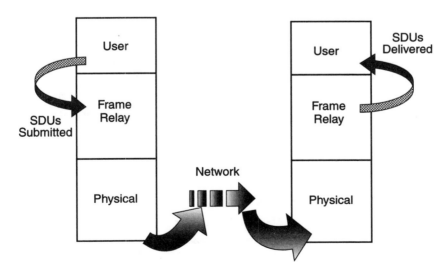

Figure 5–14   Residual error rate (RER)

know the relationship of traffic submitted to the network to that of traffic successfully delivered by the network.

The RER should be correlated with the users' actual throughput and committed burst rates. As an example, if users exceed their throughput agreement (contract), it should be expected that their traffic will be discarded and the RER will suffer. However, these matters should be examined in relation to the SLA contract. For example, if a user stays within the contract, a better RER should be expected, as well as a more attractive billing plan from the network. Conversely, the more a user violates the contract limits, the worse the RER.

EMISSION AND DISCARD PRIORITIES

Provisioning the QOS class is identical to that for a FR user-to-network (UNI) or FR network-to-network (NNI) connection. The emission priorities and discard priorities of the connection are separately provisioned to provide the QOS desired. These priorities are summarized in Table 5–4.

Other Parameters

The ITU-T has also defined other performance and QOS parameters. They are summarized in this section and in Table 5–5.

A *delivered erred frame* is defined as a frame that is delivered when the values of one or more of the bits in the frame are discovered to be in

Table 5–4   Emission and discard priorities

FR emission priority	Traffic type
Class 0	Multimedia (e.g., voice) with high emission priority
Class 1	Data with medium-high emission priority
Class 2	Data with medium emission priority
Class 3	Data with normal emission priority
FR discard priority	*Traffic type*
Class 0[1]	Control traffic (not used by Frame Relay)
Class 1	High importance
Class 2	Medium importance
Class 3[2]	Low importance

Notes
1. Not provisionable
2. Not provisionable; automatically assigned for DE = 1 traffic

Table 5–5   Other Statistics and Performance Criteria

- Delivered erred frames
- Delivered duplicate frames
- Delivered out-of-sequence frames
- Lost frames
- Misdelivered frames
- Switched virtual call establishment delay
- Switched virtual call clearing delay
- Premature disconnect
- Switched virtual call clearing failure

error. The *delivered duplicate frames* value is determined when a frame received at a destination is discovered to be the same frame as one previously delivered. The *delivered out-of-sequence frame* describes the arrival of a frame that is not in sequence relative to previously delivered frames. A lost frame is so declared when the frame is not delivered correctly within a specified time. A *misdelivered frame* is one that is delivered to the wrong destination. In this situation, DLCI interpretation may be in error, the routing table may be out of date, etc. The *switched virtual call establishment delay* and *clearing delay* refer respectively to the time taken to set up a call and clear a call. The *premature disconnect* describes the loss of the virtual circuit connection, and the *switched virtual call clearing failure* describes a failure to tear down the switched virtual call.

Other Frame Relay Specifications

Because of the rather fragmented manner in which the Frame Relay specifications developed, some of the standards define similar operations. For example, several documents define how a user device and a Frame Relay node exchange status information with "Status" and "Status Enquiry" messages. Additionally, some of them are derived from the ITU-T Q.931 Recommendation, which is the original specification for layer 3 of ISDN.

Figure 5–15 summarizes the major parts and aspects of the Frame Relay specifications. The reader should query a Frame Relay vendor carefully about that vendor's specific support for these various standards. Some of these specifications do not pertain to the subject matter of

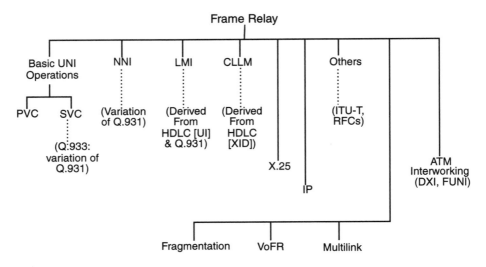

Figure 5–15   The Frame Relay specifications

this book. If you wish more details on these standards, I refer you to [BLAC98].[3]

The Consolidated Link Layer Management (CLLM) Specification

It is appropriate to examine another of the Frame Relay specifications depicted in Figure 5–15 that deals with the subject of congestion, the Consolidated Link Layer Management (CLLM) specification. Since

---

[3][BLAC98]. Black, Uyless, *Frame Relay Networks*, McGraw-Hill, 3rd Edition, 1998.

the FECN and BECN bits reside inside user frames, they cannot be issued to a user device unless user traffic is flowing to that specific device. In other words, the initial Frame Relay specification had no provision for out-of-band network management messages. Therefore, the network had no convenient method for notifying a user about congestion problems.

To solve the problem, the CLLM operation uses DLCI 1023 (as a reserved channel) to notify the user about problems. Figure 5–16 provides an example of how the CLLM message is used, both to the upstream and downstream user device.

The CLLM operation supports the following modes of operations. First, it can identify more than one DLCI, if necessary. Second, it can identify active DLCIs that are problems. Third, it can identify inactive DLCIs that should not be activated.

The CLLM Frame. Since HDLC and its subsets (for example, the link access control procedure for the D channel [LAPD]) are widely used throughout the industry, it is relatively easy to adapt parts of the protocol for use in other systems. In addition, the International Standards Organization (ISO) administers the use and registration of the exchange identification (XID) operation in HDLC, which allows XID to be applied to different network and links in a systematic and known manner. CLLM uses the XID frame to carry its information. Figure 5–17 shows the general format for the XID information and its relation to the Frame Relay frame.

The XID header contains the HDLC control field, which identifies an XID "frame." The format identifier is a registered number from the ISO. The group field is defined in ISO 8885 and, for CLLM, indicates that "private" (CLLM-specific parameters) will be contained in the parameter fields of the frame.

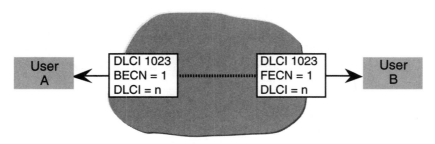

Figure 5–16 Consolidated Link Layer Management (CLLM)

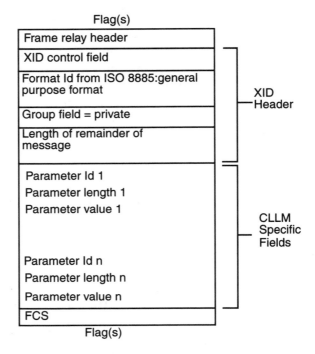

Figure 5–17   CLLM format

SWITCHED VIRTUAL CALLS (SVCs)

The Frame Relay Forum has also developed a standard for SVCs. Figure 5–18 illustrates the procedures for an SVC call establishment. SVC mapping begins with the user issuing a SETUP message to the Frame Relay network. This message contains the usual header information and the DLCI to be associated with the call. The message must also contain the called party number which is an E.164 address.

Other optional fields can be placed in the message and/or have default values established for them. The default values (for information elements) that are defined at subscription time are the transit network field and the link layer core parameters field.

Asymmetrical QOS

During the SVC procedure, the following QOS parameters may be negotiated:

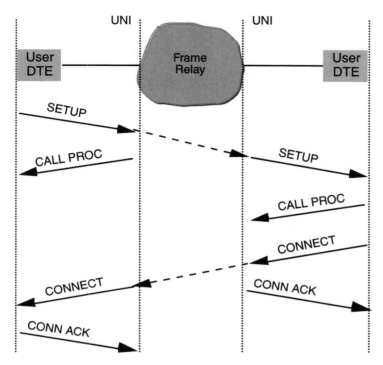

Figure 5–18 UNI SVC connection setup

- Bc
- Be
- Delay
- Throughput

These QOS parameters need not be the same values for the full-duplex virtual circuit. That is, they can differ from one direction to the other. This concept is what I call asymmetrical QOS. It can be useful, for example, in a client/server session in which more traffic is being sent by the server than the client. Consequently, the server's Bc and throughput parameters can be larger than those of the client.

Figure 5–19 shows the procedures for clearing a call. Either the user party or the network party may release the call by issuing a DISCON-NECT message. Whichever party is involved, upon the receive party receiving a DISCONNECT message, it must in turn send a RELEASE message back to the clearing party. The RELEASE message then invokes

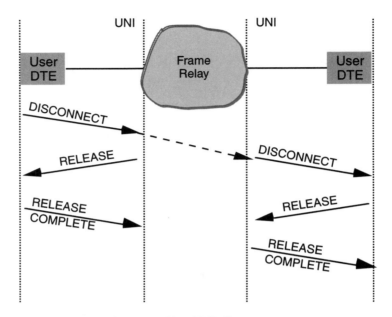

Figure 5–19   UNI disconnect

the RELEASE COMPLETE message, both at the local UNI as well as at the remote UNI.

A PROGRESS message may be sent to the calling user to inform this user that it may take a while longer to process the call. This approach would allow certain timers to be stopped, which avoids the unnecessary time-outs.

The Other SVC Messages

As mentioned earlier, Frame Relay uses the ISDN Q.931 (with modifications) specification for connection control messages. These messages are summarized in Table 5–6 and explained in this section (except those previously defined).

The ALERTING message is sent by the called user to the network and forwarded to the calling user to indicate that a call to the called user has indeed been initiated. In turn, the CALL PROCEEDING message is sent by the call user to the network and forwarded to the calling user to indicate that a call establishment procedure has been begun. It also indicates that additional call information for this call is not necessary and will not be accepted.

Table 5–6 Frame Relay connection control messages

Call Establishment	*Call Clearing*
CONNECT	DISCONNECT
CALL PROCEEDING	RELEASE
PROGRESS	RELEASE COMPLETE
CONNECT ACKNOWLEDGE	*Miscellaneous*
SETUP	STATUS
ALERTING	STATUS ENQUIRY

There are two other connection control messages that may be used for Frame Relay call management. A STATUS message invokes a STATUS ENQUIRY message, which is simply a response to the STATUS message. The STATUS ENQUIRY message can be sent by the user or the network to solicit information about various operations and procedures occurring in the Frame Relay network. STATUS and STATUS ENQUIRY messages are also used to report certain error and diagnostic messages about DLCIs and physical links.

Message Format

Now that we have developed a general understanding of the Frame Relay messages, it will be helpful to examine the contents of the fields of the messages to gain a better understanding of how the messages are used for Frame Relay connection control. Figure 5–20 illustrates the format and fields of the message.

The protocol discriminator field occupies the first octet of the message. Its purpose is to distinguish user-to-network call control messages from other messages. For Frame Relay, the protocol discriminator's value for both the ITU-T and ANSI specifications is 00001000. This value is defined in Q.931 to identify user-to-network call control messages. It is also defined in the same manner in the ITU-T and ANSI Frame Relay specifications.

The second octet contains 4 bits for the length of the call reference field. The call reference field occupies octet 3 of the message. The purpose of this field is to identify uniquely each call at the Frame Relay interface.

The last required field for all Frame Relay messages is the message type field. It occupies 7 bits of the fourth octet of the message. This field identifies the type of message that is being sent across the interface.

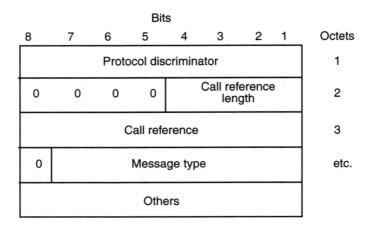

Figure 5–20   The SVC message

ADDITIONS TO FRAME RELAY OPERATIONS

During the years of 1996 to 1998, the Frame Relay Forum added three new features to Frame Relay. The following material provides a synopsis of these operations and describes the three functions: (a) PVC fragmentation, (b) voice over Frame Relay (VoFR), and (c) multilink Frame Relay (MFR). We begin this discussion with an analysis of PVC fragmentation.

Fragmentation

The fragmentation operation was developed by the Frame Relay Forum to support delay sensitive traffic such as voice connections. One approach is to multiplex the shorter frames onto the same physical interface that support longer frames. In other words, it is possible to interleave delay sensitive traffic and non-delay sensitive traffic. Obviously, this feature allows the sharing of the link by both real-time and nonreal-time traffic. The size of the fragments is implementation-specific and the fragment size can be configured based on the attributes of the line and interface as well as local clocking mechanisms, such as a channelized or an unchannelized interface. The idea is to allow each local interface to be responsible for fragmentation.

Figure 5–21 shows the format for the fragmentation header. The header is two octets in length and follows the conventional Frame Relay header. The contents of the header are as follows (beginning in octet 3 of Figure 5–21).

Bit 8	Bit 7	Bit 6	Bit 5	Bit 4	Bit 3	Bit 2	Bit 1	Octet
DLCI high six bits						C/R	0	1
DLCI low four bits				F	B	DE	1	2
0	0	0	0	0	0	1	1	3
1	0	1	1	0	0	0	1	4
B	E	C	Sequence number of high order 4 bits				R	5
Sequence number of low order 8 bits								6
Payload								5-n
Frame Check Sequence (FCS)								5-n+2

Figure 5–21   Fragmentation header

The end-to-end fragmentation also uses the multiprotocol encapsulation operation in accordance with Frame Relay Forum's specification FRF.3.1, titled "Multiprotocol Encapsulation Agreement." The unnumbered information (UI) octet (octet 3) is used for this process (0x03), and the network layer protocol ID (NLPID) value of 0xB1 (octet 4) has been assigned to identify the fragmentation header format.

- The beginning (B) bit is set to one for the first data fragment of the original frame. It is set to 0 for all other fragments of the frame. The ending (E) fragment bit is set to 1 for the last data fragment of the original data frame and it is set to 0 for all other data fragments. A data fragment can be both a beginning and ending fragment, therefore it can have both the B and E bits set to 1.
- The control (C) bit is set to 0 and is not used in the current implementation agreement. It is reserved for future operations.
- The sequence number is incremented for each data fragment transmitted on the link. A separate sequence number is maintained for each DLCI in the interfaces.

Voice over Frame Relay (VoFR)

Because of the wide-scale use of Frame Relay, some effort has been made to expand Frame Relay networks to support voice traffic. The Frame Relay Forum has published a specification for this process. It is titled, *Voice over Frame Relay Implementation Agreement—FRF.11.*

The major components of this specification deal with analog-to-digital, digital-to-analog, voice compression operations, and the transmission of the digitized images in the Frame Relay frame. In addition to the transfer of the voice traffic, the frames can also convey data and fax images, as well as the signaling needed to set up, manage, and tear down the voice and fax connection. Support is provided for dialed digits, line seizures, and other signals used in telephony, such as the ABCD signaling bits.

One of the key components of VoFR is called service multiplexing, which supports multiple voice and data channels on a single Frame Relay connection. This concept is shown in Figure 5–22. Multiple streams of user traffic (which are called subchannels) consisting of different voice and data transmission flows are multiplexed across one DLCI (DLCI n in this example). VoFR is responsible for delivering the frames to the receiving user in the order in which they were sent from the transmitting user.

Figure 5–23 shows the relationships of the subchannels to the DLCIs. The user applications at A and B are multiplexed into one virtual circuit and identified as subchannels (SCs) A and B, and also identified with DLCI 5. The user application at C is multiplexed into another virtual circuit, identified with DLCI 9 and an SC of C. It is the job of the VoFR gateway to assemble the subchannels to the Frame Relay frame. If users B and A are sending traffic that pertains to one overall traffic flow (for example, a conversation on the telephone that discusses a data flow that is exchanged and exhibited on a workstation screen), Frame Relay does not define how these two images are played out at the receiver's machines. This aspect of multiservice multiplexing is left to specific vendor implementations.

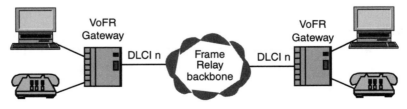

Figure 5–22   Service multiplexing

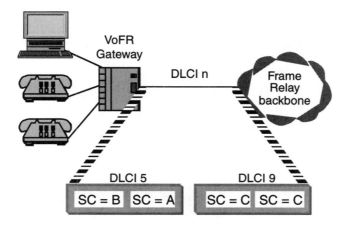

Figure 5–23   Subchannel (SC) concept

Multilink Frame Relay (MFR)

MFR is used to group or aggregate bandwidth on a set of Frame Relay links between two machines, as depicted in Figure 5–24. MFR is useful for Frame Relay customers who need to use bandwidths greater than T1 but less than T3. In addition, some customers need to aggregate multiple DS0s, and MFR provides for these features. The approach is to use software for the service in contrast to a similar solution called inverse multiplexing, which uses hardware. The software solution is considerably less expensive than its hardware counterpart.

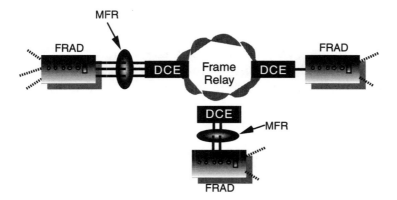

Where:
FRAD   Frame Relay access device (such as a multiplexer, router, etc.)

Figure 5–24   Multilink Frame Relay (MFR)

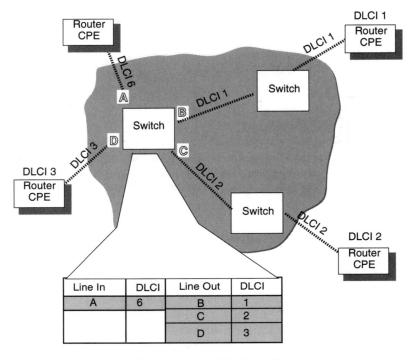

Figure 5–25   Multicasting

MULTICASTING

Some vendors are considering the support of an optional feature called *multicasting*. This is a "semi-broadcast" technology in which multiple routers are identified with one DLCI. As Figure 5–25 shows, the router need only send one copy of the frame with the reserved DLCI value in the header. The network is then required to duplicate the frame and deliver copies to a set of line-in DLCIs.

FRAME RELAY FORUM'S SERVICE LEVEL DEFINITIONS

The Frame Relay Forum publishes FRF.13, the Service Level Definitions Implementation Agreement (IA). This IA was introduced in Chapter 1 (see Figure 1–11). FRF.13 defines several metrics that can be used for the SLA between customers and Frame Relay service providers. The customers can use the parameters to compare different service providers, measure the quality of specific Frame Relay service offerings, and enforce SLA contracts. Network service providers and equipment vendors also utilize the parameters to plan, describe, and evaluate Frame Relay products and service offerings.

Figure 5–26 expands the view of Figure 1–11. The additional components in this figure are:

Frame Entry Event	Frame enters a network or end system. The event occurs when the last bit of the closing flag of the frame crosses the boundary.
Frame Exit Event	Frame exits a network or end system. The event occurs when the first bit of the address field of the frame crosses the boundary.
Traffic Policing Function	Traffic policing functions applied to an incoming frame.
Egress Queue Function	The physical interface transmission queue. All frames for all connections are queued here. Some implementations support an aggregation of connection CIR commitments in excess of the bandwidth available on an interface.

The four SLA metrics for the reference points are as follows. They are explained shortly:

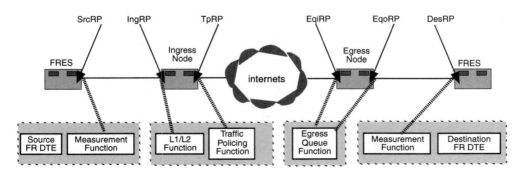

Figure 5–26   Reference points and functional entities for service levels

- Frame transfer delay
- Frame delivery ratio
- Data delivery ratio
- Service availability

SL Measurement Domains

QOS domains were discussed in Chapter 1, and the potential difficulty of a customer's UNI service provider knowing about the QOS support from the downstream providers; that is, if they meet the customer's QOS requirements. FRF.13 addresses this problem by defining measurement domains: where the measurements are taken if the service spans multiple service providers (multiple QOS domains). The idea is to be able to logically concatenate multiple QOS domains into one QOS domain, an idea also supported in DiffServ (Chapter 9). For this discussion refer to Figure 5–27.

Three monitoring domains define the scope of the monitoring operations: (a) end-to-end, (b) edge-to-edge interface, and (c) edge-to-edge (egress) queue. The end-to-end scope is applicable to the Frame Relay end stations (FRES) and all Frame Relay QOS domains between these stations. It is measured between the SrcRP and DesRP reference points. The edge-to-edge interface scope measures performance within a Frame Relay network; that is one QOS domain. It is measured between the IngRP and EqoRP reference points. The edge-to-edge (egress) queue

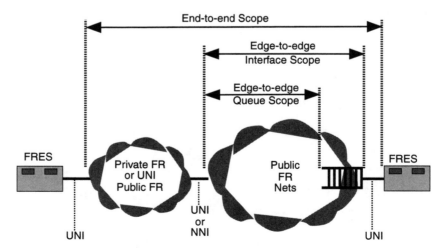

Figure 5–27   Monitoring domains

takes into account that a service provider may have no control on its emissions onto a link for which it has no control. In this example, it is the link to the destination end station. It is measured between the IngRP and EqiRP reference points.

The SL Parameters and Algorithms

This part of the discussion is divided into four parts, reflecting the four SLA definitions (metrics) and monitoring points.

Frame Transfer Delay.   The frame delay parameter reports the time required to transport traffic through the network. The value of the parameter is the difference in milliseconds between the time a frame exits a source and the time the same frame enters the destination (see Figure 5–12).

The SLA for frame transfer delay must describe:

- Which portion of the connection is measured (i.e., end-to-end or switch edge to switch edge) (See Figure 5–13)
- How delay is measured (e.g., a router ping, an external probe)
- Which connections are measured
- How often delay measurements are made
- What size frame is used to measure the delay

Frame transfer delay (FTD) is measured as: $FTD = t2 - t1$, where $t1$ is the time in milliseconds when a frame leaves the source, and $t2$ is the time in milliseconds when a frame arrives at the destination. The reference points for measuring frame transfer delay are as follows:

Measurement Domain	Source	Destination
End-to-end	SrcRP	DesRP
Edge-to-edge interface	IngRP	EqoRP
Edge-to-edge egress queue	IngRP	EqiRP

Frame Delivery Ratio.   The Frame Delivery Ratio (FDR) parameter reports the network's effectiveness in transporting an offered Frame Relay load in one direction of a connection. The FDR is a ratio of successful frame receptions to attempted frame transmissions.

The SLA must must describe:

- How the delivery ratio is measured (a router MIB, an external probe)
- Which connections are measured
- Which portion of the connection is measured (i.e., end-to-end or switch edge to switch edge)
- What adjustments are made (for example, service provider is not responsible for frames discarded because of customer node congestion)

Three frame delivery ratios are defined in FRF.13. They are as follows:

FDR   Frame Delivery Ratio:

$$FDR = \frac{(FramesDelivered_c + FramesDelivered_e)}{(FramesOffered_c + FramesOffered_e)} = \frac{FramesDelivered_{c+e}}{FramesOffered_{c+e}}$$

FDR$_c$ Frame Delivery Ratio for load consisting of frames within the committed information rate:

$$FDR_c = \frac{FramesDelivered_c}{FramesOffered_c}$$

FDR$_e$ Frame Delivery Ratio for load in excess of the committed information rate:

$$FDR_e = \frac{FramesDelivered_e}{FramesOffered_e}$$

Where,

FramesDelivered$_c$	Successfully delivered frames within committed information rate,
FramesDelivered$_e$	Successfully delivered frames in excess of CIR,
FramesDelivered$_{c+e}$	Successfully delivered total frames, including those within committed information rate and those in excess of CIR,
FramesOffered$_c$	Attempted frame transmissions within committed information rate,
FramesOffered$_e$	Attempted frame transmissions in excess of CIR, and
FramesOffered$_{c+e}$	Attempted total frame transmissions, including those within committed information rate and those in excess of CIR.

Data Delivery Ratio. The Data Delivery Ratio (DDR) parameter reports the network's effectiveness in transporting user payload (the I field of the frame) in one direction of a one connection. The DDR is a ratio of successful payload octets received to attempted payload octets transmitted, and is similar to the ITU-T and ANSI discussions in this chapter on residual error rates (see Figure 5–14).

The SLA must describe:

- How the data delivery ratio is measured
- Which connections are measured
- Which portion of the connection is measured
- What adjustments are made

Three Data Delivery Ratios are defined in FRF.13. They are as follows:

DDR   Data Delivery Ratio:

$$\mathbf{DDR} = \frac{(\mathrm{DataDelivered_c} + \mathrm{DataDelivered_e})}{(\mathrm{DataOffered_c} + \mathrm{DataOffered_e})} = \frac{\mathrm{DataDelivered_{c+e}}}{\mathrm{DataOffered_{c+e}}}$$

DDR$_c$ Data Delivery Ratio for load consisting of frames within the committed information rate:

$$\mathrm{DDR_c} = \frac{\mathrm{DataDelivered_c}}{\mathrm{DataOffered_c}}$$

DDR$_e$ Data Delivery Ratio for load in excess of the committed information rate:

$$\mathrm{DDR_e} = \frac{\mathrm{DataDelivered_e}}{\mathrm{DataOffered_e}}$$

Where,

DataDelivered$_c$	Successfully delivered data payload octets within committed information rate,
DataDelivered$_e$	Successfully delivered data payload octets in excess of CIR,
DataDelivered$_{c+e}$	Successfully delivered total data payload octets, including those within committed information rate and those in excess of CIR,
DataOffered$_c$	Attempted data payload octet transmissions within committed information rate

DataOffered$_e$ Attempted data payload octet transmissions in excess of CIR, and

DataOffered$_{c+e}$ Attempted total data payload octet transmissions, including those within committed information rate and those in excess of CIR.

Service Availability. The Service Availability parameters report the operational readiness of individual virtual connections. Included in the service availability parameters are the virtual connection availability (FRVCA), connection mean time to repair (FRMTTR) and connection mean time between service outages (FRMTBSO). Two types of outages are defined:

- *Fault outage:* Outages resulting from faults in the network and thus tracked by the Service Availability parameters
- *Excluded outage:* Outages resulting from faults beyond the control of the network as well as scheduled maintenance.

The SLA must describe:

- How connection availability is measured
- How faults are classified as qualified or excluded
- What the minimum fault outage threshold is for computing FRMTTR/ FRMTBSO
- Which connections are measured

Three service availability parameters are defined in FRF.13. They are as follows:

FRVCA   Frame Relay virtual connection availability:

$$FRVCA = \frac{IntervalTime - ExcludedOutageTime - OutageTime}{IntervalTime - ExcludedOutageTime} * 100$$

FRMTTR   Frame Relay mean time to repair for virtual connection when OutageCount > 0:

$$FRMTTR = \frac{OutageTime}{OutageCount}$$

Frame Relay mean time to repair for virtual connection when OutageCount = 0:

$$FRMTTR = 0$$

FRMTBSO   Frame Relay mean time between service outages for virtual connection when Outage Count > 0:

$$FRMTBSO = \frac{IntervalTime - ExcludedOutageTime - OutageTime}{OutageCount}$$

Frame Relay mean time between service outages for virtual connection when OutageCount = 0:

$$FRMTBSO = 0$$

Where,

IntervalTime   Time in minutes of period that availability is measured,

OutageTime   Aggregate time of all fault outages that occur during the period availability is measured,

ExcludedOutageTime   Aggregate time of all excluded outages that occur during the period availability is measured, and

OutageCount   Count of all fault outages that occur during the period availability is measured.[4]

SUMMARY

Frame Relay networks can be configured to support a variety of QOS features for the network user. The Frame Relay frame contains the bits for congestion management and traffic discards. The committed information rate (CIR) and the associated QOS parameters committed burst rate (Bc), and excess burst rate (Be) are provisioned for the Frame Relay virtual circuit. Other QOS features are provided, such as throughput and delay, as well as the rules on emission and discard priorities of the customer's traffic. Recent additions to Frame Relay, include voice over Frame Relay (VoFR). The Frame Relay Forum has published FRF.13, a valuable specification and tool for designing SLA monitors.

---

[4] This definition of Outage Count is not aligned with X.144.

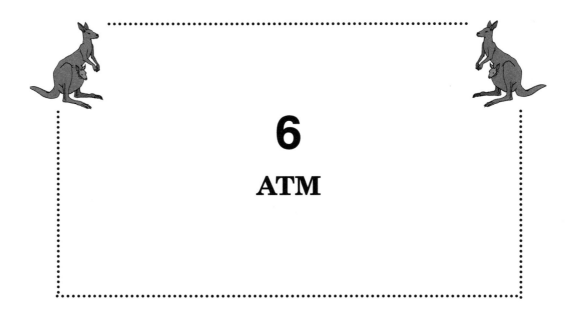

6
ATM

T his chapter describes how ATM networks can be configured to support a wide array of QOS features for the network user. We begin with an analysis of the major ATM features and a description of the ATM cell. Next, the ATM adaptation layer (AAL) is introduced and the ATM traffic classes. The QOS operations are then explained, as well as the rules for supporting synchronous real-time and asynchronous nonreal-time traffic. The chapter concludes with a look at ATM connections on demand, a tool for negotiating QOS dynamically.

ATM FEATURES

The Asynchronous Transfer Mode (ATM) forms the switching and multiplexing foundation for many broadband networks. This technology provides for demand access to a network by multiplexing user information into fixed length slots called cells. The traffic is identified and managed through virtual circuit identifiers.

ATM is a relatively new technology and is beginning to gain some market share in wide area backbone networks. Like any new technology, it takes a while for the deployment to take place, but ATM is an attrac-

Table 6–1   Asynchronous Transfer Mode (ATM) Features

Connection-oriented with virtual circuits

Connection multiplexing

Switching

Cell-based

Segmentation/reassembly

Asynchronous:
   Cells filled based on demand

Multiservice (multi-application)

Switching speed maximized with:
   (a) short headers
   (b) predefined paths
   (c) no link-to-link error recovery

tive technology, because of the features it offers. Table 6–1 lists some of the major features of ATM.

ATM SPECIFICATIONS

Multiple protocols are required to support complete ATM QOS operations. The number of protocols required depends upon where the user traffic is being transported. Figure 6–1 shows that a variety of different protocols and procedures may be invoked.

The user-to-network interface (UNI) is the most important protocol, because it defines the procedures for the operations between the user equipment and the ATM node. As the figure shows, two forms of UNI are supported: a private UNI and a public UNI. The major difference between these interfaces pertains to the physical communications links between the machines. A private UNI will likely operate on a link such as a private fiber, or twisted pair. Also, a private UNI will probably not implement formal SLA contracts, although it might implement the same monitoring and policing procedures that exist at the public UNI. A public UNI likely consists of SDH/SONET, DS3, or E3 links at the UNI. And it is at this interface that a formal SLA is established.

The network-network interface (NNI) can exist as both a public or private interface as well. It defines the interworking of the ATM network nodes. The NNI is defined by the ITU-T (for the public NNI) and the

ATM Forum (for the private NNI, called PNNI). NNI is also known as the network-node interface.

The intercarrier interface (ICI) is an internetworking protocol. As such, it defines the operations and procedures that exist between different carriers' networks.

The data exchange interface (DXI) has been developed by the ATM Forum to provide a standard procedure for the interfacing of non-ATM

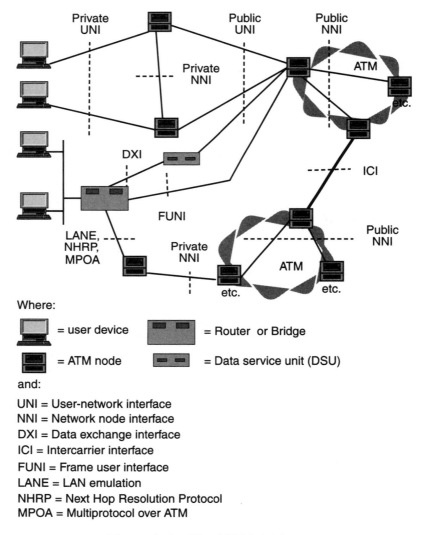

Where:

= user device   = Router or Bridge

= ATM node   = Data service unit (DSU)

and:

UNI = User-network interface
NNI = Network node interface
DXI = Data exchange interface
ICI = Intercarrier interface
FUNI = Frame user interface
LANE = LAN emulation
NHRP = Next Hop Resolution Protocol
MPOA = Multiprotocol over ATM

Figure 6–1   The ATM interfaces

equipment into an ATM node. The DXI is a very simple protocol and allows an easy migration into ATM. However, it does require the use of a data service unit (DSU). The frame UNI (FUNI) is similar to DXI, but it does not require the DSU.

Three other interfaces are now defined by the ATM forum. They are LAN Emulation (LANE), the Next Hop Resolution Protocol (NHRP), and Multiprotocol over ATM (MPOA). As a whole, they are designed to inter-network ATM hubs with LANs, and the Internet protocol stacks (IP, for example).

This chapter concentrates on the UNI, ICI, and NNI operations. The other interfaces and associated protocols are covered in the ATM Volumes I, II, and III in this series.

THE ANCHORAGE ACCORDS

One of the ongoing complaints about some of the formal ATM standards organizations is the time it takes to publish a technical specification. In addition, these specifications (standards) often are incomplete, and issues are left for "further study."

This complaint certainly cannot be levied against the ATM Forum. It has published about seventy specifications. Indeed, there have been complaints that network managers and ATM vendors cannot form a cohesive ATM "outlook," because of the profusion of information emanating from the ATM task forces. I prefer to have this overabundance of information, rather than none at all.

The ATM Forum has reached an agreement (the Anchorage Accord) that is designed to address these problems. It contains a set of specifications that are stable and provides guidance on the applicability of the specifications to six specific network environments. These environments are shown in Table 6–2 along with the applicable specifications to support each network environment [DOBR97].[1]

In a nutshell, notable progress has been made by the ATM Forum in getting ATM off-the-blocks, and other issues are being addressed, such as voice over ATM. It is the goal of the ATM Forum to complete the outstanding major specifications as soon as possible in order to facilitate the creation, implementation, and use of standardized ATM products.

---

[1][DOBR97] Dobrowski, George, and Humphrey, Marlis."The Anchorage Accord," *Business Communication Review*, June, 1997.

Table 6–2   The Anchorage Accord [DOBR97]

ATM Specification	Campus	Legacy LAN	Multimedia Desktop	Extended Campus	Legacy WAN	Multimedia WAN
ATM UNI v3.1	X	X	X	X	X	X
BICI v2.0					X	X
DXI v1.0		X				
ILMI v4.0	X	X	X	X	X	X
LANE over ATM 1.0 Includes LANE Client Management	X	X				
Network Management: Customer Network Management for ATM Public Network Service			X			
Network Management: M4 Interface Requirements & Logical MIB						X
Network Management: CMIP for the M4 Interface						X
Network Management: M4 Public Network View Requirements & Logical MIB						X
Network Management: M4 Logical MIB Addendum						X
Network Management: CES IW Requirements Logical CMIP MIB						X
Network Management: M4 Network View CMIP MIB 1.0						X

Network Management:					
AAL Management for the M4					X
PNNI v1.0		X	X	X	X
Frame UNI		X	X	X	
Circuit Emulation		X	X		X
Native ATM Services: Semantic Description	X				
AudioVisual Multimedia	X				
ATM Name System 1.0	X	X	X		X
UNI Signaling 4.0	X	X	X	X	X

From: *Business Communications Review* (BCR), June 1997, George Dobrowski and Marlis Humphrey,

THE ATM CELL

The ATM protocol data unit (PDU) is called a cell, and is shown in Figure 6–2. It is 53 octets in length, with 5 octets devoted to the ATM cell header, and 48 octets used by AAL and the user payload. Most of the values in the 5-octet cell header consist of the virtual circuit labels of VPI and VCI.

A payload type identifier (PTI) field identifies the type of traffic residing in the cell. The cell may contain user traffic or management/control traffic. The ATM Forum has expanded the use of this field to identify other payload types (OAM, control, etc.). Interestingly, the GFC field does not contain the congestion notification codes, because the name of the field was created before all of its functions were identified. The flow control fields (actually, congestion notification) are contained in the PTI field, or in a special resource management (RM) cell.

The cell loss priority (C or CLP) field is a 1-bit value. It is a tagging/marking bit. If the CLP bit is set to 1, the cell is subject to being discarded or processed at a low priority by the network. Whether or not the cell is discarded depends on network conditions and the policy of the net-

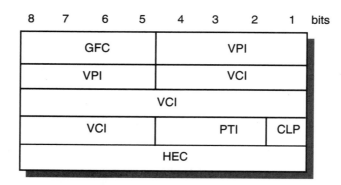

Where:
   CLP Cell loss priority
   GFC Generic flow control
   HEC Header error control
   PTI Payload type ID
   VCI Virtual channel ID
   VPI Virtual path ID

Figure 6–2   The ATM cell

work administrator. The CLP set to 0 indicates a higher priority of the cell to the network.

The header error control (HEC) field is an error check field, and also corrects a 1-bit error. It is calculated on the 5-octet ATM header, and not on the 48-octet user payload. ATM employs an adaptive error detection/correction mechanism with the HEC.

SERVICE CLASSES AND THE AAL

The ATM adaptation layer (AAL) rests on top of the ATM layer. It is organized around a concept called service classes, which are summarized in Table 6–3. The classes are defined with regards to the following QOS operations:

- Timing between sender and receiver (present or not present)
- Bit rate (variable or constant)

Table 6–3   AAL classes of traffic

Purpose:
   Aggregate different traffic into standard formats to support different applications

Class A
   Constant bit rate (CBR)
   Connection-oriented
   Timing required

Class B
   Variable bit rate (VBR)
   Connection-oriented
   Timing required

Class C
   Variable bit rate (VBR)
   Connection-oriented
   Timing not required

Class D
   Variable bit rate (VBR)
   Connectionless
   Timing not required

Class X
   Defined by the user

- Connectionless or connection-oriented sessions between sender and receiver
- Sequencing of user payload
- Flow control operations
- Accounting for user traffic
- Segmentation and reassembly (SAR) of user packets

The ITU-T also defines four classes of traffic, identified as A through D. Figure 6–3 is used for this discussion. Classes A and B require timing relationships between the source and destination. Therefore, clocking mechanisms are utilized for this traffic. ATM does not specify the type of synchronization—it could be a timestamp or a synchronous clock. This function is performed in the application running on top of AAL. Classes C and D do not require precise timing relationships. A constant bit rate (CBR) is required for class A; and a variable bit rate (VBR) is permitted for classes B, C, and D. Classes A, B, and C are connection-oriented; while class D is connectionless.

It is obvious that these classes are intended to support different types of user applications. For example, class A is designed to support a CBR requirement for high-quality video applications. On the other hand, class B, while connection-oriented, supports VBR applications and is applicable for VBR video and voice applications.

Class C services are the connection-oriented data transfer services such as X.25-type connections. Conventional connectionless services such as IP networks are supported with class D services.

Class	A	B	C	D
Timing	Synchronous		Asynchronous	
Bit transfer	Constant	Variable		
Connection mode	Connection-oriented			Connection-less
AAL Type	Type 1	Type 2	Type 3/4 Type 5	Type 3/4 Type 5

Figure 6–3   Support operations for AAL classes

THE AAL DATA UNITS

The AAL 48-byte data units are depicted in Figure 6–4. The ATM adaptation layer (AAL) uses type 1 protocol data units (PDUs) to support applications requiring a constant bit rate (CBR) transfer to and from the layer above AAL. It is also responsible for the following tasks: (a) segmentation and reassembly of user information, (b) handling the variable cell delay, (c) detecting lost and missequenced cells, (d) providing source clock frequency recovery at the receiver, and (e) correcting all 1-bit errors in the PDU and detecting of all 2-bit errors.

The AAL type 1 PDU consists of 48 octets with 47 octets available for the user's payload. The first header field is a sequence number (SN) and is used for detection of mistakenly-inserted cells or lost cells. The other header field is the sequence number protection (SNP), and it is used to provide for SN error detection and correction operations. The AAL type 1 conversion sublayer is responsible for clock recovery for both audio and video services.

AAL type 2 is employed for variable bit rate (VBR) services where a timing relationship is required between the source and destination sites. For example, class B traffic, such as variable bit rate audio or video, would fall into this category. It is responsible for handling variable cell delay as well as the detection and handling of lost or mis-sequenced cells.

The fields in the AAL2 header are as follows:

- Offset field (OSF)   Number of octets between start field and packet; acts as a pointer into the payload
- Sequence number (SN)   Sequence number of the PDU
- Parity (P)   Odd parity check on the start field
- Channel ID (CID)   Used to identify logical user channels
- Length indicator (LI)   Number of octets in payload
- User-to-user information (UUI)   A user field, transported transparently between users
- Header error control (HEC)   Error check on 3-octet packet header
- PAD (padding bytes)   To fill-out payload to 48 octets

AAL5 was conceived because AAL 3/4 was considered to contain unnecessary overhead, and it was judged that multiplexing (which AAL 3/4

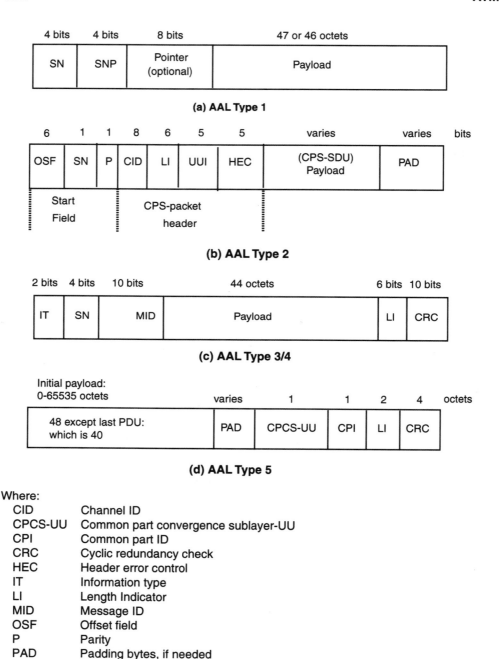

Figure 6–4   The AAL protocol data units (PDUs)

supports) could be pushed up to any upper layer, and that the some of the AAL 3/4 operations at the receiver were not needed.[2]

Figure 6–4 also shows the format of the type 5 PDU. It consists of an 8-octet trailer. The PAD field acts as a filler to fill out the PDU to 48 octets. The CPCS-UU field is used to identify the user payload. The common part indicator (CPI) has not been fully defined in ITU-T I.363. The length field (LI) defines the payload length, and the CRC field is used to detect errors in the SSCS PDU (user data).

Type 5 is used for most data applications. Although the specifications cite its support for connectionless traffic, it can be used for connection-oriented traffic as well.

VOICE SUPPORT IN ATM

Figure 6–5 provides an example of how AAL2 supports voice traffic. We assume a voice over ATM (VoATM) gateway accepts analog speech at the sender and digitizes it, thus creating G.729.A voice packets, which are presented to AAL2. At the receiving VoATM gateway, this process is reversed.

The G.729.A Recommendation is designed for low-bit rate audio coders and operates at 8 kbit/s. Each G.729.A frame is 10 octets (bytes) in length. For this example the voice packet is encapsulated with the Real Time Protocol (RTP), thus creating a 14-octet packet (the RTP header is 4 octets in length).

The offset field points to the start of the packet. This field is placed in the first octet of the 48-octet ATM-SDU. The RTP/G.729.A packet is appended with the AAL 2 packet header and these 17 octets are placed in the cell payload. The process simply loads the ATM-SDU with contiguous 17 octets until the 48 octets are filled. In this example, the third packet is placed in the last part of the first cell and the first part of the second cell (noted by the shading in the figure). The offset field in the second cell points to the first CPS packet header, which is the fourth packet in this stream. The length of the packet is indicated in the packet header, therefore, and in this example, is used to determine the remaining octets of the third packet residing in the second cell.

This example shows support of voice only, with fixed-length packets. AAL 2 can also support voice and data traffic by multiplexing these ap-

---

[2]AAL3/4 is not used much and is not discussed here.

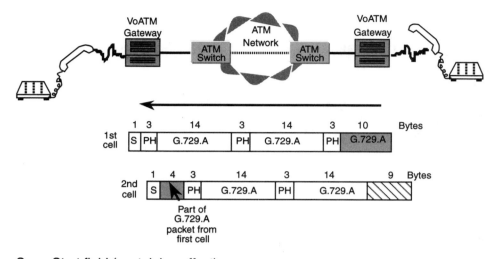

S   Start field (containing offset)
PH   Packet header

Figure 6–5   AAL 2 Support of voice traffic

plications together, and identifying each traffic stream (fixed-length voice and variable-length data) with a unique channel identifier (CID). The AAL 2 operations to handle these applications are like the example in this figure: The offset field identifies the packet boundaries. Those packets that cannot fit into one cell, are segmented and the packet's remaining octets are placed in the next cell.

PROTECTING THE CONNECTION

For large ATM networks that must support many users, the issue of network robustness is paramount, and the network provider must devise ways to ensure that the customer's traffic is delivered safely. One method for providing this service is called protection switching, which uses alternate links between ATM nodes to transmit the ATM cells, in case the primary link fails. This concept is identical to the operations shown in Figure 3–10 in Chapter 3, so we need not dwell on it further.

PERFORMANCE PARAMETERS

The ATM Forum has defined a set of ATM cell transfer performance parameters to correspond to the ITU-T Recommendation I.350. These parameters are summarized in Table 6–4. Most of them are self-descriptive, but a few more comments are in order.

For the *severely-errored cell block ratio,* a cell block is a sequence of n cells sent consecutively on a given connection. A reasonable way to measure this operation is to assume that a cell block is a sequence of cells transmitted between OAM cells, although the size of a cell block is not specified in the standards.

The *cell misinsertion rate* value is calculated as a rate and not as a ratio, since misinsertion operations are independent of the amount of traffic transmitted.

The *cell delay variation (CDV)* has two performance parameters associated with it: (a) the 1-point CDV, and (b) the 2-point CDV. The 1-point CDV describes the variability in the arrival pattern observed at a measurement point in reference to 1/T. The 2-point CDV describes variability in the arrival pattern observed at an output in relation to the pattern at an input.

Table 6–4   Cell transfer performance

Cell error ratio:
  errored cells / successfully transferred cells + errored cells

Severely-errored cell block ratio:
  severely errored cell blocks / total transmitted cell blocks

Cell loss ratio:
  lost cells / total transmitted cells

Cell misinsertion rate:
  misinserted cells / time interval

Cell transfer delay:
  elapsed time between a cell transfer

Mean cell transfer delay:
  average of number of cell transfer delays for one or more connections

Cell delay variation (CDV):
  Variability of the pattern of cell arrival for a given connection

Peak cell rate (PCR):
  permitted burst profile (an upper bound)

Sustainable cell rate is (SCR):
  permitted upper bound on average rate

The *peak cell rate (PCR)* is coded as cells per second. A further discussion of this parameter is deferred until further related definitions are clarified.

A network operator may or may not provide these services to its subscribers. However, some of these services must be implemented if the cell relay network is to operate efficiently. As examples, *peak rate traffic enforcement* and *traffic shaping* should be part of the network's ongoing functions in order to keep congestion under control.

Figure 6–6 shows some general (and not all-inclusive) examples of operations dealing with performance: (1) successfully delivered cells, (2) lost cells, (3) inserted cells, and (4) severely damaged cells.

As shown in Figure 6–6 (a), any error-free cell that arrives (Δt) before its maximum allowed time (T) is considered to be a successfully delivered cell (Δt is $< T$). This cell must be "conformant," in that it is intelligible to the receiver. Although not shown in Figure 6–6(a), a cell that arrives too early also presents problems because there may be insufficient buffer space to hold the cell. Thus these "premature" cells are also nonconformant.

Figure 6–6 (b) shows three scenarios for cell loss. In scenario 1, cell loss occurs when a cell arrives later than time T (Δt is $> T$). Even though the cell arrived safely, it is still considered lost, because in some applications, such as voice and video, a late-arriving cell is not timely enough to use it in the digital-to-analog conversion process.

In scenario 2, cell loss can also occur because of buffering problems which result in cells being discarded. Cells can also simply be lost due to mishandling by faulty software. It is also possible to experience a cell loss when an error results in the incorrect rebuilding of the header, which also results in a new VPI/VCI being injected in to the network, and a cell disappearing from the network and the virtual circuit.

In scenario 3, the cell is also defined as lost when it has an error of more than 1 bit in the header as the header error correction function cannot correct errors of more than 1 bit.

As depicted in Figure 6–6(c), a cell may be inserted into the flow due to the incorrect construction of cross-connect tables. This situation is similar to some of the problems associated with Figure 6–6(b), except this particular problem is the result of faulty configuration management practices.

In Figure 6–6(d), a severely damaged cell is one in which the user I field contains bit errors (the 48-byte portion of the ATM cell). This error is not detected by the ATM layer, which operates only on the 5-byte header. It must be checked by the AAL or the user application.

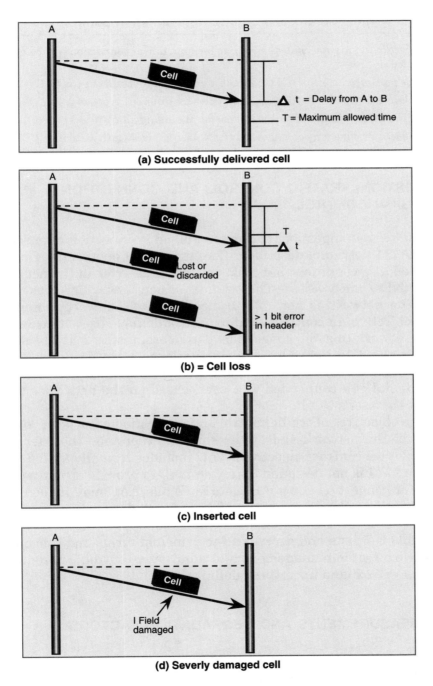

(a) Successfully delivered cell

(b) = Cell loss

(c) Inserted cell

(d) Severely damaged cell

Figure 6–6   Cell transfer performance parameters

Table 6–5   Traffic Control and Connection Admission Control

- *Connection admission control (CAC):* determine if user connection will be accepted or rejected
- *Usage parameter control (UPC):* Monitor and regulate traffic at the UNI
- *Cell loss priority (CLP):* Establish priorities for different types of traffic
- *Traffic shaping:* Establish mechanisms for managing all traffic
- *Feedback:* Provide a mechanism to inform user of bandwidth availability

---

CONGESTION, TRAFFIC CONTROL, AND CONNECTION ADMISSION CONTROL

The terms congestion, traffic control, and connection admission control in ATM networks describe different types of operations. Congestion is defined as a condition that exists at the ATM layer in the network elements (NEs) such as switches, transmission links, or cross connects where the network is not able to meet a stated and negotiated performance objective. In contrast, traffic control defines a set of actions taken by the network to avoid congestion. Therefore, traffic control takes measures to adapt to unpredictable fluctuations in traffic flows and other problems within the network. Connection admission control is the granting or denial of a connection to a user, based on the network's ability to support the user's QOS.

The objectives of traffic control and connection admission control are to protect the network and at the same time provide the user with its stated service contract objectives. This includes formally stated QOS objectives. ATM is not designed to rely on AAL to provide any type of traffic control or congestion control measures. While AAL may indeed perform these functions, the design of the ATM network does not assume this service.

Table 6–5 lists and describes the principal terms and concepts associated with traffic management and admission control. Subsequent discussions will expand upon these definitions.

QOS MEASUREMENTS AND DEGRADATION FACTORS

The performance parameters, discussed earlier, serve as the basis for measuring the QOS provided by the ATM network. The parameters in Table 6–6 are used to assess the QOS in regards to:

Table 6–6   QOS Degradation Factors

Attribute	A	B	C	D	E
Propagation delay				Y	
Media errors	Y	Y	Y		
Switch architecture		Y		Y	Y
Buffer capacity		Y		Y	Y
Number of tandem nodes	Y	Y	Y	Y	Y
Traffic load		Y	Y	Y	Y
Failures		Y			
Resource allocation		Y		Y	Y

Where:
  A: Cell error ratio
  B: Cell loss ratio
  C: Cell misinsertion rate
  D: Mean cell transfer delay
  E: Cell delay variation

Cell error ratio	accuracy
Cell loss ratio	dependability
Cell misinsertion rate	accuracy
Cell transfer delay	speed
Cell delay variation	speed

As reliable as an ATM network may be, errors will occur. Software bugs, excessive traffic, uncorrectable errors in the header, user payload corruption, etc. are examples of common problems that lead to discarded traffic. As a guideline, the ATM specifications define the relationships of several ATM "attributes" and QOS degradation factors, again shown in Table 6–6.

While the information in this table is largely self-evident, a few observations should be made. First, if possible, it is desirable to have as few as possible intermediate nodes (tandem nodes) involved in relaying the cells from the source to the destination, because each node is a potential source for the degradation of the performance parameters shown in the table. Second, traffic load (that is, excessive traffic load) is to be avoided, because it leads to the degradation of the performance parameters shown in the table. (It does not affect the cell error ratio.) Third, while propagation delay affects only the mean cell transfer delay, its effect on calculating overall delay is quite significant.

TRAFFIC SHAPING

The traffic shaping operation at an ATM node can be based on the cell emission time interval. This approach is best used for synchronous, real-time traffic, since it emits jitter-free traffic into the network. Table 6–7 shows Nortel Networks approach in supporting a virtual circuit. The Shape ID is an identifier for each cell shaping operation. Each cell shaping is based on the average cell rate (in cells/sec), and the average cell interval in μseconds (and the inverse of the cell rate). The resulting bandwidth demand (in bit/s) is shown in the last column and is derived

Table 6–7   Traffic shaping example

Shape ID	Average Cell Rate (Cells/sec)	Average Cell Interval (μsec)	Bandwidth Requirement (Bit/s)	
1	665,094	1.50	282.0	M
2	471,698	2.12	200.0	M
3	333,333	3.00	141.0	M
4	235,849	4.24	100.0	M
5	166,666	6.00	70.7	M
6	117,924	8.48	50.0	M
7	83,333	12.0	35.3	M
8	58,823	17.0	25.0	M
9	41,666	24.0	17.7	M
10	29,498	33.9	12.5	M
11	20,833	48.0	8.83	M
12	14,749	67.8	6.25	M
13	10,416	96.0	4.42	M
14	7,407	135.0	3.12	M
15	5,208	192.0	2.21	M
16	3,679	271.0	1.56	M
17	2,604	384.0	1.1	M
18	1,891	543.0	781.0	K
19	1,302	768.0	552.0	K
20	921	1085.0	391.0	K
21	651	1536.0	276.0	K
22	460	2171.0	195.0	K
23	325	3072.0	138.0	K
24	230	4342.0	97.7	K

from the average cell rate * the cell size. As an example, for Shape ID 1: 665,094 cells/sec * 53 octets per cell (424 bits per cell) = 281,999,856 bit/s.

CELL EMISSION FOR CBR TRAFFIC

The manner in which cells are emitted onto the communications channel is a proprietary operation and varies from vendor-to-vendor. The examples in Figure 6–7 show how several applications' CBR bandwidth requirements can be supported by ATM multiplexing cells into an OC-3 frame of 155.52 Mbit/s.

Example 1 is for high-quality video, which requires 135 Mbit/s of bandwidth. This application would use all the cells in an OC-3 frame (allowing for the OC-3 overhead).

Example 2 is for T1-based video. In this application, every second frame would carry one cell of the application. Some implementations will burst multiple cells of an application into the frame, and rely on the receiving machine to smooth the cells back to a synchronous flow vis-à-vis the application.

Example 3 is for heavily compressed video, which can utilize 511.7 kbit/s (depending upon the compression algorithm). This application would use one cell in every sixth OC-3 frame.

Example 4 shows that the cells from these applications can be multiplexed into one frame for transport across the communications link.

The examples are based on the following calculations:

Example One:
High-quality video can utilize 135.168 Mbit/s
Connection 7 uses almost all cells in an OC-3 frame, because:
155.52 Mbit/s - 5.76 Mbit/s (overhead) = 149.760 Mbit/s available for payload

Example Two:
T1-based video can utilize 1.536 Mbit/s
Connection 8 uses one cell in every second OC-3 frame, because:
(1 cell/2 frames) * (8000 frames per sec) * (48 bytes * 8 bits per byte) = 1.536 Mbit/s

Example Three:
Heavily compressed video can utilize 512 kbit/s
Connection 9 uses one cell in every sixth OC-3 frame, because:

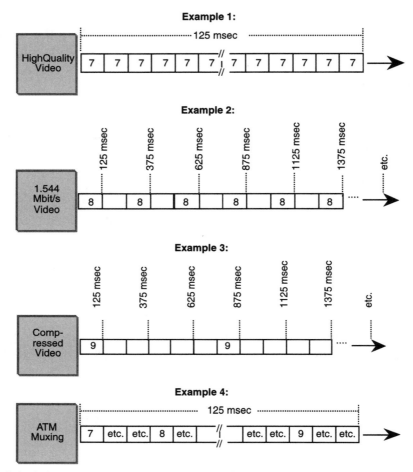

(note: Calculations assume a 48 byte cell payload)

Figure 6–7   Examples of cell loading

(1 cell/6 frames) * (8000 frames per sec) * (48 bytes * 8 bits per byte)
= 512 Mbit/s

CONNECTION ADMISSION CONTROL (CAC)

The point was made earlier that connection admission control (CAC) is a set of procedures that operate at the UNI, see Figure 6–8. CAC encompasses actions taken by the network to grant or deny a connection to

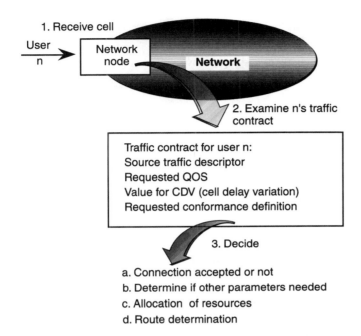

1. Receive cell

User n → Network node

Network

2. Examine n's traffic contract

Traffic contract for user n:
Source traffic descriptor
Requested QOS
Value for CDV (cell delay variation)
Requested conformance definition

3. Decide

a. Connection accepted or not
b. Determine if other parameters needed
c. Allocation of resources
d. Route determination

Figure 6–8   Connection admission control (CAC)

a user. A connection is granted when the user's traffic contract is examined, and it reveals the connection can be supported through the network at its required QOS levels.

The traffic contract should contain sufficient information to allow the network to make an intelligent decision about the granting or denial of the connection. This information includes:

- *Source traffic descriptor:* Contains values such as the peak cell rate, the sustainable cell rate, burst tolerance, etc. It may vary with each connection.

- *Quality of service (QOS) for both directions:* QOS parameters such as cell error ratio, cell loss ratio, cell misinsertion rate, etc. are supported in many networks.

- *Cell delay variation:* The amount of end-to-end variation that can occur with the cells of the connection.

- *Requested conformance definition:* Values describing the conformance of cells for the connection. Values include peak cell rate and sustainable cell rate with the cell loss priority bit (CLP) set to either 0 or 1.

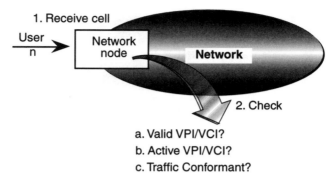

1. Receive cell

User
n

Network node

Network

2. Check

a. Valid VPI/VCI?
b. Active VPI/VCI?
c. Traffic Conformant?

Figure 6–9   Traffic policing with usage parameter control (UPC)

USAGE PARAMETER CONTROL (UPC)

After a connection is granted, and the network has reserved resources for the connection, each user's session is monitored by the network. This operation is usage parameter control (UPC), which is designed to monitor and control traffic, and to check on the validity of the traffic entering the network. UPC maintains the integrity of the network and makes sure that only valid VPIs and VCIs are "entering" the network. Figure 6–9 illustrates the concepts of UPC.

Several other features are desirable for UPC:

- The ability to detect noncompliant traffic
- The ability to vary the parameters that are checked
- A rapid response to the users that are violating their contract
- To keep the operations of noncompliant users transparent to compliant users

VIRTUAL SCHEDULING AND CONTINUOUS-STATE LEAKY BUCKET ALGORITHMS

A number of ATM implementations have adapted the continuous-state leaky bucket or virtual scheduling approach for the management of CBR traffic. The virtual schedule and the leaky bucket monitoring information is maintained at the UNI network side for each connection. Shortly, the specific algorithms published by the ITU-T and the ATM

Forum are explained. For this introduction, we take a generic approach, based on some of Bellcore's ideas about leaky buckets.

Basic Concepts of the Leaky Bucket

Periodically, a token generator at the ATM node issues values called tokens. These tokens are placed into a token pool. The token generator can be thought of as a credit accrual timer in that its invocation gives the user credits (rights) to send cells to the network.

When cells are sent to the network, the token pool is reduced for the respective connection by the number of cells that were sent, see Figure 6–10. If the user sends excessive traffic (beyond the service contract), the token pool is exhausted; that is, the user has "used up" its tokens, or the "bucket is overflowing." In such a situation, (a) the cell may have its CLP bit set to 1 by the network and passed into the network, or (b) the cell may be dropped at the UNI without further processing. These decisions depend upon the actual implementation of the specific network.

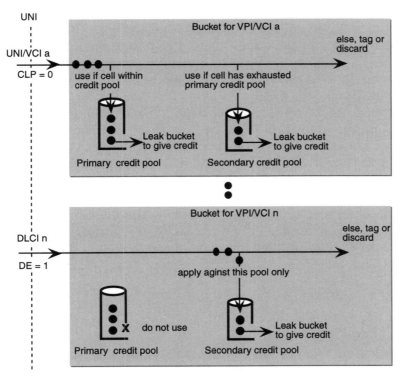

Figure 6–10   The leaky bucket approach (generic example)

The bucket "leaks" a certain amount over a specific time in order to allow the user to send more cells (that is, to fill in the bucket).

Some systems specify two token pools for each connection. One pool is debited for cells in which the CLP bit is set to 0 by the user (a primary pool). Another pool is debited for cells in which the CLP bit is set to 1 by the user (a secondary pool). This approach gives the user some control on which cells may be dropped by the network, because the cells with CLP = 1 are not debited from the primary pool.

Generic Cell Rate Algorithm (GCRA)

The generic cell rate algorithm (GCRA) is employed in traffic policing and may be part of the user/network service contract. In the ATM Forum specification, the GCRA consists of two parameters: (1) the increment I, and (2) the limit L. The notation GCRA (I, L) means the generic cell rate algorithm with the increment parameter set to I and the limit parameter set to L. The increment parameter affects the cell rate. The limit parameter affects cell bursts.

The GCRA allows, for each cell arrival, a one unit leak out of the bucket per unit of time. In its simplest terms, the bucket has finite capacity, and it leaks out at a continuous rate. Its contents can be filled (incremented) by I if L is not exceeded. Otherwise, the incoming cell is defined as nonconforming. This idea is shown in Figure 6–11.

Figure 6–12 shows the two algorithms available for the GCRA, which is implemented as a virtual scheduling algorithm, or a continuous-state leaky bucket algorithm. The two algorithms serve the same purpose: to make certain that cells are conforming (arriving within the bound of an expected arrival time), or nonconforming (arriving sooner than an expected arrival time).

First, two definitions are needed: the theoretical arrival time (TAT) is the nominal arrival time of the cell from the source, assuming the source sends evenly spaced cells. Additionally, the parameter k is the kth cell in a stream of cells on the same virtual connection.

Given these definitions, the virtual scheduling algorithm operates as follows:

- After the arrival of the first cell, $t_a(1)$, the TAT is set to the current time; thereafter,
- If the arrival time of the kth cell is after the current value of TAT (in the flowchart: TAT < $t_a(k)$), then the cell is conforming and TAT is updated to $t_a(k)$, plus the increment I.

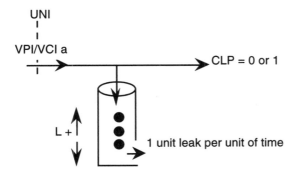

UNI

VPI/VCI a

→ CLP = 0 or 1

L +

1 unit leak per unit of time

Generic cell rate algorithm, GCRA(I,L):

I = increment parameter, affects cell rate

L = limit parameter, affects cell bursts

Leaky bucket:
- Finite-capacity bucket
- Contents leak out at a continuous rate of 1 per unit time
- Contents are incremented by I, if L is not exceeded

Figure 6–11   The generic cell rate algorithm

- If the kth cell's arrival time is greater than or equal to TAT – L but less than TAT [in the flow chart: TAT > $t_a(k)$ + L], then the cell is once again conforming and TAT is incremented to I.
- The cell is nonconforming if the arrival time of the kth cell is less than TAT – L [if TAT is greater than $t_a(k)$ + L]. In this situation the TAT is unchanged.

The continuous state leaky bucket algorithm is viewed as a finite-capacity bucket, whose content drains out at a continuous rate of 1 unit of content per time unit. Its content is increased by the increment I for each conforming cell. Simply stated, if at cell arrival, the content of the bucket is less than or equal to the limit L, the cell is conforming. Otherwise, it is nonconforming. The bucket capacity is L + I (the upper bound on the counter).

The continuous state leaky bucket algorithm operates as follows:

- At the arrival on the first cell $t_a(1)$, the content of the bucket X is set to 0, and the last conformance time (LCT) is set to $t_a(1)$.

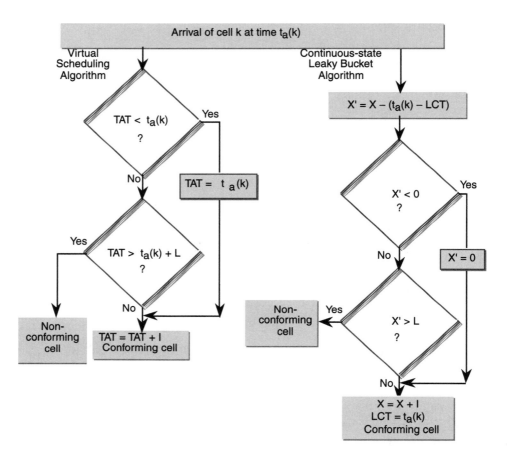

Where:
  TAT = theoretical arrival time
  ta(k) = time arrival of a cell
  X = value of leaky bucket counter
  X′ = auxiliary variable
  LCT = last compliance time
  I = increment
  L = limit

Figure 6–12   The generic cell rate algorithm (GCRA)

- At the arrival of the kth cell, $t_a(k)$. the content of the bucket is up-dated to the value X′. With this update, X′ equals the content of the bucket X, after the arrival of the last conforming cell minus the amount the bucket has drained since that arrival (in the flow chart: $X' = X - t_a(k) - LCT$).

- The content of the bucket is not allowed to negative (in the flow chart: $X' < 0$, then $X' = 0$).
- If X' is less than or equal to the limit value L, then the cell is conforming, and the content of the bucket X is set to $X' + I$ for the current cell, and the LCT is set to current time $t_a(k)$.
- If X' is greater than L, then the cell is nonconforming and the values of X and LCT are not changed.

Examples of the Leaky Bucket Operation

Figure 6–13 shows three examples of how the leaky bucket GCRA is applied [ATM94a]. The vertical arrows connote the arrival of a cell across the UNI. The horizontal arrows connote time. The variables t- and t+ mean the following:

t-: State of bucket just before the arrival of a cell

t+: State of bucket just after the arrival of a cell

In Figure 6–13(a) the CBR cell rate is 1.5 cell units, which describes the cell interarrival time. The bucket depth is 2 cell units. This example is constructed to show a poor way to implement the leaky bucket for synchronous traffic, because of its variable drain rate. At each time, the bucket drains by a variable increment. To aid in following the example, the drain rate is as follows for Figure 6–13(a):

- time 2: drain of 1 cell unit
- time 3: drain of .5 cell units
- time 4: drain of 1.5 cell units
- time 5: drain of 1 cell unit

In time 1, 1.5 cell units arrive at the bucket. The entire cell unit increment can be added to the bucket, because the bucket depth is 2. The bucket does not overflow, so the cell units are conforming. Each cell time t, the bucket drains by variable cell units. At time 2, the bucket has drained to .5 cell units, so another 1.5 cell units can be added to the bucket. At time 3, the bucket cannot hold the 1.5 cell units, because its drain is only .5. Therefore, the cells are nonconforming. How these cells are handled is not defined in the standards and is left to the specific implementation. For times 4 and 5, the bucket is able to hold the 1.5 cell units. In time 4, the drain is 1.5 cell units; in time 5, the drain is 1 cell unit.

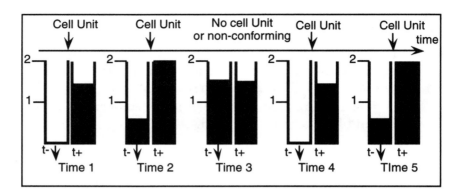

(a) CBR with variable leak

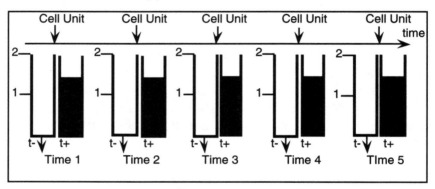

(b) CBR with fixed leak

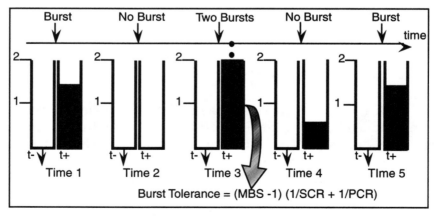

Burst Tolerance = (MBS -1) (1/SCR + 1/PCR)

(c) VBR with fixed leak

Figure 6–13 Examples of the continuous-state leaky bucket

This example is not a very smart way to handle CBR traffic. Since the traffic is predictable, synchronous, and the user is adhering to its SLA. The better approach is to guarantee a bucket depth and a drain rate that never marks the cells as nonconforming. Indeed, the rules for the continuous-state leaky bucket stipulate a drain at a continuous rate of 1 unit of content per time unit.

Figure 6–13(b) shows a better approach to managing the CBR traffic. The bucket depth, the arrival rate, and the drain rate are working harmoniously to provide the customer support for the traffic flow. All traffic is conforming; the arrival rate is consistent with the drain rate; the arrival rate and the drain rate are 1.5 cell units.

Figure 6–13(c) shows another example of the leaky bucket operations. Traffic is burst into the switch at times 1, 3, and 5. The bursts are in 1.5 cell units, the bucket depth is 2 cell units, and the drain rate is 1.5 cell units. In time 3, two bursts arrive, but only one can be accommodated.

Notice the equation for burst tolerance in the figure. It defines the bucket depth. The formula includes the sustainable cell rate (SCR) and the peak cell rate (PCR), as well as the maximum burst size (MBS). The burst tolerance is not just the maximum burst size, because the bucket is draining. This drain rate is modeled as the SCR. Therefore, the formula for the burst tolerance takes into account the MBS as well as the arrival rate of the cells (PCR), while draining out at the SCR rate.

THE ARB AND UBR SERVICE CLASSES

The initial ATM specifications and standards published by the ITU-T focused on constant bit rate (CBR) and variable bit rate (VBR) applications. As more experience was gained with the ATM technology, it became evident that other "bit rate" classes should be defined, as well as techniques to handle these other classes.

Two more service classes are now defined by the ATM Forum: (a) unspecified bit rate (UBR), and (b) available bit rate (ABR). UBR is the lowest quality of service that an ATM network offers. A UBR user takes what bandwidth is left on the channel after CBR and VBR have had their go. As some people have phrased it, UBR is like flying standby. UBR provides no way for a user to negotiate with the network, and the network provides no guarantee that the user's traffic will be delivered.

UBR+ is discussed in some literature, but it is not defined as part of the formal ATM specifications. The idea behind UBR+ is not to throttle completely UBR traffic, even when CRB, VBR, and ARB queues have cells in them. This concept translates into the servicing of UBR+ queues "on occasion."

ABR is somewhat similar to UBR in that the user is not given as much preferential treatment as the users of the CBR and VBR services. However, the network provides enough bandwidth to keep the user application up-and-running (a minimum cell rate, or MCR). Additionally, flow control mechanisms are available to throttle the user's ABR traffic in the event of problems.

Figure 6–14 compares these classes of service in relation to bandwidth guarantee, delay variation guarantee, throughput guarantee, and congestion feedback.

Figure 6–15 shows Cisco's view of the relationships of the ATM QOS categories and possible pricing for obtaining services in those categories. Reasonably enough, the pricing increases as a customer uses the ATM

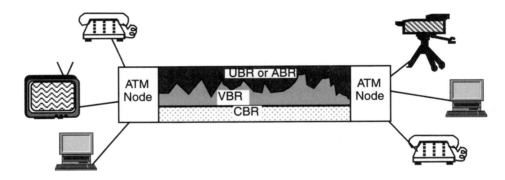

In order of priority:

Constant bit rate (CBR):	Assured steady supply of bandwidth
Variable bit rate (VBR):	Assured supply of bandwidth with: rt = real time, and nrt = nonreal time
Available bit rate (ABR):	Bandwidth to keep application running
Unspecified bit rate+ (UBR+)	Bandwidth to prevent queue buildup behind CBR, VBR, and ABR
Unspecified bit rate (UBR):	Bandwidth as available with no assurance

Quality of Service:

Service	Bandwidth Guarantee	Delay Variation Guarantee	Throughput Guarantee	Congestion Feedback
CBR	Yes	Yes	Yes	No
VBR-rt	Yes	Yes	Yes	No
VBR-nrt	Yes	No	Yes	No
ABR	Yes	No	Yes	Yes
UBR+	Yes	Upper bound	Somewhat	Yes
UBR	No	No	No	No

Figure 6–14   Service classes

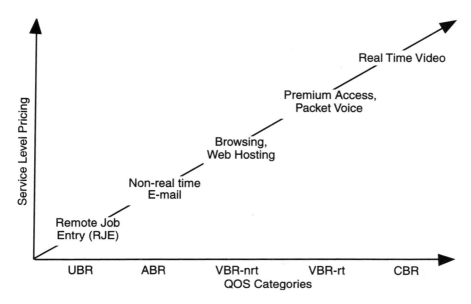

Source: Cisco marketing material

Figure 6–15   Pricing versus QOS categories

QOS categories that require more bandwidth and more dedicated resources to support the resources to support the bandwidth.

Interestingly, the CBR service category, while granted a higher priority for use of the network's bandwidth, is easier to manage than "lesser" QOS categories, because CBR is designed to avoid feedback loops, such as congestion notification. Traffic monitoring and metering is straightforward with CBR as well.

Even though the ABR QOS category is not considered high in the ATM QOS category hierarchy, it is a difficult traffic type to manage, because of its asynchronous, bursty, and somewhat unpredictable nature. Coupled with these attributes is the fact that ABR traffic is granted a guarantee of a minimum cell rate (MSR) through the QOS domain. It can be seen that ABR may not warrant a big chunk of the revenue pie, relative to CBR and VBR categories, but it does require a lot of attention. Later discussions in this chapter will expand on these ideas.

Approaches to ABR Implementations

Vendors have taken different approaches to the implementation of ABR. The choices revolve around two approaches (with variations and combinations of these approaches):

1. Rate-based schemes
    a. Credits for each connection
    b. Credits aggregated for all connections
2. Explicit congestion notification (ECN) based schemes
    a. ECN established for each connection
    b. ECN established for all connections

The rate-based scheme can operate on a hop-by-hop basis for each connection (see Figure 6–16[a]), or on a hop-by-hop basis for all connections (see Figure 6–17[a]). The explicit congestion notification also can operate on each connection on a hop-by-hop basis (see Figure 6–16[b]), or on all connections (see Figure 6–17[b]).

With the rate-based scheme, downstream nodes send rate-parameters (credits to increase or reduce the send window of the sending node) to upstream nodes all the way to the source of the traffic. These parameters regulate the sending node's traffic emission rate to a destination note, as well as each node on the path.

The ECN scheme is quite similar to the Frame Relay congestion notification operations. An ATM node can send the destination a forward congestion notification (FCN) signal. The destination user, in turn, sends to its source a backward congestion notification (BCN) signal and through some algorithm, the source will back off from sending cells.

Both approaches have their advantages and disadvantages. Rate-based schemes are much more effective in regulating bandwidth immediately but they have more overhead. ECN-based schemes are cheaper to implement but the latency of acting upon forward and backward congestion notification could result in some oscillating behavior in the network.

The granularity of feedback is also a very important consideration in ABR. This feedback may be aggregated on each connection (see Figure 6–16), or over multiple connections, as shown in Figure 6–17. Obviously, the advantages and disadvantages for these operations are that aggregate feedback does not permit monitoring individual connections. Consequently, cells might be marked as congestion even though they may not be part of the problem. The per-connection feedback selects only those connections that are contributing to the problem.

In addition to the granularity and feedback, granularity of buffering is also an important consideration. Granularity of buffering simply means that connections are aggregated in one buffer or an individual buffer is reserved for each connection.

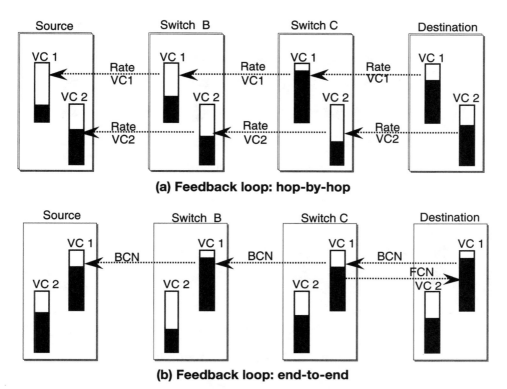

(a) Feedback loop: hop-by-hop

(b) Feedback loop: end-to-end

Note: Dashed lines in figure (b) show logical flow of feedback

Figure 6–16   Feedback on each connection

ATM Forum ABR Operations

The ABR QOS category uses several parameters in its operations. Table 6–8 lists these parameters, describes their functions, and notes their units and (possibly) ranges. Several of these parameters are carried in resource management (RM) cells that are exchanged between ATM nodes. Others parameters are variables that are employed at the user nodes and switches to keep track of the traffic on each connection.

The following signaled parameters are negotiated during the connection establishment procedure. They are listed here, along with their negotiation options, and their default values. The first list is the required parameters and the second list is the optional parameters:

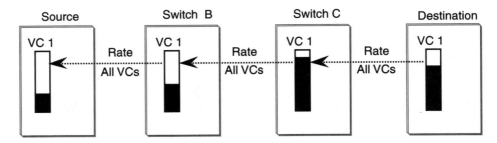

(a) Feedback loop: hop-by-hop

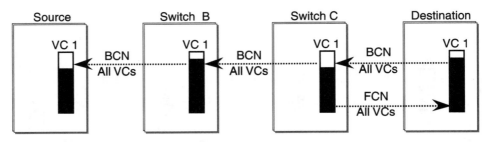

(b) Feedback loop: end-to-end

Figure 6–17   Aggregate feedback

Required Parameter Name	Negotiation	_Default Value_
PCR	Down	Mandatory
MCR	Down to MCRmin if MCR min is signaled, else no	0
ICR	Down	PCR
TBE	Down	16,777,215
FRTT	Accumulated	Set by source
RDF	Down	1/16
RIF	Down	1/16
Optional Parameter Name	Negotiation	_Default Value_
Nrm	No	32
Trm	No	100
CDF	Up	1/16
ADTF	Down	0.5

Table 6–8   The ABR Parameters

Label	Description of Label	Units and Range
PCR	Peak cell rate: rate source cannot exceed	Cells/sec
MCR	Minimum cell rate: rate source can always send	Cells/sec
ICR	Initial cell rate: rate source initially sends	Cells/sec
RIF	Rate increase factor: rate source may increase sending of cells	Power of 2, range:1/32768 to 1
Nrm	Maximum number of cells source can send for each forward RM cell	Power of 2, range: 2 to 256
Mrm	Controls bandwidth allocation between RM cells and data cells	Constant value of 2
RDF	Rate decrease factor: controls rate of decrease of cell transmission rate	Power of 2, range 1/32768 to 1
ACR	Allowed cell rate: rate source is allowed to send	Cells/sec
CRM	RM cell count: Limit to number of forward RM cells sent	Implementation specific
ADTF	ACR decrease time factor: time between sending RM cells before rate is decreased to ICR	Seconds, range: .01 to 10.23
Tm	Upper bound on time between forward RM cells	Milliseconds, $100*2^{-7}$ to $100*2^{0}$
FRTT	Fixed round trip time: fixed RTT between source and destination	Microseconds, range: 0 to 16.7 sec
TBE	Transient buffer exposure: Cell send limit during startup	Cells, range: 0 to 16,777,215
CDF	Cutoff decrease factor: Controls decrease in ACR associated with CRM	0, or power of 2, range: 1/64 to 1
TCR	Tagged cell rate: limits out-of-rate RM cells	10 cells per sec

After the call setup these parameters are computed as follows:

$$\text{CRM} = \left\lceil \frac{\text{TBE}}{\text{Nrm}} \right\rceil \text{ and ICR} = \min \left(\text{ICR}, \frac{\text{TBE}}{\text{FRTT}} \right)$$

Explicit Rate (ER).   In the ATM Forum deliberations on flow control, attention focused on several techniques which are variations of those just described. The ATM Forum chose a rate based method for flow control, also called the Explicit Rate (ER) algorithm.

As shown in Figure 6–18, with the ER technique, resource management (RM) cells are sent by the source of the traffic cells through intermediate nodes (switches) to the end receiver for each connection. The RM cells contain values that describe the allowed cell rate (ACR) the sender is transmitting cells (measured in cells per second), the ACR value is carried in the current cell rate (CCR) field in the RM cell. The cell also contains the rate that the sender would like to increase this allowance; this request is placed in the explicit rate (ER) field in the RM cell. (The ACR and ER are set up during the establishment of the session.) Any node that processes this RM cell (intermediate nodes or the end node) can reduce the requested rate (ER) (this value cannot be increased).

The source end system (SES) sends cells at the allowed cell rate (ACR), which is set initially to the initial cell rate (ICR) and the current cell rate (CCR). Periodically (every Nrm –1 data cells), the SES first

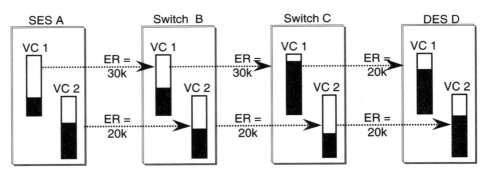

(a) Source node sends forward-RM cells

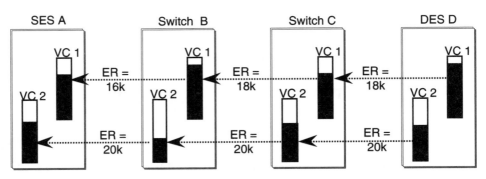

(b) Downstream nodes return backward-RM cells

Figure 6–18   ATM Forum Explicit Rate (ER) Approach

sends a forward RM-cell. In the cell is the ER field, and it can be modified by all nodes that process the cell.

The destination end system (DES) reverses the RM cell, which is
sent back to the originator, and is now called a backward-RM cell. See
Figure 16–18(b). During the journey to the end node, any node can reduce further the requested cell rate (ER). The final arbiter is the node
next to the originating node, and if this node reduces the requested rate,
the sending node must so comply, regardless of the actions at the other
nodes.

Figure 6–18 depicts two active virtual connections, VC1 and VC2.
VC2's ER remains the same in the forward direction and backward direction. VC1's ER is changed both in the forward direction and in the backward direction. In the forward direction, switch C reduces the ER from
30 kcells/sec to 20 kcells/sec. In the backward direction, DES D reduces
the 20 kcells/sec rate to 18 kcells/sec, and switch B further reduces the
18 kcells/sec rate to 16 kcells/sec. Consequently, SES A has had its bandwidth for the session reduced by almost half.

The user stations as well as the switches use the parameters discussed earlier to coordinate their activities with each other. The fields
that are of interest here are (a) congestion indication (CI), (b) rate decrease factor (RDF), (c) minimum cell rate (MCR), (d) no increase (NI), (e)
peak cell rate (PCR), (f) explicit forward congestion indication (EFCI) and
(g) rate increase factor (RIF).

This part of our analysis will concentrate on the actions the SES,
DES, and the switches take when they receive forward or backward
RM-cells.[3]

Actions at the Destination End Station (DES).   As depicted in Figure 6–19, the destination end station D (DES D) receives a forward RM
cell from the source end station (SES). Based on its condition when it receives the forward RM cell, it can set CI = 1, NI = 1, and alter the ER
field. It may use the CCR field to decide what value to place in the ER. If
it receives the forward RM cell with EFCI set, then it must set CI = 1 in
the backward RM cell.

---

[3]I am summarizing the actions of the user stations and the switches in this discussion. The ABR operation stipulates additional rules for its implementation, but the major
aspects of the ABR behavior are covered in this overview. For all the rules, see Sections
5.10.4, 4.10.5, and 5.10.6 of the ATM Forum Traffic Management Specification Version
4.0, document number af-tm-0056.000, January, 1997.

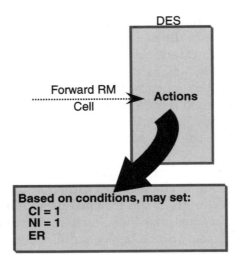

Figure 6–19   Actions at the destination end station (DES)

Actions at the Switch.   Any switch in the path between the SES and DES is allowed to perform the following actions, and illustrated in Figure 6–20 with Switch D:

- Set the EFCI in the cell
- Set CI or NI to 1

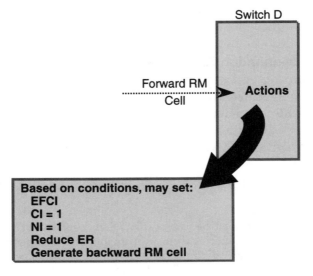

Figure 6–20   Switch reaction to the forward RM cell

- Reduce ER
- Generate a backward RM cell

Actions at the Source End Station (SES). The actions at the source end station A (SES A) upon receiving a backward RM-cell are shown in Figure 6–21. If the SES receives the backward RM-cell with the CI = 1, then it must reduce the value of its ACR by ACR * RDF, unless this reduction would result in the ACR at a lower value than MCR. If this is the case, the ACR is set to the MCR. If the backward RM-cell has both CI = 0 and NI = 0, then the ACR may not be increased by more than RIF * PCR, and to a rate not greater than PCR. If the backward RM-cell has NI = 1, the ACR cannot be increased.

After ACR has been adjusted as discussed in the previous paragraph, ACR is set to the minimum of the adjusted ACR value and the ER field, but no lower than MCR.

Implications of ER operations. Although the intermediate nodes participate in the ER operations, the operations at these nodes are not

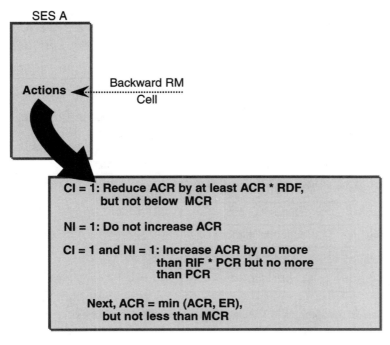

Figure 6–21   SES reaction to the backward RM cell

burdensome. They may choose to participate in the RM cell operations, or they may not participate. Therefore, the approach is attractive to switch vendors. Conceptually, only the source and destination nodes need keep bookkeeping operations. The transit nodes need not keep information about each VC, but simply modify the ER value, and the CI and NI fields in the RM cell as appropriate.

Thus, the ER mechanism has an end-to-end significance (certainly, more so than a hop-to-hop flavor). Most of the work is at the SES.

The ABR RM-cell. Figure 6–22 shows the format and the fields of the ABR RM cell. Here is a description of how the fields are used.

- *Header:* The RM cell is identified with a PTI = 110 for a VCC and additionally, a VCI = 6 for a VPC. The CLP bit = 0 for an in-rate cell and 1 for an out-or-rate cell

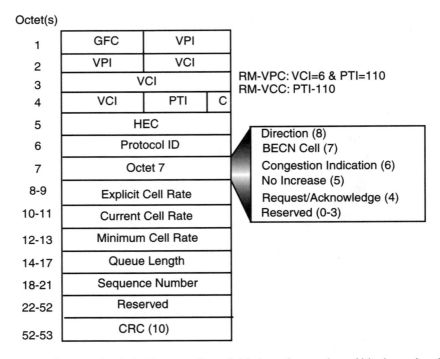

Note: Numbers in parenthesis in Message Type field show the number of bits in each sub-field.

Figure 6–22   The resource management (RM) cell

- *Protocol ID:* Assigned by the ITU-T as 1 to identify the ABR service using the RM cell
- *Direction (DIR):* Set to 1 for a forward RM cell and a 1 for a backward cell
- *BECN (BN):* BN = 1 indicates a backward explicit congestion notification (BECN) cell, generated by a nonsource node. BN = 0 indicates a source generated cell
- *Congestion indication (CI):* Indicates congestion when set to 1. It requires the source to decrease its ACR
- *No increase (NI):* Prevents a source from increasing its ACR, but does not require a decrease
- *Request/acknowledge (RA):* Not used by the ATM Forum
- *Explicit cell rate (ER):* Limits ACR value. Set by source as a requested rate
- *Current cell rate (CCR):* Set by source to its current ACR. Can be used by ABR node to compute a value for a new ER
- *Minimum cell rate (MCR):* Conveys the connection's minimum cell rate
- *Queue length and sequence number:* Not used by the ATM Forum
- *Cyclic redundancy check (CRC):* The error check computed on the RM cell payload

PERFORMANCE MANAGEMENT

Performance management entails the periodic evaluation of ATM equipment and software. The goal is to assess the ATM system in a systematic way in order to determine how the network is performing, if components are deteriorating, and if error conditions are acceptable. VPC and VCC monitoring can be performed end-to-end, or on VPC/VCC segments. Recall that a segment represents one part of a connection, such as one network provider (say, out of several that are part of the virtual circuit).

Performance management consists of:

- Forward monitoring: Generating cells from one network element to a receiving network element.
- Backward monitoring: At the receiving network element, checking the cells and reporting back to the generating network element.

- Monitoring/reporting: Storing the results of the monitoring activities based on filtering selected parameters and thresholds.

Figure 6–23 depicts the performance monitoring operations. A block of cells on one connection are sent to an endpoint. These cells are bounded by OAM cells, which are not part of the block. Each user cell in the block has a BIP-16 calculation performed on the user payload. An OAM cell (a forward monitoring cell), which contains the same VPC/VCC as the user cells, is inserted behind the block of cells which contains the result of the BIP-16 calculation, as well as other information (explained shortly). In addition, the OAM cell contains a count of the number of user cells in the block. The blocks can vary in size, and an OAM cell can be inserted at times that do not interfere with ongoing operations.

The receiving network element receives the user and OAM cells and compares the BIP-16 value in the forward monitoring OAM cell to a BIP-16 calculation it executed over the user cells. It also counts the number of cells in the block and compares this count with the count in the OAM header to determine if any cells have been lost or if extra cells have been inserted. This information is stored and later sent back to the originator in the form of a backward reporting OAM cell.

These operations may occur in both directions, if the performance management system has been so-configured.

Figure 6–24 shows the format for an OAM performance monitoring cell. The OAM cell type is coded as 0010; the OAM function type is coded as 0000, 0001, 0010. The 360 bits specific to the OAM type are divided into the following fields:

- *Monitoring sequence number:* A sequence number in forward monitoring cells to detect missing of inserted cells.

- *Total cell number:* Number of user cells in the block sent before this OAM cell

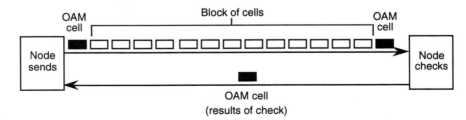

Figure 6–23   Performance monitoring

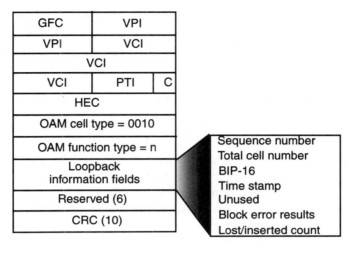

Figure 6–24   The OAM performance monitoring cell

- *BIP-16 value:* Value of the BIP-16 calculation on the user cells, that have been sent since the last OAM cell.
- *Timestamp:* An optional field to indicate when the OAM cell was inserted.
- *Unused:* Not used, and coded to all 0x6A.
- *Block error results:* Used in backward reporting cell to indicate how many errored parity bits were received in the forward monitoring OAM cell.
- *Lost or inserted count:* Used in backward reporting to indicate how many cells were lost or inserted.

USING CONNECTIONS ON DEMAND TO NEGOTIATE QOS

Most of the initial ATM deployments have been with PVCs. This approach means the bandwidth, connections, QOS, etc. are provisioned once, and "nailed-up" permanently. Switched virtual calls (SVCs), also known as "connections on demand" allow users to access the network as needed, and use the SVC procedures to negotiate QOS on a session-by-session basis.

ATM Volume II of this series devote several chapters to the subject of ATM SVCs. Therefore, the approach in this discussion is to provide a general description of ATM SVCs, and how they support QOS negotiations between the users and the QOS service provider.

Connection Management Messages

The ATM connection establishment procedures begin by a user issuing the SETUP message, as shown in Figure 6–25. This message is sent by the calling user to the network and is relayed by the network to the called user. This message contains several information elements (fields) to identify the message, specify various AAL parameters, calling and called party addresses, requirements for QOS, selection of the transit network (if needed), and a number of other fields.

Upon receiving the SETUP message, the network returns a CALL PROCEEDING (CALL PROC) message to the initiating user, forwards the SETUP message to the called user, and waits for the called user to return a CALL PROCEEDING message. The CALL PROCEEDING mes-

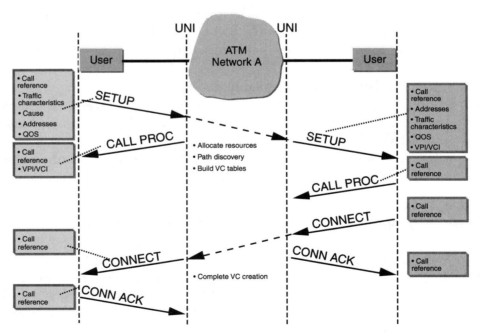

Figure 6–25   Connection Setup

sage is used to indicate that the call has been initiated and no more call establishment information is needed, nor will any be accepted.

The called user, if it accepts a call, will then send to the network a CONNECT message. This CONNECT message will then be forwarded to the calling user. The CONNECT message contains parameters that deal with some of the same parameters in the SETUP message such as call reference, message type, etc. as well as the accepted AAL parameters and several other identifiers that are created as a result of the information elements in the original SETUP message.

Upon receiving the CONNECT messages, the calling user and the network return the CONNECT ACKNOWLEDGE to their respective parties.

Figure 6–26 illustrates how a disconnect occurs. Either user can initiate a disconnect operation. To do so requires the user to send to the network the RELEASE message. The effect of this message clears the end-to-end connection between the two users and the network. This message only contains the basic information to identify the message across the network. Other parameters are not included because they are not needed to clear the state tables for the connection.

The receiving network and receiving user are required to transmit the RELEASE COMPLETE message as a result of receiving the RELEASE message.

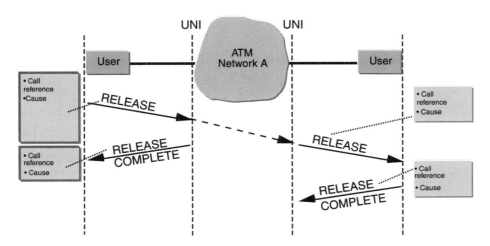

Figure 6–26   Connection release

Other Signaling Messages

This section provides a summary of the other ATM signaling messages. As you will see, most of them are identical to Frame Relay messages. Also, I will bring timers into the discussion; they are used for all signaling message exchanged, including those just described. I explained the above examples without timers for the purpose of simplicity.

Restart. The network or user can initiate restart operations for any number of reasons. Failure of any component can result in the restart procedure being invoked, and information elements in the header cite the reason for the restart. The field in the RESTART message labeled restart indicator determines if an indicated virtual channel is to be restarted or all channels controlled by this layer 3 entity are to be restarted.

Status Inquiry. The status inquiry procedure is invoked by either the network or the user to determine the state of a connection, such as the call state, the type of connection being supported, the end state of a point-to-multipoint connection, etc. Timer T322 controls this procedure. Either party may invoke the STATUS INQUIRY message, the user or the network.

Status inquiry operations are effective tools to help manage the network's virtual circuits. They serve as PVC provisioning and OAM tools to assist the network and customer in the following activities:

- Adding a PVC
- Deleting a PVC
- Providing for notification of UNI failures
- Providing for notification of PVC segments (portions of an end-to-end PVC)
- Providing for notification of NNI failures

Add Party/Drop Party. Because of the importance and wide use of conference calls, multicasting data traffic, and video conferencing operations, ATM defines procedures to support these types of applications.

This capability is implemented through the add-party procedure as shown in Figure 6–27. This illustration shows the addition of only one party, but multiple parties may be connected with this operation. The originating site issues an ADD PARTY message across the UNI to the

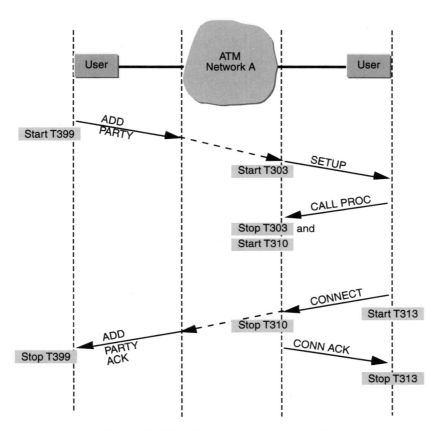

Figure 6–27   The add-party procedure

network. The network forwards this message to the destination in which the destination network node, issues a SETUP across the UNI to the destination user. The SETUP message is used if procedures must begin from scratch. That is to say, this UNI is currently not participating in the call. Not shown in this figure is the possibility of issuing the ADD PARTY message across the remote UNI for situations where a call is already in place and another calling party needs to be added.

The operation is controlled with a timer at the sending site. This timer is turned off upon receiving a CONNECTION ACKNOWLEDG-MENT, an ADD PARTY, ADD PARTY ACK, REJECT, or a RELEASE. In this example, the remote side uses the initial setup operation, discussed earlier. The point-to-multipoint operation is also controlled by party-states. These states may exist on the network side or the user side of the interface. They are summarized as follows:

- *Null:* A party does not exist; no endpoint allocated.
- *Add party initiated:* An ADD PARTY message or a SETUP message has been sent to the other side of the interface for this party
- *Add party received:* An ADD PARTY message or a SETUP message has been received by the other side of the interface for this party
- *Drop party initiated:* A DROP PARTY message has been sent for this party
- *Drop party received:* A DROP PARTY message has been received
- *Active:* On the user side of the UNI, an active state is when the user has received an CONNECT ACKNOWLEDGE, ADD PARTY ACKNOWLEDGE, or a CONNECT. On the network side an active state is entered when it has sent a CONNECT, CONNECT ACKNOWLEDGE or an ADD PARTY ACKNOWLEDGE; or when the network has received an ADD PARTY ACKNOWLEDGE from the user side.

As the reader might expect, the drop party procedure provides the opposite function of the add party procedure discussed in the previous section. With this operation, one party or multiple parties can be dropped from the connection. The activity is controlled by the T398 and T308 timers. RELEASE and RELEASE COMPLETE messages are used at the remote side. Under certain conditions the drop party is also activated at the remote side.

Figure 6–28 shows a point-to-multitpoint operation. These table entries are set up to support the ATM add party procedures. The concept is quite simple. The cross-connect table contains multiple entries. In this example, an incoming cell is sent to two output ports. The table contains the mapping values to change the VPI and VCI values in the cell headers.

Although not shown in the figure, the cross-connect table could have bi-directional significance. That is, the cells labeled VPI = 8, VCI = 5 and VPI = 2 and VCI = 9 could be mapped to a cell labeled VPI = 6 and VCI = 4.

The Q.2931 Message Structure. The ATM call and connection control are derived from the Q.931 protocol, the layer 3 specification for ISDN. The purpose of Q.931 is to establish connections for B channels at the ISDN basic rate interface (BRI). Q.2931 is used to set up and tear down a connection through the ATM network.

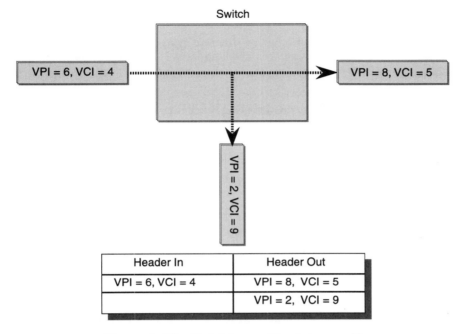

Figure 6–28   Point-to-multipoint operation

The messages contents vary, depending on the class of traffic to be supported, and the QOS that is needed within the class.

Figure 6–29 shows the basic organization of the Q.2931 message. The protocol discriminator field can be coded to identify the Q.2931 message, or other layer 3 protocols, such as ISDN Q.931, a Frame Relay SVC

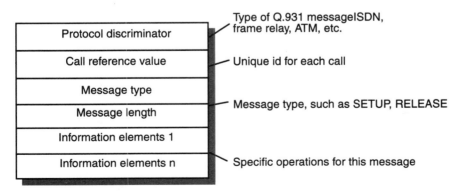

Figure 6–29   Contents of the Q.2931 message

Table 6–9   Functions of the information elements

Protocol discriminator	Distinguishes different types of messages within ITU-T standards and standards bodies throughout the world
Call reference	Uniquely identifies each call at the UNI
Message type	Identifies type of message, such as SETUP, STATUS, etc.
Message length	Length of message excluding the three elements above and this element
AAL parameters	AAL parameters selected by user
ATM user cell rate	Specifies set of traffic parameters
Broadband bearer capability	Indicates several network bearer services (end-to-end timing, CBR, VBR, point-to-point, multipoint services)
Broadband high layer information	End-user codes, passed transparently through ATM network; identifies upper layer protocols or a vendor-specific application
Broadband repeat indicator	Used to allow repeated information elements to be interpreted correctly
Broadband low layer information	End-user codes, passed transparently through ATM network; identifies lower layer protocols/configurations
Called party number	Called party of the call
Called party subaddress	Called party subaddress
Calling party number	Origin party number
Calling party subaddress	Calling party subaddress
Call state	One of twelve values describing status of a call (active, call initiated, etc.)
Cause	Diagnostic codes
Connection identifier	The VPI and VCI for the call
QOS parameter	QOS class
Broadband sending complete number	Indicates the completion of the called party
Transit network selection	Identifies a transit network (an IXC in the U.S.)
Endpoint reference	Identifies endpoints in a point-to-multipoint connection
Endpoint state	Indicates state of each endpoint (add party initiated, received, active, etc.)
Restart indicator	Identifies which virtual channels are to be restated

message in a Frame Relay network. Obviously, it is coded in this protocol to identify Q.2931 messages.

The call reference identifies each call and is assigned by the originating side of the call (the user at the local side, and the network at the remote side). Its purpose to keep the different calls uniquely identified.

The message type identifies the specific type of message, such as a SETUP, ADD PARTY, etc.

The information elements contain the fields that are used to control the connection operation. They contain information of the AAL and QOS operations that are to be supported during the connection.

The Information Elements. The functions of the information elements are summarized in Table 6–9. The entries listed are briefly explained, and *ATM Volume II* of this series describes each in detail.

SUMMARY

ATM networks can be configured to support a wide array of QOS features for the network user. The support of CBR traffic is accomplished with the ITU-T's rules for CAC, UPC, and GRCA operations. The support of VBR traffic is supported through the ATM Forum's rules for ABR and UBR operations. ATM connections on demand provide a tool for negotiating QOS dynamically, with the Q.2931 protocol.

7

Internet QOS Protocols

This chapter describes the operations of the Internet protocols used to support QOS. The emphasis is on QOS in a wide area network. We start with an examination of IPv6 and the revised and expanded IP address. I do not spend much time describing IPv4 since its QOS features are very limited. Next, IPv6 operations are described, concentrating on the IPv6 header extensions. The next part of the chapter is devoted to TCP and how it accounts for user traffic, and manages flow control operations between applications. UDP is also explained, but the explanation is terse, reflecting the paucity of functions provided by this protocol.

The last part of the chapter introduces four more protocols that have been around for several years. They are described in a general way in this chapter because other books in this series describe them in detail. However, to help you in understanding these protocols (and if you don't want to buy another book), Appendix A provides tutorials on (a) multicasting, (b) the Real Time Protocol (RTP), (c) the Real Time Control Protocol (RTCP), and (d) the Resource Reservation Protocol (RSVP).

WHY IPv6?

IPv4 (version 4) is the current IP employed in the industry. It is an old protocol, conceived over twenty years ago. It is remarkable that it has performed so well for so long a time. But with the changing technology, IPv4 now exhibits a number of deficiencies.

First, of course, is the limited IP address space. Various estimates have been made about when the 32-bit space will be exhausted. Christian Huitema [HUIT96][1] provides an estimate that the 32-bit maximum address space will be exhausted between the years 2005–2015. Regardless of the exact time of IP address space exhaustion, it will indeed become exhausted. IPv6 stipulates an address of 128 bits (which should be sufficient for a while).

Second, a number of operations in IPv4 are inefficient. Consequently, since the changing of IP's address requires the changing of the IP protocol, it makes sense to change other aspects of IPv4 as well.

IPv6 is designed to overcome the limitations of IPv4. As we mentioned earlier, the major design philosophy behind IPv6 is to extend the IP address space and, at the same time, make the protocol simpler to use and more efficient in its operations. Clearly, its intent is to migrate from a data-specific protocol to a multiservice protocol. However, it was emphasized throughout the design process that IPv4 had been quite successful, and many of its characteristics have been retained. Additionally, IPv6 is designed to complement other related protocols which have been developed or are in development at the writing of this book. These protocols concern themselves with the support of either voice, video, or data traffic as well as QOS operations. They are explained in Chapters 8, 9, and Appendix A.

Before the analysis of IPv6 is undertaken, it is useful to pause and describe the rationale for the very large address of 128 bits. Many proposals pertaining to the size of the address were placed before the task force. These deliberations have continued since 1992, with the final completion of the specification in 1995. In essence, the IPv6 designers held fast to the notion that the Internet should be able to support anyone on earth who wishes to connect to it. Since IPv6 is positioned for the future, various estimates were made as to how many people would be on the planet in the next century. The study projected the population growth to

---

[1][HUIT96] Huitema, Christian, IPv6: *The New Internet Protocol*, Prentice Hall, 1996

2020. In addition, with the proliferation of computers into many people's lives, it was essential that the IP address accommodate the probability that one person would utilize multiple computers. Some studies hypothesize that in the future perhaps a use of 100 computers per person could occur. This may seem far-fetched but remember that computers are inculcating themselves into almost every facet of our lives. Computers operate our watches; computers run in our automobiles; LANs even operate underneath our automobile hood. All these components need addresses in order to function properly. At any rate, the value of 2^{128} was believed to be sufficient for a long-term growth to accommodate approximately all the people on earth.

SCARCITY OF QOS IN IPv4 AND IPv6

I have made the point earlier in the book that IPv4 was not designed for the support of many QOS features; it was designed as a best-effort forwarding protocol. With some exceptions (explained later in this chapter), IPv6 uses the same approach. It is still a connectionless, best-effort forwarding protocol. Then how can feature-rich QOS, such as guaranteed bandwidth and delay, be obtained in an IP-based internet? The answer is in several of the supporting protocols to IPv6 which have been developed (or are being developed) to provide the QOS features.

IPv4 and IPv6 can be implemented with or without these supporting protocols. This design philosophy gives the network operator considerable flexibility in how (and to what extent) IP-based QOS domains are established. The back part of this chapter and Chapters 8 and 9 explain these protocols, as does Appendix A (which, as stated earlier, is an abbreviated summary of the protocols that are covered in a companion book to this series, titled "Advanced Features of the Internet").

SUMMARY OF CHANGES

Table 7–1 provides a summary of the major changes made to IPv6 in relation to IPv4 and the reasons for the changes. The changes are significant, to the extent that IPv4 and IPv6 cannot interwork with each other unless conversions are made between the two. In some instances, conversions cannot be made, since IPv6 offers features that cannot be mapped to IPv4.

Table 7-1   Aspects of the Change

- Ethertype value is $86Dd_{hex}$
- These fields are eliminated: (a) header length, (b) TOS, (c) identification, (d) flags, (e) fragment offset, (f) header checksum
- These fields are renamed (and redefined somewhat): (a) length, (b) protocol type, (c) time to live
- Options fields are redone completely
- Two fields are added: (a) priority, (b) flow label
- Header is a fixed format
- Hop-to-hop fragmentation is not permitted

THE IPv6 ADDRESS

The convention for writing the IPv6 address is as 4-bit integers, with each integer represented by a hexadecimal (hex) digit. The address is clustered as eight 16-bit integers (four hex digits), separated by colons, as in this example:

```
68DA:8909:3A22:FA64:68DA:8909:3A22:FACA
```

It is unlikely that initial implementations will use all 128 bits, and some of them will be set to 0, as in this example:

```
68DA:0000:0000:0000:68DA:8909:3A22:FACA
```

This notation can be shortened by substituting 0s in the hex 16-bit cluster as follows:

```
68DA:0:0:0:68DA:8909:3A22:FACA
```

In addition, if more than one consecutive hex cluster of 16 bits is null, they can be replaced by two colons, as in this example:

```
68DA::68DA:8909:3A22:FACA
```

Since the notation the IPv4 address is in decimal, dot form, IPv6 allows an IPv4 address to have the following notation:

```
::47.192.4.5
```

Hierarchical addresses are preferable to flat addresses, and IPv6 stipulates a hierarchical address format. The format of the address is coded with a prefix, and five hierarchical subfields, in the order shown in Table 7–2(a). Currently, the registry ID is set up to identify IP registration authorities. There are three registrations identified for North America, Europe, and Asia. These registrations dole out Provider IDs to ISPs. In the initial allocation, the ISPs assign the addresses (subnetwork ID and interface ID) to their subscribers, who can use these bits to their own preferences. Several special addresses are provided in IPv6 (which includes the standard prefix of 010). The coding rules for these addresses are provided in Table 7–2(b).

An unspecified address consists of all 0s. One (1) can be coded in a source address, and is used in situations where a station has not been configured with an address. A loopback address is 0:0:0:0:0:0:0:1, and it allows a node to send a datagram to itself; for example, when the source and destination application reside in the same node.

OSI network service access points (NSAPs) and Novell IPX addresses are supported in IPv6 because of their wide use in other systems.

The site local address prefix is used if an organization wishes to set up its own private addresses in its internet, which cannot be employed in the Internet. Additionally, a node can be given a link local address if it has not been assigned a link local address or a provider-based address.

Like IPv4, the IPv6 also supports unicasting and multicasting, and IPv6 adds additional functionality to multicasting. For example, the multicast address contains a field to limit the scope of the multicast operation to a local site, a local link, global, etc.

Table 7–2(a)   Address Hierarchy

Prefix, Registry ID, Provider ID, Subscriber ID, Subnetwork ID, Interface ID
Where:

Prefix: 010	Provider-based addresses
Registry ID:	Registry in charge of allocating
Provider ID:	Internet service provider (ISP)
Subscriber ID:	Subscriber ID, which is obtained from the ISP
Subnetwork ID:	Subnetwork of the subscriber
Interface ID:	Host address on the subnetwork

Table 7–2(b)   IPv6 Special Addresses

	Allocation
	Reserved
	Unassigned
0000 001	ISO/ITU-T NSAP addresses
0000 010	IPX addresses
0000 011	Unassigned
0000 1	Unassigned
0000 10	Unassigned
0001	Unassigned
001	Unassigned
010	Provider- based unicast addresses
011	Unassigned
100	Geographic-based unicast addresses
101	Unassigned
110	Unassigned
1110	Unassigned
1111 0	Unassigned
1111 10	Unassigned
1111 110	Unassigned
1111 1110 0	Unassigned
1111 1110 10	Link local addresses
1111 1110 11	Site local addresses
1111 1111	Multicast addresses

THE IPv6 DATAGRAM

This section provides a description of each field in the datagram, and the next section compares the IPv6 fields with the fields in the IPv4 datagram.

Figure 7–1 illustrates the format of IPv6 datagram (also called a packet in some literature). The header consists of 64 bits of control field followed by a 128-bit source address and a 128-bit destination address. The initial 64 bits are:

- Version field, 4 bits
- Priority field, 4 bits

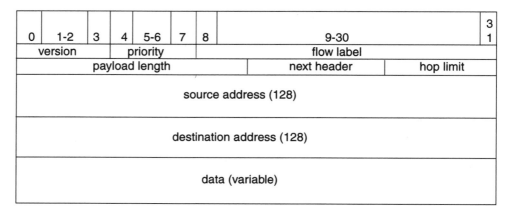

0	1-2	3	4	5-6	7	8	9-30	3 1

Figure 7–1 shows the IPv6 datagram structure with fields: version, priority, flow label, payload length, next header, hop limit, source address (128), destination address (128), and data (variable).

Figure 7–1   The IPv6 datagram

- Flow label field, 24 bits
- Payload length, 16 bits
- Next header type, 8 bits
- Hop limit, 8 bits
- Addresses, 128 bits each

The *version* field identifies the version of the protocol. For this implementation, the code is 6 (0110) for the 4-bit field.

The *priority* field is a new field. It can be coded to indicate 16 possible values and is intended to play a similar role as the precedence field of IPv4. The IPv6 priority field is used to support different types of traffic, from synchronous real time video to asynchronous data.

Table 7–3 shows the permitted values for the IPv6 priority field and what types of traffic the priority values identify. The smaller numbers identify low-priority traffic, such as email, bulk-file transfers, etc. The values 9–14 were set aside with the original publication of IPv6. The standards groups are in the process of defining some of these values for traffic, such as voice.

RFC 1883 sets these rules for the priority field: Values 0–7 are used to specify the priority of traffic for which the source is providing congestion control. Values 8–15 are used to specify the priority of traffic that does not back off in response to congestion, real-time voice, or video packets being sent at a constant rate.

For noncongestion-controlled traffic, the lowest priority value (8) should be used for those packets that the sender is most willing to have

Table 7–3   IPv6 priority field

0	Uncharacterized traffic
1	"Filler" traffic (news)
2	unattended data transfer (e-mail)
3	Reserved
4	Bulk traffic (file transfer)
5	Reserved
6	Interactive traffic (...Telnet)
7	Control traffic (..OSPF,SNP)
8	High-fidelity video
9–14	Reserved
15	Low-fidelity video

discarded under conditions of congestion (e.g., high-fidelity video traffic), and the highest value (15) should be used for those packets that the sender is least willing to have discarded (e.g., low-fidelity audio traffic). There is no relative ordering implied between the congestion-controlled priorities and the noncongestion-controlled priorities.

The *flow label* field is also a new field in contrast to IPv4. Like the priority field, it is also designed to handle different types of traffic, such as voice, video, or data. The flow label field is a special identifier that can be attached to the datagram to permit it to be given special treatment by a router. It is called the flow label field because its intent is to identify traffic in which multiple datagrams are "flowing" from a specific source address to a specific destination address. The flow label field can be used in place of the IP destination address fields, but its specific use is implementation-specific. Section 6 of RFC 1883 provides guidance on the use of flow labels.

The *payload length* field identifies the length of the payload. Since its length is 16 bits, the payload size is limited to 64 kbytes. However, the protocol does provide for the support of larger packets by utilizing the next header field.

The *next header* field represents one of the major changes of the protocol. First, it replaces the IPv4 options field and, for usual implementations, it identifies the next header to be TCP or UDP. This means that the first part of the payload is carrying TCP or UDP traffic. However, other headers can be placed in the payload. They are called extension headers and reside between the IP header and the TCP or UDP header and payload. This approach simplifies the processing of a packet at a node, since the basic header is now a fixed length.

The *hop limit* field reflects how many hops the datagram is permitted to traverse during its stay in an internet. This implementation is specific to the needs of the application.

The IP address fields are the last fields in the IP header. Each address is 128 bits in length, which allows for significant growth in the Internet.

IPv4 AND IPv6 HEADERS

This section is an extension to the previous discussion. It compares the headers of IPv4 and IPv6. This comparison will allow us to move into another level of detail about IPv6. The approach taken here is to start with the IPv4 header fields and to explain their fate in IPv6. To aid in this analysis, Figure 7–2 provides an illustration of the IPv4 datagram.

The *version* field is retained with the value of 6.

The *IPv4 header length* field is eliminated, and the IPv4 total length field is replaced by the IPv6 payload length. This latter field defines the contents of only the data (and not the header) field.

The *IPv4 type of service (TOS)* field is eliminated in IPv6, and parts of its contents (and functions) are placed in the IPv6 priority and flow label fields.

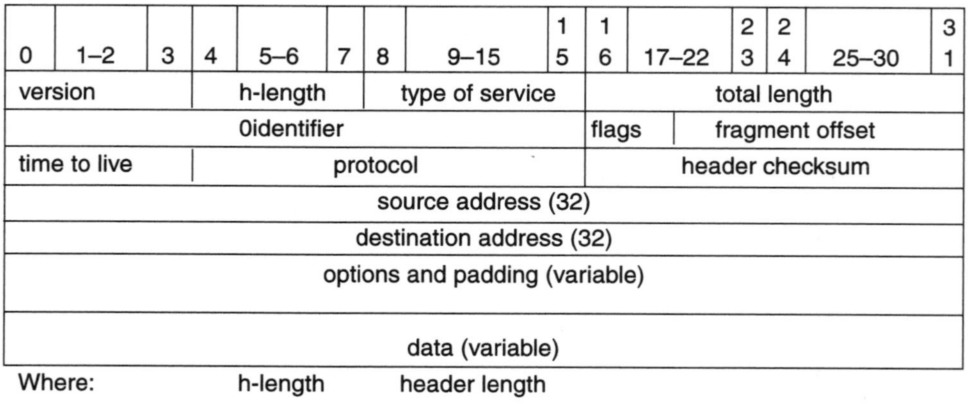

0	1–2	3	4	5–6	7	8	9–15	1 5	1 6	17–22	2 3	2 4	25–30	3 1
version			h-length			type of service			total length					
0identifier								flags		fragment offset				
time to live			protocol					header checksum						
source address (32)														
destination address (32)														
options and padding (variable)														
data (variable)														

Where: h-length   header length

Figure 7–2   The IPv4 datagram

The *identifier, flags,* and *fragment offset* fields in IPv4 are removed and similar functions are placed in an optional header extension.

The *IPv4 time-to-live (TTL)* field is renamed the hop limit field in IPv6. But with the revision, the field's name is now accurate, because IPv6 uses it as a count of the number of hops the IP datagram has traversed.

The *IP protocol* field is removed, and its function is retained in yet another extension header.

The *header checksum* field is eliminated in IPv6. This removal reflects the fact that the vast majority of communications systems in operation today perform error checks at the lower layers; that is, the layers below IP.

The *options* field in IPv4 is not used much. It is awkward to implement, and in some cases leads to considerable overhead in processing its contents because the field requires the execution of special routines in the IP software. It is replaced with IPv6 header extensions, discussed next.

IPv6 EXTENSION HEADERS

The approach in IPv6 is to use extension headers, with each extension header stipulating what is in effect an option. As Figure 7–3 shows, the header extension describes a header that is inserted between the internet header and the user payload (data field). Indeed, there may be

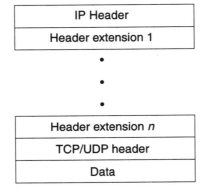

Figure 7–3   Example of the IPv6 extension header layout

more than one header inserted here with the fields coded to identify each successive header. In effect, a header is identified by its header type which also carries a header type of the next header in the chain (if any exist).

The IPv6 RFC describes six extension headers:

- Fragment header
- Hop-by-hop options header
- Authentication header
- Encrypted security payload header
- Routing header
- Destination options header

With one exception, extension headers are not examined by any node along the delivery path. The node identified in the destination address of the header examines the next header field to determine if an extension header is present, or if the upper layer header is present. The hop-by-hop options is the exception, and it is processed by every node on the path. The specification supports variable length extensions, if necessary.

Fragmentation Header

IPv4 permits the fragmentation of large packets into smaller datagrams. This operation is useful, but it leads to considerable overhead in an internet. Consequently, IPv6 nodes will not fragment large packets once the traffic enters the network. In effect, the system reacts as if the IPv4 "don't fragment bit" is turned on. IPv6 does permit the packets to be fragmented before they are sent into the network. In addition, the fragments can be sent independently through an internet and arrive at different times and in different sequences at the receiver. The fragmentation operations of IPv6 are similar to those in Pv4. However, fragmentation is performed only by the source node; intermediate nodes on the path are not allowed to fragment packets.

Hop-by-Hop Options Header

The destination options header (discussed later) is used at the final destination. However, it may be important that intermediate nodes (hops) be able to execute some operations to process the datagram. Functions that come to mind are ongoing debugging or network management operations. Therefore the hop-by-hop options extension header is used for these purposes. The contents of the hop-by-hop options header must be defined based on the individual implementation, with one exception, the jumbo payload option. This option permits large PDUs to be sent whose length exceeds that encoded in the 16-bit length field. When this option is implemented, the IPv6 length field is set to all 0s. The processing node must then use a field in the hop-by-hop options to understand how to process the PDU.

Security Extension Headers

The IPv6 security features are provided by the *authentication header* and the *encrypted security payload header*. This section summarizes the IPv6 security features. More information is provided in RFCs 1825, 1826, 1827, 1828, and 1829.

Both authentication and encryption require that the sending and receiving parties agree on a key and a specific authentication or encryption algorithm. Other parameters are set up as well, such as the lifetime of the key.

The fields in the header are:

- *Authentication data:* Implementation-specific
- *Security Parameter Index (SPI):* Identifies the security association for the security operation

The format for the header is quite simple. It contains the next header indicator in the daisy chain of headers, the length of the header in multiples of 32 bits, a 16-bit reserved field that is currently set to 0s, the 32-bit SPI, and authentication data also coded in 32-bit word increments. The contents of the authentication data field depends on the specific encryption/authentication algorithm and the types of keys that are used.

The encrypted security payload header is the last header in the daisy chain of headers. The SPI is an Internet security concept that identified the security association for a particular packet, including:

- Destination IP address
- Security protocol that is to be used, which defines if the traffic is to be provided with integrity as well as secrecy support. It also defines the key size, key lifetime, and cryptographic algorithms
- Secret keys to be used by the cryptographic operations

- Encapsulation mode which defines how the encapsulation headers are created and which part of the user traffic is protected during the communicating process.

Routing Header

The routing header is similar to the source routing option in the options field of IPv4. Like its predecessor, the IPv6 routing header carries a list of intermediate IP addresses through which the IP datagram is relayed.

Destination Options Header

In many systems, it is desirable to relay information transparently through an internet to be used only by the receiving end station. The IPv6 destination options header provides for this service. It contains an options field within the header which is acted upon by the end-user application. If the options field is not recognized by the destination, then this feature provides the ability to generate an ICMP report stipulating the problem that has occurred by receiving an unrecognized option.

INTERNET CONTROL MANAGEMENT PROTOCOL (ICMP) FOR IPv6

Since ICMP uses IP addresses, it too must be revised to operate with IPv6. In addition, the IPv4 Internet Group Membership Protocol (IGMP) was incorporated into ICMP.

The IPv6 ICMP messages have the same general format as the IPv4 ICMP messages including a type field, a code field, a checksum, and a variable length data part. The IPv6 ICMP also defines ICMP type messages which are similar to IPv4 messages. Currently, there are fourteen different types defined and they are listed here:

1	=	destination unreachable
2	=	packet too big
3	=	time exceeded
4	=	parameter problem
128	=	echo request
129	=	echo reply
130	=	group membership query

131 = group membership report

132 = group membership termination

133 = router solicitation

134 = router advertisement

135 = neighbor solicitation

136 = neighbor advertisement

137 = redirect

INTERWORKING IPV4 AND IPV6

As of this writing, it is clear that people other than the IPv6 developers are aware that IPv6 must be dealt with. A number of organizations are beta testing IPv6 in test networks.

A key issue in the use of IPv6 is how to get there from IPv4. The Internet Working Groups have published RFCs to guide the network administrator through the transition maze. I refer you to RFCs 1933 and 2185, and the book in this series titled, *Advanced Features of the Internet*.

TCP AND ITS EFFECT OF QOS

The Transmission Control Protocol (TCP) significantly impacts the quality of service an application obtains in an internet. To see why, take a look at Figure 7–4. The QOS domain does not encompass the TCP operations and has nothing to do with TCP; that is, the QOS and TCP entities do not communicate with each other. But notice the horizontal arrow in the figure. Using conventional OSI Model notations, this arrow means that the two TCP modules, residing outside the QOS domain are exchanging packets with each other. The packets' contents are not of interest to the QOS domain, they are acted upon by the TCP modules in the source end system (SES) and the destination end system (DES). Therefore, TCP has the ability to affect the following QOS features on an end-to-end basis:

- Acknowledgments of packets
- Retransmissions of missing, erred, or out-of-sequence packets
- Controlling rate of packet flow between the TCP modules

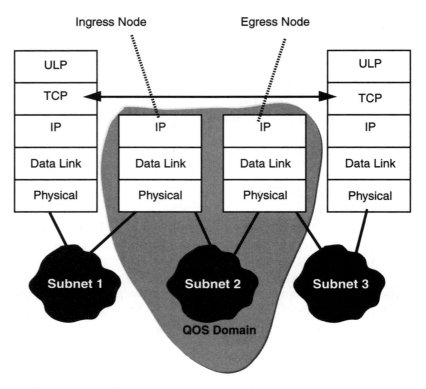

Figure 7–4   Relationship of transport layer to other layers

Notwithstanding, TCP may be placed in the QOS nodes, and in practice it is. The reasons for this placement vary. As one example, TCP is used in some routers for router-to-router acknowledgment.

Many of the TCP functions (such as flow control, reliability, sequencing, etc.) could be handled within an application program. But it makes little sense to code these functions into each application. Moreover, applications programmers are usually not versed in error-detection and flow control operations. The preferred approach is to develop generalized software that provides community functions applicable to a wide range of applications, and then invoke these programs from the application software. This allows the application programmer to concentrate on solving the application problem, and it isolates the programmer from the nuances and problems of network QOS activities.

HOW TCP HANDLES USER TRAFFIC

TCP acknowledges segments for both interactive traffic and bulk data traffic.[2] However, TCP varies in how these acknowledges occur. The variability depends on the operating system through which TCP executes, as well as the options chosen for a TCP session. In essence, there is no "standard" TCP operating profile.

Notwithstanding these comments, TCP does use many common procedures that are found in most TCP implementations and versions. This part of the chapter provides a survey on them.

Interactive Traffic

For interactive traffic (using Rlogin as examples), TCP may use a delayed acknowledgment (ACK) operation. Some implementations hold back the ACK for a brief time (usually 200 ms) and attempt to piggyback the ACK onto an Rlogin echo segment in order to reduce the amount of traffic sent onto the network. TCP does not send the ACK immediately after receiving data, but waits before sending, with the expectation that the Rlogin echo is placed in the TCP segment. However, TCP will not wait the 200 ms if it has data to send; in this situation, it sends data immediately, and piggybacks the TCP ACK on this segment.

TCP also supports the Nagle algorithm, which states that the TCP connection is allowed only one Rlogin byte (or any application's small segment) to be outstanding (not ACKed). The result is that data is collected by the sending TCP module while awaiting the ACK to the single segment. This approach allows the sending of more than one byte in the next transmitted segment.

For TCP support of interactive traffic (and bulk data), TCP will send an ACK if the data is acceptable, even though the data has not yet been passed to the application.

Bulk Traffic

For the support of bulk traffic, the delayed ACK is also supported, which was described earlier. In addition, a common approach to bulk data ACKs is the acknowledgment of every other segment. This operation is designed to conserve bandwidth on the channel. TCP uses an in-

---

[2]The term segment is used to describe the TCP protocol data unit.

clusive acknowledgment approach to ACKs, which allows one ACK segment to acknowledge multiple data segments.

Another approach to TCP bulk data traffic management is called the slow start. Used by itself, it is not a slow start, but an exponential start. But other TCP operations will mitigate its exponential behavior. The slow start states that each received ACK will increase the TCP's ability to send segments in an exponential manner. This operation proceeds, up to a point, at which time TCP resorts to an additive (linear) mode which is based on the round-trip time (RTT) of the received ACKs. That is, the time it took to receive an ACK for a transmitted segment.

If TCP receives ACKs that indicate a missing contiguous segment, it resends the missing segment and all other succeeding segments that were sent after this "first" missed segment. However, this GO-BACK-N (go back to segment N and resend all segments of larger sequence numbers) may not occur if TCP receives three ACKs for the same segment. In this situation, TCP resends only the one segment in question.

The RTT is computed on the received ACKs, based on several simple algorithms, which account for the round trip time as well as: (a) the possibility of receiving duplicate ACKs on one segment and (b) the variability in time in receiving the ACKs (the RTT values are smoothed).

Example of TCP Traffic Accounting Operations

TCP has a unique way of accounting for traffic on each connection. Unlike many other protocols, it does not have an explicit *negative acknowledgment (NAK)*. Rather, it relies on the transmitting entity to issue a time-out and retransmit data for which it has not received a *positive acknowledgment (ACK)*. This concept is illustrated in Figure 7–5, which shows eight events labeled with numbers (1 through 8). Each of these events will be described in order. Note that this example assumes the receiver is sending its ACKs back to the sender with a credit window that permits the sender to continue sending segments.

Event 1: TCP A sends a segment to TCP B. This example assumes a segment size of 300 octets. The sequence (SEQ) number contains the value of 3. As indicated in this event, 300 bytes are sent to TCP B.

Event 2: TCP B checks the traffic for errors and sends back an acknowledgment with the value of 303 [remember, this value is an inclusive acknowledgment which acknowledges all traffic (all bytes in the segment) up to and including 302: SEQ number 3–302]. As depicted by

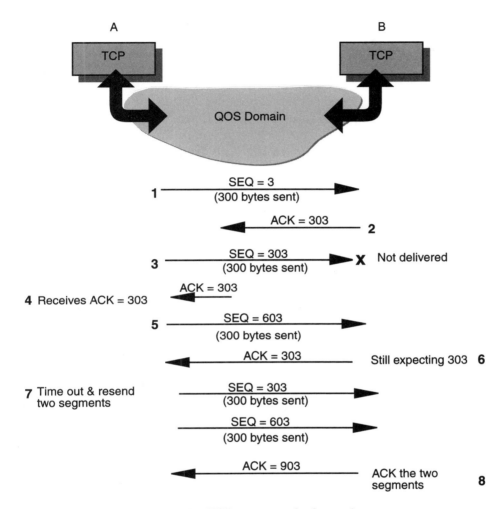

Figure 7–5   TCP retransmission schemes

the arrow in event 2, this segment has not yet arrived at TCP A when
event 3 occurs. (The tip of the arrow is not at A's location.)

Event 3: Because TCP A still has its window open, it sends another
segment of data beginning with number 303. However this traffic segment is not delivered to TCP B, either because IP discards it, or because
TCP detects a problem with its checksum operation.

Event 4: The acknowledgment segment transmitted in event 2 arrives at TCP A stipulating that TCP B is expecting a segment beginning
with number 303. At this point, TCP A cannot know if the traffic trans-

mitted in event 3 was not delivered or simply has not yet arrived due to variable delays in an internet. Consequently, it proceeds with event 5.

Event 5: TCP A sends the next segment beginning the number 603. It arrives error-free at TCP B.

Event 6: TCP B successfully receives segment number 603, which was transmitted in event 5. However, TCP B sends back a segment with ACK 303 because it is still expecting segment number 303 and is not allowed to ACK out-of-sequence traffic. The frequency of sending ACKs varies, but a common practice is to send ACKs every 200 ms.

Event 7: Eventually, TCP A must time out and resend the segments for which it has not yet had an acknowledgment. In this example, it must resend to TCP B the segments beginning with numbers 303 and 603. Of course, the idea depicted in event 7 has its advantages and disadvantages. It makes the protocol quite simple, because TCP simply goes back to the last unacknowledged segment number and retransmits all succeeding segments. On the other hand, it likely retransmits segments which were not in error; for example, the segment beginning with number 603 which had arrived error-free at TCP B. Nonetheless, TCP operates in this fashion at the risk of some degraded throughput for the sake of simplicity. Moreover, if TCP A receives three successive ACKs with the same sequence number, it is smart enough to resort to a "selective retransmission" and resend only one segment.

Event 8: All traffic is accounted for after TCP B receives and error checks segments 303 and 603 and returns an ACK value equal to 903.

The TCP Timer

An approach for controlling traffic emission into the network is to utilize adjustable timers at the network or transport layers in the end-user machine. These operations are built on retransmission timers that are turned on when traffic is sent to the network. Assume the timer is initially set to expire in n seconds. Upon expiration, if an acknowledgment has not been returned from the receiver to the sender, the sender will time-out and resend the traffic, perhaps adjusting the timer to reflect nonreceipt of the ACK to the transmitted segment. The timer does not change with every retransmission; rather the transmitter builds a profile of the delays encountered for a number of ACKs in order to account for the variability of the delay sending the data and receiving the ACK.

We assume that responses are returned from the end user in a timely manner. The first transaction's round-trip delay is n milliseconds, which is well within the bounds of retransmission timer T. The transmitting entity maintains the same time-outs, of say m milliseconds.

As we learned, profiles are built on response times. In the event that network congestion begins to occur, resulting in increased delays, the replies will arrive beyond the bound on T. After the appropriate time-outs occur and the traffic is resent, the sending entity will adjust its timer to a longer value. In this manner, the traffic is not sent to the network as often, and the network can begin to adjust and drain its buffers.

The transmitter changes its timer and continues to build profiles on the responses. As congestion diminishes and the round-trip delay decreases, the retransmission timer maintains or decreases its current value. The timers can even decrease further as delay lessens.

Timer Values

Choosing a value for the retransmission timer is not an easy task. The reason for this complexity stems from the fact that (a) the delay of receiving acknowledgments from the receiving host varies in an internet; (b) segments sent from the transmitter may be lost in the internet which obviously invalidates any round-trip delay estimate for a nonoccurring acknowledgment; (c) (and in consonance with b) acknowledgments from the receiver may also be lost, which also invalidates the round-trip delay estimate.

Because of these problems, TCP does not use a fixed retransmission timer. Rather, it utilizes an adaptive retransmission timer that is derived from an analysis of the delay encountered in receiving acknowledgments from remote hosts.

The round-trip time (RTT) is derived from adding the send delay (SD), the processing time (PT) at the remote host, and the receive delay (RD). If delay were not variable, this simple calculation would suffice for determining a retransmission timer. However, as stated earlier, delay in the internet is often highly variable so other factors must be considered.

Several aspects of Figure 7–6 should be emphasized: (1) In most systems, timing is performed by incrementing a 500-ms step counter. In this example, even though the ACKs arrive at 1.11 and 0.78 sec, they are recorded as increments of 500 ms. (2) The timer is turned off when the ACK arrives. (3) The system remembers the starting sequence number of the transmitted segment and knows which ACK pertains to this seg-

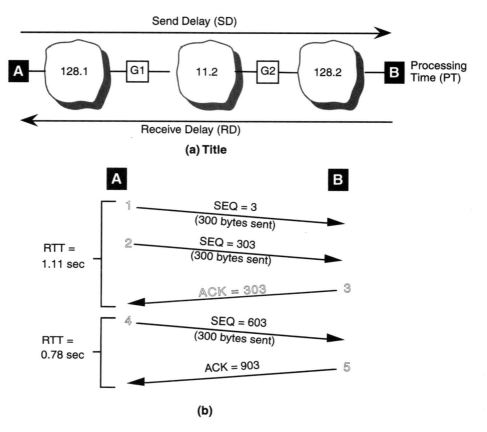

Figure 7–6   Round-trip delay (RTT)

ment. (4) Only one timer per connection is used. Therefore, the segment in event 2 is not timed.

The Nagle Algorithm

With the Rlogin operation, 1 byte is sent at a time from the client to the server. Thus 20 bytes are sent for the TCP header, 20 bytes for the IP header, 4–8 bytes for the layer 2 header—all to transport the 1 byte of Rlogin traffic.

To alleviate this problem, RFC 896 defines a mechanism called the Nagle algorithm. Its operation is shown in Figure 7–7. It requires that a TCP connection can have only one unacknowledged small segment, and so other segments can be sent until this segment is ACKed, and the ACK is received correctly at the TCP module.

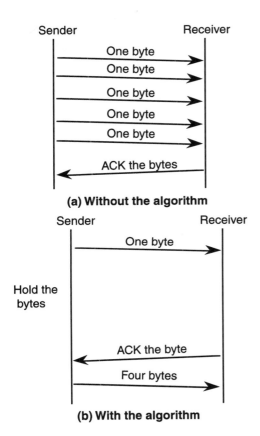

(a) Without the algorithm

(b) With the algorithm   **Figure 7–7   Nagle's algorithm**

The effect of this rule is that the small segments are collected into one TCP segment until the sending TCP receives an ACK from the peer TCP. So, on a fast network, the ACKs are received quickly, and the data are then sent quickly. This is the situation in a fast and uncongested network. However, in a congested network, the ACKs arrive more slowly, and fewer 1-byte segments are sent. This Nagle algorithm is elegantly simple and helps solve the 1-byte transmission. The Nagle algorithm does not have to be executed. It can be turned off for applications that need very fast response time and very low delay.

Slow Start

TCP implements an operation called the slow start. Slow start uses a variable called the congestion window (*cwnd*). The sending TCP module is allowed to increment *cwnd* when it receives acknowledgments of previously transmitted segments.

Figure 7–8 shows, upon initialization, TCP A sends one segment; and at this time *cwnd* = 1. In event 2, TCP B acknowledges TCP A's segment 1 which allows TCP A to increment *cwnd* = 2. In event 3, it sends two segments numbered 2 and 3.

Notice in Figure 7–8 that slow start is really not a slow start but an exponential start. In event 4, TCP B acknowledges segments 2 and 3 which allows TCP A to increment *cwnd* to a value of 4 and sends the four segments shown in event 5.

This exponential increase in the transmission of segments from TCP A is constrained by its transmit window, which of course is governed by TCP B.

One point is noteworthy here. The variable *cwnd* will not continue to be increased exponentially; if a time-out occurs and the TCP sending module must resend segments. In this situation, *cwnd* is set to one segment, which is in harmony with the slow start concept: Take it easy and don't send traffic if the network is congested.

The example in Figure 7–9 shows that TCP supports the rule that the sending TCP module will not send traffic continuously at an expo-

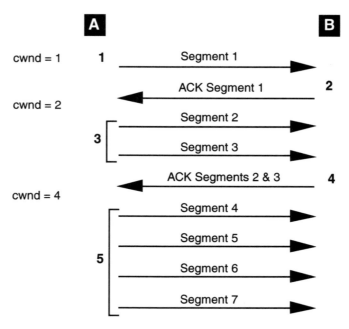

Figure 7–8   The slow start and the congestion window (*cwnd*)

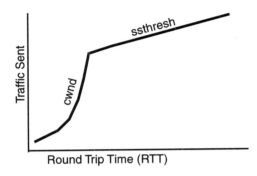

Figure 7–9 Congestion window (*cwnd*) and threshold size (*ssthresh*)

nential rate if the ACKs to the segments are delayed. In essence, a point is reached where the sending TCP backs off its sending of segments.

Two TCP variables are pertinent here: (a) *cwnd* and (b) *ssthresh*. The operation proceeds as follows. If the TCP module detects congestion, either through a time-out or through the reception of duplicate acknowledgments, a value is saved in *ssthresh*. This value must be one half of the current window size, but can be at least two segments. Moreover, if a time-out occurs, *cwnd* is reset to the value of 1 which reinitializes the slow start operation.

Therefore, congestion avoidance requires that *cwnd* must be incremented by 1/*cwnd* each time an ACK is received. Consequently, for this situation, this results in a linear increase in the traffic sent.

ROLE OF UDP IN THE QOS PICTURE

The User Datagram Protocol (UDP) is sometimes used in place of TCP in situations where the full services of TCP are not needed. For example, the Trivial File Transfer Protocol (TFTP), and the Remote Procedure Call (RPC) use UDP. So do voice and video applications.

UDP serves as a simple application interface to the IP. Since it has no reliability, flow control, nor error-recovery measures, it serves principally as a multiplexer/demultiplexer for the receiving and sending of IP traffic.

Like TCP, UDP uses the port concept to direct the user packets to the proper upper-layer application. The UDP datagram contains a destination port number and a source port number. The destination number is used to deliver the traffic to the proper recipient.

ROLE OF MULTICASTING, RTP, RTCP, AND RSVP IN THE QOS PICTURE

Other protocols have been used in the past to support IP in providing QOS features to the user. They are covered in other books in this series, and Appendix A summarizes their operations for the newcomer who has not read these other books. In this part of the chapter, I will explain how they can jointly provide a powerful QOS platform for IP-based networks.

Figure 7–10 shows the operations of the following protocols to provide these QOS functions to users. You may notice that I have not included DiffServ in this example because it is explained in Chapter 8. Also, the exact order in which these protocols are invoked can vary; for example, the distribution of labels can occur before or after QOS is set up for the session. The important point is that the network operator and customer must coordinate how these protocols are invoked (and in what order) to support the session:

- Internet Group Management Protocol (IGMP): Manages the multicasting group.
- *Multiprotocol Label Switching (MPLS)*: Sets up label tables for the multicasting session.

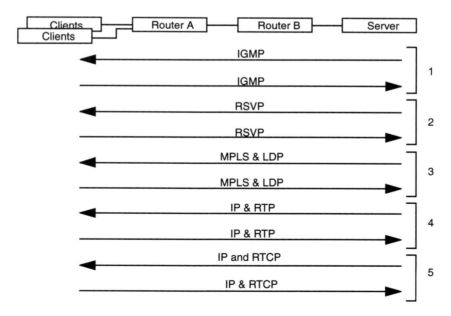

Figure 7–10   Example of IP-based QOS operations

- *Label Distribution Protocol (LDP)*: Distributes the labels within the multicasting group.
- *Resource Reservation Protocol (RSVP)*: Reserves resources for the session.
- *IPv6:* Forwards multicasting traffic through the QOS domain, using the IPv6 flow label field.
- *Real Time Protocol (RTP)*: Provides encapsulation and timestamping support for multicast traffic.
- *Real Time Control Protocol (RTCP)*: Provides an end-to-end feedback mechanism between the multicasting parties.

Let us assume that the session example is a videoconference, with the principal sources of the conference information streams (videos, slide shows, etc.) located at the node labeled "server" in Figure 7–10. Most of the transmissions will emanate from the server node. The clients will also participate in the conference, but their QOS requirements will not be as demanding. For example, the server will be showing high-quality, real-time animations to the clients. The clients will send back only questions or comments about the animated show; so they do not need as much bandwidth as required by the server.

The IGMP is invoked by the server in event 1 to allow the server to advertise a multicast address for the videoconference. These "query" packets are sent to the clients, who if they wish to participate in the conference, return IGMP "report" packets to the server. During this process the parties are assigned an IP multicast address (which was obtained previously from the Internet).

The IGMP operations do not set up the QOS resources for the conference. This is the responsibility of RSVP. In event 2, the server sends out a RSVP "path" message to the multicast group. This message must also be processed by routers A and B, because they too must reserve resources for the session. The clients respond in event 2 with a RSVP "reservation" message.

These messages may contain many fields, depending on the nature and level of QOS that is to be provisioned for the conference. As examples, the RSVP message contains the IP destination address, the IP protocol ID, and a destination port, to define a specific session for the other packets that follow. The messages provide information about the data packets that should receive the desired QOS, as well as the traffic characteristics of the server's flow. Another important piece of information that might be coded in the RSVP message deals with the QOS scope. For

RSVP, this "scope" information is a list of nodes toward which the RSVP path message must be forwarded. This list could have been derived from the IGMP operations in event 1, or it might be preconfigured.

After the QOS features have been reserved for the videoconference, labels must be assigned for the ongoing exchange of traffic. RSVP could be used for this operation, but there is more interest in the protocols shown in event 3. The label assignment operation is executed in event 3 with the Multiprotocol Label Switching (MPLS) protocol and the Label Distribution Protocol (LDP). The exact manner in which MPLS and LDP interwork with RSVP is still being worked out in the Internet task forces. These two protocols must support RSVP, but there will probably be restrictions on multicasting, which is one aspect of this example.

However, RSVP will interwork with MPLS and the LDP, and these protocols are responsible for the distribution of routing labels between neighbor label switching routers (LSRs), shown as routers A and B in our example.

MPLS does not make a forwarding decision with each L3 datagram. That operation will remain with IPv6 (in event 4). Instead, a forwarding equivalency for the videoconferencing traffic is determined and a fixed-length label is negotiated (using the LDP) between neighboring routers along label switch paths (LSPs) from ingress to egress; through routers A and B, and perhaps the clients and servers in Figure 7–10. I say "perhaps" because it is likely that the clients and server will not invoke the MPLS procedures. Rather they will sit outside the QOS domain, and routers A and B will act as the edge devices into and out of the domain.

After the labels are set up, and the label tables have been constructed, IPv6 is used to forward the traffic between the server and the clients, shown in Figure 7–10, as event 4. This event provides us the opportunity to introduce the Real Time Protocol (RTP).

RTP is designed for the support of real-time traffic, that is traffic that needs to be sent and received in a very short time period. Two real-time traffic examples are (a) the video stream from the server in our example and (b) the questions and comments from the clients.

RTP is also an encapsulation protocol in that the real-time traffic runs in the data field of the RTP packet, and the RTP header contains information about the type of traffic that RTP is transporting. RTP also has a timestamp field in its header, which can be used to synchronize the traffic play-out to the receiving application.

IPv6 comes into play in the example, because the labels that were assigned in event 3 can be carried in the IPv6 flow label field. Thus, the per-datagram forwarding process through the QOS domain is reduced to label-lookup, label swapping and a forwarding selection.

During the videoconference, each router sends LDP notification messages to each of its neighbors. This message is sent periodically to maintain the neighbor relationship.

Event 5 in Figure 7–10 is an optional operation using the Real Time Control Protocol (RTCP). This protocol is responsible for the management of the real-time session between sending and receiving applications. The protocol is designed to allow senders to inform receivers about the RTP traffic that they should have received from the sender and it also allows the receiver of the traffic to generate reports back to the sender. This idea has been found to be quite useful in IP multicasting because it is used to troubleshoot faults in packet distribution.

SUMMARY

Neither IPv4 nor IPv6 implement many QOS features. IPv6 certainly provides more than does IPv4 with its priority, flow label fields, and its extension headers. This approach is not one of short-sightedness, but one that permits IP-based networks to avail themselves and the IP users to QOS features by implementing and executing several supporting QOS protocols, such as RTP, RTCP, RSVP, and DiffServ. The latter protocol is the subject of the next chapter.

8

Differentiated Services (DiffServ)

This chapter examines the Internet QOS protocol, Differentiated Services (DiffServ or DS). The principal DiffServ traffic conditioning operations of metering, marking, shaping, and policing are explained. DS domains are introduced, as well as per hop behavior (PHB)—a method of configuring QOS in the DS domain.

DIFFSERV ARCHITECTURE

DiffServ provides a framework that enables service providers to offer each customer a range of services that are differentiated on the basis of performance (and perhaps an associated price). The customer and provider negotiate an SLA describing the customer's packet rate submittal, and the provider's support of the customer's packet rate. If the customer submits traffic in excess of the SLA, that traffic need not be given the service established in the SLA. Table 8–1 provides a summary of the DiffServ features.

DiffServ is designed to scale to large networks and a large customer population. It forces many of the QOS operations out of the network and to the nodes surrounding the network (edge nodes). These nodes do not affect the overall performance of the network core, and even though they

Table 8–1   Differentiated Services (DiffServ or DS) features

- Services differentiated by performance (and maybe price)
- Service on a packet-by-packet basis
- Does not define a control plane (a control or signaling protocol)
- Attempts to force complexity out of network to edges
- Concerned with:
  Traffic classification
  Traffic conditioning
- Relies on IP header to contain a label (a codepoint) to identify traffic type
- Traffic conditioning is the enforcement of rules for
  Metering: measuring traffic rates
  Marking: setting/changing codepoint
  Shaping: controlled traffic emission
  Policing: traffic discarding
- Rules are called: Traffic Conditioning Agreement (TCA)

themselves may experience problems, those problems affect only the customers at that node and not the customer "universe" inside the network.

The key ideas of DiffServ are to: (a) classify traffic at the boundaries of a network, and (b) condition this traffic at the boundaries. The classification operation entails the assignment of the traffic to *behavioral aggregates*. These behavioral aggregates are a collection of packets with common characteristics, as far as how they are identified and treated by the network. They are defined as a collection of packets with the same DS codepoint crossing a link in a particular direction. The classification operation in a DS network classifies the packets based on the content of the packet headers, and at least a codepoint.

A codepoint is the DS packet identifier, and is similar to a label in the Frame Relay or ATM technologies. The identified traffic is assigned a value (a differentiated services [DS] codepoint, DCSP). For IPv4, the codepoint is in the TOS field; for IPv6, the codepoint could be the flow label field.

The idea of the codepoint is similar to ATM labels, but it is not the same. First, a codepoint does not identify a virtual circuit, and therefore can operate in a native mode with IP-based connectionless networks. Second, since the codepoint does not identify a virtual circuit, there is no need to map VPI/VCI labels from the incoming interface to the outgoing interface (Chapter 2, Figure 2–16). The codepoint can remain unaltered as the packet makes its journey to the end user.

After the packets have been classified at the boundary of the network, they are forwarded through the network based on the DS codepoint. The forwarding is performed on a per-hop basis; that is, the DS node alone decides how the forwarding is to be carried-out. This concept is called per-hop-behavior (PHB). The PHB is the observable forwarding behavior of a DS node.

In order to provide a controlled environment and prevent congestion, the traffic conditioning functions must enforce rules on the influx of traffic into and out of the DS domain. These rules are known collectively as the traffic conditioning agreement (TCA). They govern how the user packet stream is treated within the SLA.

DiffServ: Control Plane and Data Plane

DiffServ is different from most of the QOS protocols discussed in this book because it does not define a control plane. A control plane is a stack of protocols that provide signaling, such as the Frame Relay and ATM switched virtual call (SVC) protocols. DiffServ relies on the data plane for its information, that is, the ongoing user data packets. Nothing precludes the use of a control protocol to assist the service provider in provisioning the QOS nodes. As examples, RSVP or LDP could serve this purpose. Alternately, the DiffServ configurations can be performed manually, by crafting commands.

COMPARISON OF QOS TECHNOLOGIES

We are nearing the end of our analysis of the QOS protocols used in wide area networks. Now is an appropriate time to pause and reflect on some of the key concepts covered in the previous chapters. This pause will also present the opportunity to explain why DiffServ represents a different approach to many of the other QOS architectures that have been discussed thus far.

Figure 8–1 compares differentiated services (DS) with guaranteed services (GS), such as ATM's CBR, VBR, and ABR operations, as well as RSVP, and some of the Frame Relay operations [BACA98].[1] These operations have been discussed in the appropriate chapters, but a few more observations are appropriate.

---

[1][BALA98] Balakrishnan, Meera, and Venkateswaran, Ramanathan. "QOS and Differentiated Services in a Multiservice Network Environment," *Bell Labs Technical Journal,* October–December, 1998.

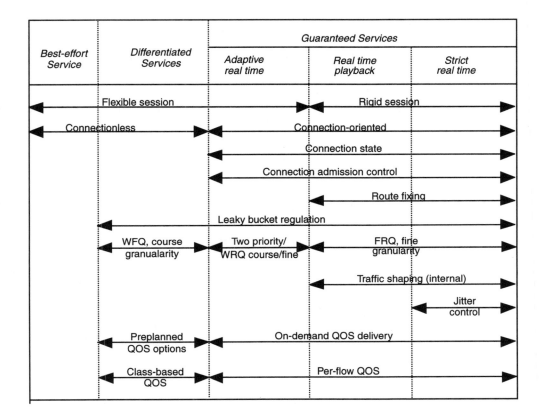

Figure 8–1   Best-effort versus DiffServ versus guaranteed services [BALA98]

The services and operations associated with GS vary among Frame Relay, ATM, RSVP, and IPv6. Most of them are offered in ATM and Frame Relay, some are available in RSVP.

IPv6 still fits into the best-effort service category; none of the guaranteed services shown in Figure 8–1 are available in IPv6 (or IPv4). But they are not supposed to be part of these protocols. DiffServ, RSVP, and other systems serve as supporting partners to IP to obtain some of these GSs.

Figure 8–1 shows DS and GS using leaky buckets and weighted fair queuing. As a general statement, these services do indeed use these techniques. But they need not implement them as shown in the Figure 8–1. Also, DS is based on the idea of preplanned QOS options, and does not define a procedure for setting up QOS features between DS nodes. Once again, I see no reason why DS cannot be used with (say) Multiprotocol Label Switching (MPLS) and the Label Distribution Protocol (LDP), which would provide tools for label distribution.

Notwithstanding these comments, the figure is a useful model of the subject.[2] Now let's take a look at the specific operations of DiffServ, as defined in the Internet standards and drafts.

DS DOMAINS

DiffServ uses the idea of a DS domain for its TCA operations (see Figure 8–2). It is a network or a collection of networks operating under an administration with a common provisioning policy. It is responsible for meeting the SLA between the user and the DS domain service provider.

The DS domain consists of a contiguous set of nodes that are DS-compliant, and agree to a common set of service provisioning policies. The DS domain also operates with common per-hop-behavior (PHB) definitions. The PHB defines how a collection of packets with the same DS codepoint are treated.

A common example of PHB behavior is how packets are forwarded by a DS node. If one behavioral aggregate is used on a link, the operation is simple: The loading of the link determines the PHB behavior. When more than one behavior aggregate compete for link resources, the PHB is used to allocate resources to the behavior aggregates. Thus, the PHB provides a hop-by-hop resource allocation and allows the support of differentiated services.

The manner in which PHBs are specified and implemented varies. They can be set up in terms of resource allocation of the QOS relative to other PHBs, for example. Recent work of the IETF is also focusing on guaranteed services, similar to the ATM class A traffic.

A PHB group is a set of one or more PHBs. The PHB group allows a set of related forwarding behaviors to be specified together. For example, a PHB group may specify more than one dropping priority.

The DS domain contains DS boundary nodes that are responsible for the classifying operations and the possible conditioning of ingress traffic.

---

[2]I would alter this figure to include the traffic shaping and jitter control services as part of DiffServ.

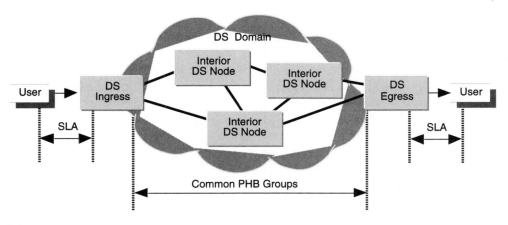

Where:
DS   DiffServ
PHB   Per-hop-behavior
SLA   Service level agreement

Figure 8–2   The DS domain

I will have more to say about conditioning later. For this introduction, it consists of controlling the traffic to make sure it "behaves" according to the rules of the DS domain (and, one hopes, the desires of the user).

Once past the ingress node, and inside the DS domain, the internal nodes continue to forward packets based on the DS codepoint. Their job is to map the DS codepoint value to a supported PHB. Thus, there are DS boundary nodes and DS interior nodes. The DS boundary nodes connect the DS domain to other DS domains or noncompliant systems. There is no restriction on what type of machine executes the boundary or interior node operations. For instance, a host might play the role of a DS boundary node.

Here is a brief summary of the key DS terms and concepts:

- *Boundary link:* a link connecting the edge nodes of two DS domains
- *DS boundary node:* a DS node that connects a DS domain to a node
- *DS-capable:* capable of implementing differentiated services
- *DS ingress node:* a DS boundary node in its role in handling traffic as it enters a DS domain
- *DS egress node:* a DS boundary node in its role in handling traffic as it leaves a DS domain
- *DS interior node:* a DS node that is not a DS boundary node

DS REGIONS

Regardless of what machine runs the DS boundary node functions, it must act as an ingress node and egress node for traffic flowing into and out of the DS domain. It is responsible for supporting traffic conditioning agreements (TCAs) with other domains. Traffic conditioning means the enforcement of rules dealing with traffic management and includes four major operations: (a) metering, (b) marking, (c) shaping, and (d) policing. These concepts are shown in Figure 8–3.

Metering entails measuring the rate of a stream of traffic, in bit/s, packets per second, bursts of packets over time, etc. Marking entails setting the DS codepoint. Shaping entails the emission of traffic (perhaps the delaying of traffic) to meet a defined traffic emission profile. Policing entails discarding packets (based on the state of the meter) to enforce a defined traffic profile.

Multiple DS domains constitute a DS region, also shown in Figure 8–3. These regions support differentiated services along paths in the domains that make up the DS region. One advantage to defining a DS region is that DiffServ allows the DS domains in the DS region to support different PHB groups. For example, a DS domain on a college campus may have different PHB groups than a DS domain in a corporate net-

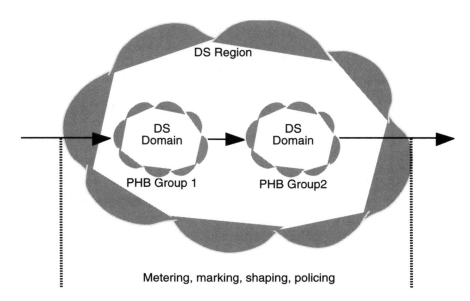

Figure 8–3   DS domains and DS regions

work. Yet these two "peering" domains must be able to interwork in a predictable and structured manner. They must define a peering SLA that establishes a TCA for the traffic that flows between them.

TRAFFIC CLASSIFICATION AND CONDITIONING

The DS node must provide traffic classification and conditioning operations, as shown in Figure 8–4. The job of packet classification is to identify subsets of traffic that are to receive differentiated services by the DS domain. Classifiers operate in two modes: (a) the behavior aggregate classifier (BA) classifies packets only on the DS codepoint, (b) the multifield classifier classifies packets by multiple fields in the packet, such as codepoints, addresses, and port numbers.

The classifiers provide the mechanism to guide the packets to a traffic conditioner for more processing. The traffic stream selected by the classifier is based on a specific set of traffic profiles, such as variable or constant bit rates, jitter, delay, etc.

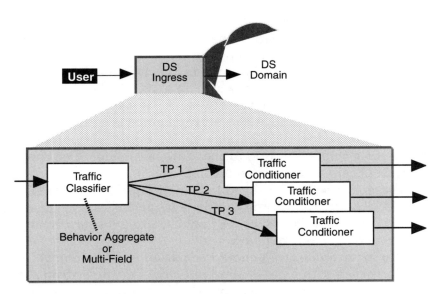

Note: Traffic classifiers can also be located at egress boundary nodes, or within the interior of
    the DS domain
Where: TP = traffic profile

Figure 8–4   DiffServ Classifiers and Conditioners

The packets that are presented to a specific traffic conditioner constitute a traffic profile (TP) and may be in-profile or out-of-profile. In-profile means the packets are "conformant" to the user-to-network SLA. Out-of-profile packets are outside an SLA, or because of network behavior, they arrive at the traffic conditioner at a rate that requires the conditioner to condition them (delay their delivery, drop them, etc.).

As a general practice, classification and conditioning operations take place at the network boundaries. But nothing precludes the internal nodes from invoking these operations, but their classification and conditioning operations are probably more limited than the boundary nodes.

Figure 8–5 shows a logical view of the relationships of the key DS functions for DS packet classification and traffic conditioning operations. The packets that exit the DS node in this figure must have the DS codepoint set to an appropriate value, based on the classification and traffic conditioning operations.

A traffic stream is selected by a classifier and sent to a traffic conditioner. DiffServ uses the term traffic conditioning block (TCB) to describe the overall conditioning operations. If appropriate, a meter is used to measure the traffic against a traffic profile. The results of the metering procedure may be used to mark, shape, or drop the traffic, based on the packet being "in-profile" or "out-of-profile." The classifiers and meters can operate as a "team" to determine how the packet is treated with regard to marking, shaping, and dropping.

The packet marking procedure sets the DS field of a packet to a codepoint, and adds the marked packet to a specific DS behavior aggregate. The marker can be configured to mark all packets to a single codepoint which are steered to it. Alternately, the marker can mark a packet to one of a set of codepoints. The idea of this configuration is to select a PHB in a PHB group, according to the state of a meter. The changing of the codepoint is called packet re-marking.

The shaping procedure is used to bring the packet stream into compliance with a particular traffic profile. The packet stream is stored in the shaper's buffer, and a packet may be discarded if there is not enough buffer space to hold a delayed packet.

The dropping procedure polices the packet stream in order to bring it into conformance with a particular traffic profile. It can drop packets to adhere to the profile. The figure shows the shaper and dropper as one entity because a dropper can be implemented as a special case of a shaper.

The originating node of the packet stream (the DS source domain) is allowed to perform classification and conditioning operations. This idea is called pre-marking and can effectively support the end application's view of the required QOS for the packet stream. The source node may

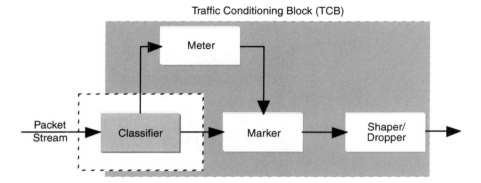

Traffic Conditioning Block (TCB)

- Operations may be at:
  Source
  Ingress node
  Egress node
  Interior node
- TCB may or may not include a classifier

Figure 8–5   The DS traffic classification and conditioning model

mark the codepoint to indicate high-priority traffic. Next, a first-hop router may mark this traffic with another codepoint, and condition the packet stream.

I stated that the collective operations of metering, marking, shaping, and dropping are known as the traffic conditioning block (TCB). The classifier need not be a part of the TCB, because it does not condition traffic. However, the classifiers and traffic conditioners can certainly be combined into the TCB. These options are shown in Figure 8–5 with the dashed lines.

The next part of this chapter goes into more detail on the classifiers and traffic conditioners. This material is available from the Internet draft authored by [BERN99]:[3]

CLASSIFICATION OPERATIONS

The main job of the classifier is to accept a packet stream (unclassified traffic) as input and generate separate output streams (classified traffic). This output is fed into the metering or marking functions.

---

[3][BERN99] Bernet, Y., et al., A Conceptual Model for DiffServ Routers, draft-ietf-fiddserv-model-00.txt, June, 1999.

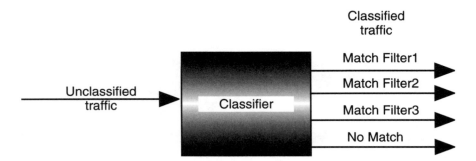

Figure 8–6   Example of the classifier's filtering operations

As mentioned earlier, the classifier operates as a behavior aggregate (BA) classifier or as a multifield (MF) classifier. The BA classifier uses only the DS codepoint to sort to an output stream, whereas the MF classifier uses other fields in the packet stream, such as a port number, or an IP protocol ID.

The BA or MF classifier checks are performed by filters, which are a set of conditions that are matched to the relevant fields in the packet to determine onto which output stream the packet is placed. This idea is shown in Figure 8–6. Unclassified traffic is flowing into an interface and passed to the classifier. The filtering operations output the packets into four streams for the traffic conditioning operations. The first three filters are exact matches on the BA or MA values. The no match is a default filter to handle any packet types that have not been provisioned at the QOS node.

METERING OPERATIONS

After the packets have been classified, the meter monitors their arrival time in the packet stream to determine the level of conformance to a traffic profile. The profile has been pre-configured, perhaps based on an SLA contract.

Figure 8–7 is a functional diagram of the metering operation. The unmetered traffic is input to the metering function. This function is implemented with one or several types of meters defined in [BERN99], but others can be used: (a) the average rate meter, (b) the exponential weighted moving average meter, (c) the token bucket meter.

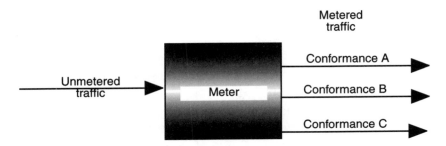

Figure 8–7   Example of the metering operations

Average Rate Meter

This meter measures the rate that packets are submitted to it over a specified time interval, for example 1000 packets per second for a 1-second interval. If the total number of packets that arrive between the current time T, and T-1 second do not exceed 1000, the packet under consideration is conforming. Otherwise, the packet is nonconforming

Exponential Weighted Moving Average (EWMA) Meter

The EWMA meter is expressed as follows:

$$\text{avg} (n + 1) = (1 - \text{Gain}) * \text{avg} (n) + \text{Gain} * \text{actual} (n + 1)$$

$$t (n + 1) = t (n) + \Delta$$

Where n is the number of packets, actual (n) and avg (n) measure the number of bytes in the incoming packets in a small sampling interval, Δ.

Gain controls the frequency response of a low-pass filter operation. An arriving packet that pushes the average rate over a predefined rate Average Rate is nonconforming.

So, for a packet arriving at time $t (m)$:

```
if (avg (m) > AverageRate)
      non-confoming
   else
      conforming
```

Token Bucket Meter

The token bucket meter is similar to the ATM token bucket (Chapter 6, Figure 6–10), and the continuous-state leaky bucket (Chapter 6,

Figure 6–12). Let's review the token bucket (TB) meter as defined in [BERN99]:

- The TB profile contains three parameters: (a) an average rate, (b) a peak rate, and (c) a burst size.
- The meter compares packet arrival rate to average rate, as byte tokens accumulate in the bucket at the average rate.
- Byte tokens accumulate in the bucket at the average rate, up to a maximum burst size (a credit).
- Arriving packets of L length are conforming if L tokens are available in the bucket at the time of packet arrival .
- Packets are allowed to the average rate in bursts up to the burst size, as long as they do not exceed the peak rate, at which point the bucket is drained.
- Arriving packets of L length are nonconforming if insufficient L tokens are in the bucket upon the packet arrival.

It is possible to implement token bucket models that have more than one burst size and conformance levels; for example two burst sizes and three conformance levels. This concept is known as two-level token bucket meter, and is similar to Frame Relay's Bc and Be profiles (Chapter 5, Figure 5–5), and Bellcore's ATM (Chapter 6, Figure 6–10).

Representations of the Meters

The following definitions represent the meters just described. I quote directly from [BERN99]:

Simple Token Bucket Meter
Meter1:

Type:	SimpleTokenBucket
Profile1:	output A
NonConforming:	output B

Profile1:	
Type	SimpleTokenBucket
AverageRate:	100 Kbps
PeakRate:	150 Kbps
BurstSize	100 Kb

EWMA Meter
Meter2:

Type:	ExpWeightedMovingAvg
Profile2:	output A
NonConforming:	output B

Profile2:	
Type:	ExpWeightedMovingAvg
Gain:	1/16
Δ:	10us
AverageRate:	200 Kbps

Two-level Token Bucket Meter
Meter3:

Type:	TwoLevelTokenBucket
Profile3:	output A
Profile4:	output B
NonConforming:	output C

Profile3:	
Type:	SimpleTokenBucket
AverageRate:	100 Kbps
PeakRate:	150 Kbps
BurstSize :	50 Kb

Profile4:	
Type:	SimpleTokenBucket
AverageRate:	120 Kbps
PeakRate:	150 Kbps
BurstSize:	100 Kb

Average Rate Meter
Meter4:

Type:	AverageRate
Profile5:	output A
NonConforming:	output B

Profile5:	
Type:	AverageRate
AverageRate:	120 Kbps
Δ:	100us

MORE IDEAS ON MARKING AND SHAPING OPERATIONS

We learned earlier that markers set the DS codepoint (DSCP) in the IP header. They may also mark a DSCP that is set to 0, or change a previously marked DSCP. Certain DS codepoints are reserved. For example, RFC 2597 defines an assured forwarding PHB group in which user packets are guaranteed a certain level of QOS. For this PHB, twelve codepoints are reserved. They are discussed later in this chapter.

We also learned that the shapers condition or shape traffic to a certain temporal profile. In the previous example, the 1001st arrival of a packet within the 1-second interval would require the packet to be held in buffer until it becomes conforming.

Shaping operations can be complex. They must be able to prevent a "rogue" flow from seizing more QOS resources that it is allowed. Also, they must not allow conformant flows to be compromised by the rogue flows. In many instances, the shaping operations depend on the size of buffers, and queue depths. However, the shaper's individual actions are straightforward, with the use of token buckets.

ANOTHER LOOK AT THE TRAFFIC CONDITIONING BLOCK (TCB)

Figure 8–8 shows a likely implementation of the TCB, and in this example, the TCB includes the classifier. The main point to Figure 8–8 is that the conditioning elements may be included or excluded from processing the packet. In addition, they may drive other TCBs on other interfaces or on the same (egress) interface.

In this example, the BA classifier operates with four filters A, B, C, and D (D is a no-match). Initially, the packet is associated with the DSCP's PBH. As long as the packet is conforming to its profile (shown as Profile1, Profile2, and Profile3 in the figure) it will be given service in accordance with the SLA.

There is a meter instantiation for each DSCP and PHB. Based on the packet and its profile, the meter judges the packet to be conforming or nonconforming. Then, the actions on the packet can vary. A dropper may discard the packet, a shaper may shape the packet to a different profile, or a marker may remark the packet's DSCP. Finally, based on these operations, the packet is either discarded, or sent to an appropriate queue for transferal onto an egress interface for this TCB.

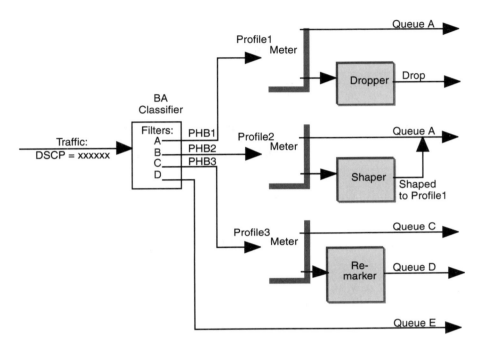

Figure 8–8   The TCB in more detail

THE DS CODEPOINT (DSCP)

The DS field in the IP datagram is the IPv4 type of service (TOS) field. It is called the DS codepoint (DSCP). This IPv4 8-bit field is shown in Figure 8–9, along with the redefinition according to the DS specifications.

The IPv4 *type of service (TOS)* field, shown in Figure 8–9(a), can be used to identify several QOS functions provided for an Internet application. Transit delay, throughput, precedence, and reliability can be requested with this field.

The TOS field contains five entries consisting of 8 bits. Bits 0, 1, and 2 contain a precedence value which is used to indicate the relative importance of the datagram. The next 3 bits are used for other services and are described as follows: Bit 3 is the *delay bit (D bit)*. When set to 1 this TOS requests a short delay through an internet. The aspect of delay is not defined in the standard, and it is up to the vendor to implement the service. The next bit is the *throughput bit (T bit)*. It is set to 1 to request for high

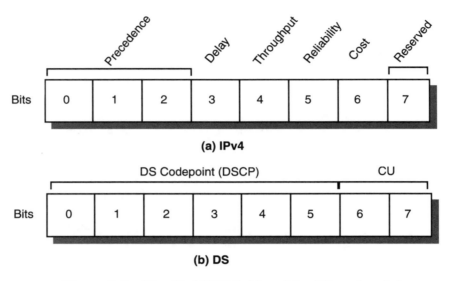

Figure 8–9   The IPv4 TOS field and the DS codepoint

throughput through an internet. Again, its specific implementation is not defined in the standard. The next bit used is the *reliability bit (R bit)*, which allows a user to request high reliability for the datagram. The last bit of interest is the *cost bit (C bit)*, which is set to request the use of a low-cost link (from the standpoint of monetary cost). The last bit is not used at this time.

The DSCP is 6 bits in length, as depicted in Figure 8–9(b). The remaining two bits of the TOS field are currently unused (CU). The DSCP notation is *xxxxxx,* where *x* may be a 1 or 0. The left-most bit signifies bit 0 of the field, and the right-most bit signifies bit 5. The entire 6-bit field are used by DS nodes as an index into a table to select a specific packet handling mechanism.

The codepoints are related to the PHBs, and the PHBs include a default codepoint. A default configuration contains a recommended codepoint-to-PHB mapping. The default PHB is the conventional best-effort forwarding operation that exists today and is standardized in RFC 1812. When a link is not needed to satisfy another PHB, the traffic associated with the default PHB should be placed onto the link. RFC 2474 states that a default PHB should not be subject to bandwidth starvation, and should be given some bandwidth, but the manner in how the bandwidth is provided is implementation-specific. The ABR operation in ATM is a good model to use for this implementation (Chapter 6, Figure 6–18). The default codepoint for the default PHB is 000000.

Table 8–2   Codepoint Assignments

Pool	Codepoint space	Assignment Policy
1	xxxxx0	Standards Action
2	xxxx11	EXP/LU
3	xxxx01	EXP/LU (*)

(*) may be utilized for future allocations as necessary

The recommended codepoints may be amended or replaced with different codepoints, at the discretion of the service provider. Even if the same PHBs are implemented on both sides of a DS boundary, the DSCP still may be re-marked.

If a DS node receives a packet containing an unrecognized codepoint, it simply treats the packet as if it were marked with the default codepoint. This rule means the DS node may examine other fields in the IP header (or layer 4 header) in order to know about the default codepoint. I make this point because this rule implies that a DS node must be able to review fields other than the codepoint. Strictly speaking, the fewer fields examined the better. If only the codepoint is examined, the operation can be very efficient, similar to ATM label switching.

The DSCP field can convey 64 distinct codepoints, as depicted in Table 8–2. The codepoint space is divided into three pools for the purpose of codepoint assignment and management. A pool of 32 codepoints (Pool 1) is assigned by Standards Action as defined in the ongoing Internet standards. A pool of 16 codepoints (Pool 2) are reserved for experimental or local use (EXP/LU), and a pool of 16 codepoints (Pool 3) which are initially available for experimental or local use. The DS standards state that Pool 3 should be preferentially utilized for standardized assignments if Pool 1 is exhausted.

DS GUARANTEED RATE (GR)

An Internet Networking Group has been working on specifications to define a DS guaranteed rate PHB [WORS98],[4] see Figure 8–10. The concepts revolve around nonreal-time traffic with a guaranteed rate

---

[4][WORS98]. Worster, Tom, and Wentworth, Robert, Guaranteed Rate in Differentiated Services, draft-worster-diffserv-gr-00.txt, June, 1998.

(GR). This rate is also defined in ATM, as part of the available bit rate (ABR) service. One difference between the ATM and DS approaches is that ATM is constrained to defining a successful delivery as one in which all the bits in the user frame are delivered successfully, which may entail more than one successfully-delivered cell. This distinction is avoided in DS because the DS operations are defined at the L_3 IP level. The following is an overview of the DS GR, as defined in [WORS98].

The GR service provides transport of IP data with: (a) a minimum bit rate guarantee under (b) the assumption of a given burst limit.

GR implies that if the user sends bursts of packets, that in total do not exceed the maximum burst limit, then the user should expect to see all of these packets delivered with minimal loss. GR also allows the user to send in excess of the committed rate and the associated burst limit, but the excess traffic will only be delivered within the limits of available resources.

For excess traffic, each user should have access to a fair share of available resources. The definition of fair share is network specific and is not specified by either the GR PHB or service. The DS GR uses the term service representation (SR) to describe a guaranteed minimum rate and the packet characteristics to which the DS GR service commitment applies. The guaranteed minimum rate uses the generic packet rate algorithm (GCRA) leaky bucket with the rate and credit parameter: GPRA (x, y), where x is the rate parameter is bytes/s, and y is the credit limit parameter in bytes.

The SR is defined by (S, CR, BL), where S is the set of characteristics of the packet stream to which the service is being committed. The guaranteed minimum rate specification is defined as GPRA (CR, BL) where CR is the committed rate in bit/s and BL is the burst limit in bytes.

The interpretation of the SR is: The network commits to transporting with minimal loss at least those packets belonging to the stream specified by S that pass a hypothetical implementation of the GPRA (CR, BL) located at the network's ingress interface.

The following theorem ensures a DS GR level of service that is always at least R as defined in the GR PHB, and I quote directly from Worster [WORS98]:

> Let a_j be the arrival time of the start of packet j, let t_j be the time when the start of packet j is transmitted, and let TL_j be the total length of packet j. Suppose the transmission times satisfy $s_j < t_j < s_j + T_2$, where $s_{(j+1)} - s_j \le (TL_j/R)$, and also suppose that if a packet arrives when no other packets in

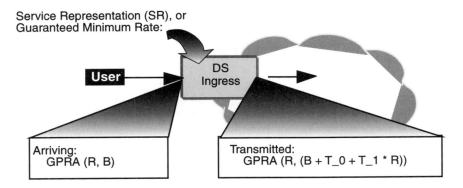

Service Representation (SR), or
Guaranteed Minimum Rate:

User → DS Ingress →

Arriving:
   GPRA (R, B)

Transmitted:
   GPRA (R, (B + T_0 + T_1 * R))

- GR given if user:
    Sends bursts < maximum burst limit
- And:
    User can send in excess of limit...
    With service within available resources

Figure 8–10   DiffServ guaranteed rate (GR)

the stream are awaiting transmission, then $a\_j + T\_0 <= s\_j < a\_j + T\_0 + T\_1$. T_0, T_1, and T_2 are, respectively, the fixed empty-queue packet latency, the maximum variation in the empty-queue packet latency, and the scheduling tolerance. Then, if the arriving packets all pass GPRA(R, B), the transmitted packets will all pass GPRA(R, (B + (T_0 + T_1)*R))

The proof for this theorem is found in an ATM Forum paper by [WENT97].[5]

Though perhaps not all "guaranteed rate" nodes will schedule packets in a way that fits this form, the preceding theorem suggests that it is reasonable to expect that a significant class of such devices would have the ability to guarantee that if the input packet stream satisfies GPRA(R, B) then the output packet stream will satisfy GPRA(R, B + BTI) where BTI is the devices burst tolerance increment for the stream in question. This result allows us to consider several possible schemes by which an edge-to-edge guaranteed rate service commitment may be made. For example, if we know that each node has a BTI that does not exceed BTI_max then we can establish GR service with parameters {S, CR, and BL} by provisioning a GR PHB with parameters {S, R = CR, and B = BL + BTI_max} along the stream's path though the network. We do not attempt to specify the rules by which a network operator should distribute appropriate GR PHB parameters. To some extent the appropriate scheme will depend on char-

---

[5][WENT97] Wentworth, R., ATM Forum Contribution 97-0980, December, 1997.

Table 8–2   Assured Forwarding (AF) Codepoints, Classes, and Drop Preferences

	Class 1	Class 2	Class 3	Class 4
Low Drop Prec	001010	010010	011010	100010
Medium Drop Prec	001100	010100	01110	100100
High Drop Prec	001110	010110	011110	100110

acteristics of the implementation of the GR PBH in network nodes. It may also depend on limitations of the protocol used to distribute the parameters. GR service can also be supported across concatenated GR diff-serv networks.

ASSURED AND EXPEDITED FORWARDING PHBS

The Internet Network Working Group has recognized that additional PHBs must be defined for DiffServ nodes to support a diverse user community. To that end [JACO99][6] has authored the RFC 2598 titled "An Expedited Forwarding (EF) PHB," and [HEIN99][7] has authored the RFC 2597 titled "Assured Forwarding PHB Group".

The codepoint for the expedited forwarding (EF) is 101110. The DS traffic conditioning block must treat the EF PHB as the highest priority of all traffic. However, EF packets are not allowed to preempt other traffic. Consequently a tool, such as a token bucket, must be part of the DS features. RFC 2598 includes an appendix (Appendix A) that explains the results of some simulations of models to support EF PHB. I found this information to be very useful in my work, and I have included this information as Appendix 8A at the back of this chapter. Please note the Internet Society copyright statements pertaining to this information.

RFC 2597 defines the assured forwarding (AF) PHB. It enables a DS domain to support different levels of forwarding assurances for IP traffic that is received from a customer. Four AF classes are defined in relation to three drop precedences. In case of congestion, the drop precedence for the packet determines its relative importance within the AF class. The classes, drop precedences, and associated codepoints are shown in Table 8–2.

---

[6][JACO99].   Jacobson, V, et al., RFC 2598,"An Expedited Forwarding PHB," June 1999.

[7][HEIN99].   Heinanen, J, et al., RFC 2597, "Assured Forwarding PHB Group," June, 1999.

SUMMARY

Differentiated Services (DS) is a new protocol. Its deployment is quite limited, but it will grow in use. Interest is keen on DS, due to its efficiency, flexibility, and scalability. Its basic standards are in place with RFCs published by the IETF. Other issues and subjects about DiffServ are being addressed in the Internet working group studies.

APPENDIX 8A   DIFFERENTIATED SERVICES (DIFFSERV)

This material is Appendix A of RFC 2598. The main body of this RFC is discussed in this chapter.

Network Working Group
Request for Comments: 2598
Category: Standards Track

V. Jacobson
K. Nichols
Cisco Systems
K. Poduri
Bay Networks
June 1999

An Expedited Forwarding PHB

Appendix A: Example use of and experiences with the EF PHB

A.1   Virtual Leased Line Service

A VLL Service, also known as Premium service [2BIT], is quantified by a peak bandwidth.

A.2   Experiences with its use in ESNET

A prototype of the VLL service has been deployed on DOE's ESNet backbone. This uses weighted-round-robin queuing features of Cisco 75xx series routers to implement the EF PHB. The early tests have been very successful and work is in progress to make the service available on a routine production basis (see ftp://ftp.ee.lbl.gov/talks/vj-doeqos.pdf and ftp://ftp.ee.lbl.gov/talks/vj-i2qos-may98.pdf for details).

A.3   Simulation Results

A.3.1   Jitter variation

In section 2.2, we pointed out that a number of mechanisms might be used to implement the EF PHB. The simplest of these is a priority queue

(PQ) where the arrival rate of the queue is strictly less than its service rate. As jitter comes from the queuing delay along the path, a feature of this implementation is that EF-marked microflows will see very little jitter at their subscribed rate since packets spend little time in queues. The EF PHB does not have an explicit jitter requirement but it is clear from the definition that the expected jitter in a packet stream that uses a service based on the EF PHB will be less with PQ than with best-effort delivery. We used simulation to explore how weighted round-robin (WRR) compares to PQ in jitter. We chose these two since they're the best and worst cases, respectively, for jitter and we wanted to supply rough guidelines for EF implementers choosing to use WRR or similar mechanisms.

Our simulation model is implemented in a modified ns-2 described in [RFC2415] and [LCN]. We used the CBQ modules included with ns-2 as a basis to implement priority queuing and WRR. Our topology has six hops with decreasing bandwidth in the direction of a single 1.5 Mbps bottleneck link (see figure 6). Sources produce EF-marked packets at an average bit rate equal to their subscribed packet rate. Packets are produced with a variation of +−10% from the interpacket spacing at the subscribed packet rate. The individual source rates were picked aggregate to 30% of the bottleneck link or 450 Kbps. A mixture of FTPs and HTTPs is then used to fill the link. Individual EF packet sources produce either all 160 byte packets or all 1500 byte packets.

Though we present the statistics of flows with one size of packet, all of the experiments used a mixture of short and long packet EF sources so the EF queues had a mix of both packet lengths.

We defined jitter as the absolute value of the difference between the arrival times of two adjacent packets minus their departure times, $|(aj-dj) - (ai-di)|$. For the target flow of each experiment, we record the median and 90th percentile values of jitter (expressed as % of the subscribed EF rate) in a table. The pdf version of this document contains graphs of the jitter percentiles.

Our experiments compared the jitter of WRR and PQ implementations of the EF PHB. We assessed the effect of different choices of WRR queue weight and number of queues on jitter. For WRR, we define the service-to-arrival rate ratio as the service rate of the EF queue (or the queue's minimum share of the output link) times the output link bandwidth divided by the peak arrival rate of EF-marked packets at the queue. Results will not be stable if the WRR weight is chosen to exactly balance arrival and departure rates thus we used a minimum service-to-arrival ratio of 1.03. In our simulations this means that the EF queue gets at least 31% of the output links. In WRR simulations we kept the link full with other traffic as described above, splitting the non-EF-marked traffic among the non-EF queues. (It should be clear from the experiment description that we are attempting to induce worst-case jitter and do not expect these settings or traffic to represent a "normal" operating point.)

Our first set of experiments uses the minimal service-to-arrival ratio of 1.06 and we vary the number of individual microflows composing the EF aggregate from 2 to 36. We compare these to a PQ implementation with 24 flows. First, we examine a microflow at a subscribed rate of 56 Kbps sending 1500 byte packets, then one at the same rate but sending 160 byte packets. Table 1 shows the 50th and 90th percentile jitter in percent of a packet time at the subscribed rate. Figure 1 plots the 1500 byte flows and figure 2 the 160 byte flows. Note that a packet-time for a 1500 byte packet at 56 Kbps is 214 ms, for a 160 byte packet 23 ms. The jitter for the large packets rarely exceeds half a subscribed rate packet-time, though most jitters for the small packets are at least one subscribed rate packet-time. Keep in mind that the EF aggregate is a mixture of small and large packets in all cases so short packets can wait for long packets in the EF queue. PQ gives a very low jitter.

Table 1: Variation in jitter with number of EF flows: Service/arrival ratio of 1.06 and subscription rate of 56 Kbps (all values given as % of subscribed rate)

# EF flows	1500 byte packet		160 byte packet	
	50th %	90th %	50th %	90th %
PQ (24)	1	5	17	43
2	11	47	96	513
4	12	35	100	278
8	10	25	96	126
24	18	47	96	143

Next we look at the effects of increasing the service-to-arrival ratio. This means that EF packets should remain enqueued for less time though the bandwidth available to the other queues remains the same. In this set of experiments the number of flows in the EF aggregate was fixed at eight and the total number of queues at five (four non-EF queues). Table 2 shows the results for 1500 and 160 byte flows. Figures 3 plots the 1500 byte results and figure 4 the 160 byte results. Performance gains leveled off at service-to-arrival ratios of 1.5. Note that the higher service-to-arrival ratios do not give the same performance as PQ, but now 90% of packets experience less than a subscribed packet-time of jitter even for the small packets.

Table 2: Variation in Jitter of EF flows: service/arrival ratio varies,
8 flow aggregate, 56 Kbps subscribed rate

WRR	1500 byte pack.		160 byte packet	
Ser/Arr	50th %	90th %	50th %	90th %
PQ	1	3	17	43
1.03	14	27	100	178
1.30	7	21	65	113
1.50	5	13	57	104
1.70	5	13	57	100
2.00	5	13	57	104
3.00	5	13	57	100

Increasing the number of queues at the output interfaces can lead to
more variability in the service time for EF packets so we carried out an
experiment varying the number of queues at each output port. We fixed
the number of flows in the aggregate to eight and used the minimal 1.03
service-to-arrival ratio. Results are shown in figure 5 and table 3. Figure
5 includes PQ with 8 flows as a baseline.

Table 3: Variation in Jitter with Number of Queues at Output Interface:
Service-to-arrival ratio is 1.03, 8 flow aggregate

# EF	1500 byte packet	
flows	50th %	90th %
PQ (8)	1	3
2	7	21
4	7	21
6	8	22
8	10	23

It appears that most jitter for WRR is low and can be reduced by a proper
choice of the EF queue's WRR share of the output link with respect to its
subscribed rate. As noted, WRR is a worst case while PQ is the best case.
Other possibilities include WFQ or CBQ with a fixed rate limit for the EF
queue but giving it priority over other queues. We expect the latter to have
performance nearly identical with PQ though future simulations are
needed to verify this. We have not yet systematically explored effects of
hop count, EF allocations other than 30% of the link bandwidth, or more
complex topologies. The information in this section is not part of the EF
PHB definition but provided simply as background to guide implementers.

A.3.2   VLL service

We used simulation to see how well a VLL service built from the EF
PHB behaved, that is, does it look like a 'leased line' at the subscribed

rate. In the simulations of the last section, none of the EF packets were dropped in the network and the target rate was always achieved for those CBR sources. However, we wanted to see if VLL really looks like a 'wire' to a TCP using it. So we simulated long-lived FTPs using a VLL service. Table 4 gives the percentage of each link allocated to EF traffic (bandwidths are lower on the links with fewer EF microflows), the subscribed VLL rate, the average rate for the same type of sender-receiver pair connected by a full duplex dedicated link at the subscribed rate and the average of the VLL flows for each simulation (all sender-receiver pairs had the same value). Losses only occur when the input shaping buffer overflows but not in the network. The target rate is not achieved due to the well-known TCP behavior.

Table 4: Performance of FTPs using a VLL service

% link	Average delivered rate (Kbps)		
to EF	Subscribed	Dedicated	VLL
20	100	90	90
40	150	143	143
60	225	213	215

Full Copyright Statement

THE INFORMATION HEREIN WILL NOT INFRINGE ANY RIGHTS OR
ANY IMPLIED WARRANTIES OF MERCHANTABILITY OR FITNESS FOR
A PARTICULAR PURPOSE.

Acknowledgement

Funding for the RFC Editor function is currently provided by the Internet Society.

9

IP-Based Layer 2 and 3 Switching and Routing

The ability of a QOS service provider to provide effective services to the customer depends on a number of factors such as the bandwidth capacity of the QOS domain, and the ability to forward the customer's traffic quickly to the end user. This latter operation is the subject of this chapter: the forwarding of packets through the QOS domain. This subject encompasses many procedures and protocols, some are proprietary; some are standardized. It is also of such scope to warrant a separate book, one of which is being written for this series. Our approach in this chapter is to provide an overview of the subject.

The standards on switching and routing use the term "port" or "interface" to describe the physical connection of the communications link to a router or a user device. This chapter uses these terms synonymously.

LABEL SWITCHING

Label, tag, or codepoint switching is a topic of considerable interest in the Internet.[1] The interest stems from the fact that traditional software-based routing is too slow to handle the large traffic loads in the

---

[1]For simplicity, I use the term "label" for the terms "tag" and "codepoint."

Internet or an internet, see Table 9–1. Even with enhanced techniques, such as a fast-table lookup for certain packets, the load on the router is often more than the router can handle. The result may be lost traffic, lost connections, and overall poor QOS performance in the IP-based network. Label switching, in contrast to IP routing, is proving to be an effective solution to the problem.

Several methods are employed to implement label switching. For this chapter, we examine those that are now deployed and also under consideration for deployment. As we will see, many of them are similar—variations on the same theme.

Some techniques use the concept of a flow (introduced in Chapter 1, see Figure 1–2), which is a sequence of user packets sent from one source machine or application to one or more machines or applications. For a "long" flow (many packets flowing between these entities), a router can cache information about the flow and circumvent the traditional IP routing mechanisms (subnet masking, search on longest subnet mask, and so on) by storing the routing information in cache, thus achieving high throughput and low delay.

As shown in Figure 9–1, a label switch also performs multiplexing functions. The information from the ingress interface ports are multiplexed onto the egress interface ports. The operations also include switching; the traffic from the ingress interface ports is switched to the egress interface ports. While the packets are switched through the switching fabric from input-to-output interfaces, their label values are also translated from the incoming label to another outgoing label.

Figure 9–1 shows that a label switch is performing space switching by moving traffic from incoming interface ports a, b, c, d to outgoing interface ports w, x, y, z. The switch is also performing header translation, which is sometimes called header switching, or label mapping. This fig-

Table 9–1   Label/tag/codepoint switching

Why?

    Conventional IP routing is slow

    Requires many operations (masking, best match)

    Enhance with high-speed label/tag switching

What?

    Correlate IP addresses, ports, etc. to simple label

    Use label as index to cache for routing information

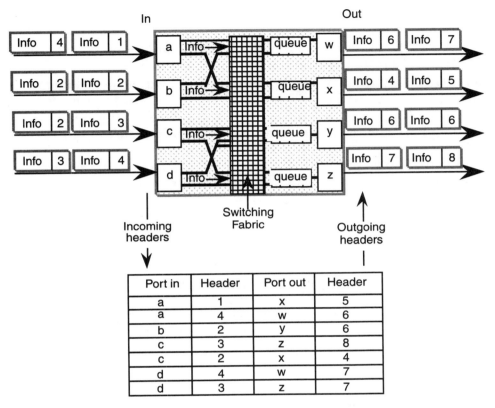

Figure 9–1   Forwarding and header translation

Port in	Header	Port out	Header
a	1	x	5
a	4	w	6
b	2	y	6
c	3	z	8
c	2	x	4
d	4	w	7
d	3	z	7

ure also shows the use of queues (in this example, they are called output queues because they exist at the outgoing interfaces). These buffers are used to assure that packets do not contend for the same egress interface at the same time.

Figure 9–1 also depicts how the labels in the packet headers are used to determine the output interface port for the incoming cell. For example, a cell with label 1 arrives at interface a. Forwarding operations reveal that the packet is to be relayed to output interface x, and its label changed to 5. As another example, a packet with label 3 arrives at interface c. It is relayed to output interface z and its label is mapped to label 8.

ASSIGNING LABELS

One of the key aspects of high-speed forwarding systems is the assignment of a label to identify the traffic. Figure 9–2 depicts these operations. The assignment of the value to a packet varies, depending on the vendor's approach and/or the standard employed (an Internet RFC, for example). This part of the chapter introduces the concepts of label allocation (binding), and in later discussions, we focus on more detailed examinations.

Figure 9–2(a) shows an example binding operations. The local label allocation at a node (local binding) refers to the operation in which the local node sets up a label relationship with QOS features. It can set this relationship up as it receives traffic, or it can set it up as it receives control information from an upstream or downstream neighbor. Remote binding is an operation in which a neighbor node (upstream or downstream) assigns a binding to the local node. Typically, binding is performed with control messages, such as a set up message.

Downstream label allocation refers to a method in which the label allocation is done by the downstream label switching router (LSR). Upstream label allocation is done by the upstream LSR.

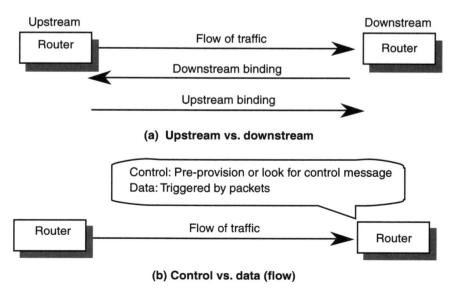

(a) Upstream vs. downstream

(b) Control vs. data (flow)

Figure 9–2. Assignment and binding operations

The broad category of control versus flow-driven binding is distinguished by control binding being set up in advance with control messages or pre-provisioning craft commands to the node. See Figure 9–2(b). Flow control binding (also called data binding) occurs dynamically, based on an analysis of the flow of the streaming packets.

A SWITCHING/ROUTING TAXONOMY

One of the most confusing aspects of modern switching and routing techniques is discerning exactly what the terms *switching* and *routing* mean. Figure 9–3 is my attempt at classifying these techniques. The term routing initially referred to making relaying decisions that were performed in a machine typically based with software programs and routing tables stored in conventional RAM. In contrast, switching referred to relaying decisions with the support functions consisting principally in hardware, with specialized processors,[2] and special compilers.

In addition, the term routing traditionally referred to using a destination layer 3 address to make the relaying decisions, whereas switching traditionally referred to using a layer 2 address to perform the relaying operations. In most instances, the layer 2 address was (and still is) a 48-bit IEEE MAC address. For layer 3 operations, the address traditionally has been the IP address or an IPX address.

In the past few years, a number of approaches have emerged that use these techniques or combinations of these techniques and append different names to them. The most common names currently in the industry are described next. Be aware that many of these techniques are quite similar to each other. Figure 9–3 should help you during this discussion

- *Layer 2 switching:* This operation uses conventional LAN bridges, and switches the traffic based on a 48-bit LAN media access control (MAC) address.
- *Layer 3 routing*: This operation uses a conventional router, and routes the traffic based on say, a 32-bit IP address.
- *Label switching*: As the figure indicates, label switching is a catchall term that encompasses a wide range of relaying tech-

---

[2]These definitions were used, but they were not correct. The X.25-based packet switches, built almost thirty years ago, performed "packet switching" in software.

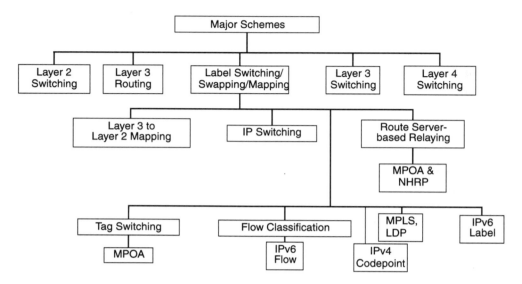

Figure 9–3   Layer 2 and 3 switching and routing categories

niques. Other terms used are swapping and mapping. But whatever the technique employed, we learned earlier that label switching entails the use of a value that is associated with (and part of the header of) a packet. It is not an address; it does not have any topological or geographical significance. It is simply a number that is reserved to identify a specific flow of packets from a sender to a receiver, or receivers. Its most common implementation is in the form of a virtual circuit number, such as: (a) a Frame Relay Data Link Connection Identifier (DLCI), (b) an ATM Virtual Path ID/Virtual Channel ID (VPI/VCI), an X.25 Logical Channel Number (LCN), or an IP codepoint.

- *Layer 3 to Layer 2 mapping:* This approach is quite similar to flow classification and IP switching, with the layer 3 address being mapped to a layer 2 address or virtual circuit ID. The mapping can be to the ATM VPI/VCI or a Frame Relay DLCI. The mapping typically occurs by a router or switch that sits at the edge of the network. Implementations for this method are fairly wide spread including Cisco's tag switching, IBM's ARIS, Cascade's IP Navigator, as well as Cabletron's Secure Fast Virtual Networking.

- *IP switching:* This term was coined by Ipsilon and refers to the association of an IP address with an ATM VPI/VCI; thereafter, the IP traffic is encapsulated in ATM cells and the ATM VPI/VCI is used for the relaying decisions.

- *Route server-based relaying:* This approach is quite similar to the layer 3 to layer 2 address mapping. The main difference is that a designated machine performs route calculations in contrast to the layer 3 to layer 2 operation where the translation is performed in the same machine. Examples of this operation are Multiprotocol over ATM (MPOA) and the Next Hop Resolution Protocol (NHRP). The route-server based operations still perform layer 3 to layer 2 address translations, it is simply done in a different machine (a server).

- *Tag switching:* This technique is also a form of label switching. The concepts are derived largely on Cisco's research. It is based on using a label (a tag) in place of an address for the relaying decision. The ATM Forum's Multiprotocol Over ATM (MPOA) is one example of a tag switching specification. Notice that MPOA also falls under more than scheme.

- *Flow classification:* Flow classification is also utilized in Ipsilon's IP switching (and other venders, as well). A long-term flow (many packets going to the same destination) has the IP address in these packets correlated to an ATM VPI/VCI with the resulting encapsulation of the IP packets into the ATM cells. MPOA also fits into this category.

- *IPv6 Flow:* This category is a flow classification scheme, and uses the flow label is the IPv6 datagram header.

- *IPv4 Codepoint:* This category uses the codepoint of the revised IPv4 type of service field (TOS) as a label, then uses the label for forwarding decisions.

- *MPLS (Multiprotocol label switching), and the Label Distribution Protocol (LDP):* MPLS is a form of label switching which is based on Cisco's tag switching specifications. The idea of MPLS is to use an operation at the edge of the network to assign labels to each packet. These labels, in turn, or used to route the traffic from the source to the destination. In addition, it is anticipated that commercial implementations will see MPLS over ATM where the MPLS traffic is mapped onto an ATM VPI/VCI. The LDP is used to distribute the labels on behalf of MPLS.

- *IPv6 Label:* This simply uses the IPv6 flow label field in the header. I place this category separately from the "IPv6 Flow" category because the label need not be associated with a flow (but in practice, it probably is).

- *Layer 3 switching:* This technology is a newer method now emerging in the industry. The distinguishing attribute of layer 3 switching is that the relay functions are performed in hardware through the use of applications specific integrated circuits (ASIC), or specially designed hardware. They differ from some of the other implementations just discussed in that they do not perform any label mapping nor do they necessarily rely on ATM/Frame Relay-based switching fabrics, and the ATM/Frame Relay virtual circuits IDs. Instead, they use an IP address.

• *Layer 4 switching:* This technique uses information in the layer 4 header for part of the label identifier. The most common practice is to use TCP or UDP source and destination port numbers. The term layer 4 switching is not accurate because the operation also uses a layer 3 address, and perhaps the IP TOS and Protocol ID fields for making the forwarding decision.

What Is Next?

It is obvious from reading the last few paragraphs that these various operations have many overlapping characteristics. Indeed, some of them are more similar to each other than they are different. Nonetheless, each one has its own personality and each one has different backers in the industry. How these technologies will fare in the market has yet to be decided. However, as of this writing, some form of ATM-based label switching has become a popular approach. But for the future, considerable progress is being made on layer 3 switching with high-speed processors using the IP address, and/or the TOS and Protocol ID fields for the relaying decisions.

There are problems with the ATM-based approach, principally the use of a small payload of 48 bytes, and a large header of 5 bytes. In the past, this small traffic unit was necessary to support the need for fast processing at a switch, as well as insuring that a loss of a traffic unit did not result in the loss of a significant amount of the user payload. With the introduction of high-speed switches that can switch at wire-speed, and the use of optical fiber with very low bit error rates, the argument for cell-based networks is subject to doubt.

POSITION OF PROTOCOLS

It is likely you have seen a semblance of Figure 9–4 in other writings. We will use it as a review and also to introduce some new ideas. The major change in the layered structure is the "Mapping/Header Alteration and Encapsulation" layer. These two operations need not operate

Application Layer (L_7)
TCP/UDP
IP, IPX, Appletalk, XNS, SNA, DECnet
Mapping/Header Alteration and Encapsulation
Ethernet, Token Ring, FDDI, ATM, Frame Relay, PPP, X.25
Physical Layer (L_1)

Figure 9–4 Examples of positions of protocols

as a combined layer entity, but they are invoked in operations that occur between the network layer (IP, IPX, Appletalk, etc.), and layer 2 (Ethernet, ATM, Frame Relay, Token ring, etc.).[3]

The mapping/header alteration operations involve: (a) label translation and swapping (changing the label as it traverses from the input interface to the output interface), or (b) header alteration [a native IP address is used, but the header (say, a hop count field) is altered as it traverses from the input interface to the output interface].

The encapsulation operations entail placing a header in front of the layer 3 protocol data unit (PDU), principally to identify the type of packet. For example, the header is coded differently if the packet is an IP datagram, of an SNA packet. This header is called an encapsulation header, a shim header, or a tunneling header.

ENCAPSULATION HEADERS

It is not uncommon for a network to support different kinds of traffic. For example, a Frame Relay network might transport both IP datagrams and IPX packets back-and-forth between end users. In order to relay this traffic, the network must have some means of identifying each protocol data unit, as shown in Figure 9–5.

In traditional voice networks, the digital voice images are multiplexed onto a physical link with time-division multiplexing techniques (TDM).

---

[3]Notice that I have placed X.25 in the same layer as Ethernet, ATM, etc. We know from Chapter 4 that X.25 consists of three layers (physical, data link, and network), and the X.25 virtual circuits are managed in the network layer. However, I have chosen to show X.25 at layer 2, because it is viewed as a basic bearer service, like Frame Relay, ATM, and the others shown in this figure.

For example, a DS1 link carries 24 64 kbit/s voice channels, and each channel (a DS0 channel) is identified by its temporal position in the TDM frame. That is, each DS0 channel is identified by its time-position in the DS1 frame. Therefore, the DS0 channels (voice PDUs) *do not need* a header to identify them. We do not deal with TDM systems here, but with statistical time-division multiplexing systems (STDM) in which the traffic appears on the physical link in an asynchronous, bursty fashion. Since the user packets cannot be identifed by a set time slot on the channel, the traffic is identified with either an address (such as a L_2 MAC or a L_3 IP address), or a label such as an X.25 LCN, or a Frame Relay DLCI.

In addition, a network often multiplexes more than one user onto a virtual circuit (such as a Frame Relay PVC or SVC). A common practice is to append to each user's packet another header or headers to: (a) distinguish that user from others, and/or (b) to distinguish the type of traffic from others (for example, TCP vs. UDP traffic).

The term encapsulation refers to an operation in which a transport network, such as Ethernet, ATM, or Frame Relay, carries packets from other protocols through the transport network. The other protocols could be IP, AppleTalk, SNA, DECnet, etc. that operate at the upper layers of the OSI layered model, typically at layer 3 and above. The transport network performs lower layer bearer services, typically at layers 1 and 2, and perhaps layer 3 of the model (but not always ... nothing is simple in internetworking).[4]

If possible, the transport network does not become involved with either the syntax or the format of the transported traffic. The term encapsulation refers to the notion of the interworking unit (say, a router) "wrapping" the *transport* packet around the *user* packet, without considering its contents.

Some people use the terms encapsulation and tunneling synonymously. Others use the term tunneling to describe the notion of sending traffic (say a car) through a "tunnel," and periodically stopping the car, rolling down the windows of the car and checking the contents in the passenger space. In other words, some definitions of tunneling suggest that the contents of the PDU may be examined during the transport operations. I disagree: The tunnel ends when the tunneled traffic is examined. I use the term encapsulation to describe both concepts just cited.

---

[4]Bearer services is a term used by most standards bodies to describe the basic telecommunications services that are available to the user of a network. They support services such as throughput (in bit/s), delay (in ms), etc.

To invoke encapsulation operations, the user must furnish the network with a specific identifier to distinguish the type of traffic that is to be sent through the transport network. This identifier is important, because the router and the receiving user machine must invoke support procedures that apply to the specific type of traffic; that is, a specific protocol family, such as X.25, IP, SNA, etc. After all, a router cannot process the PDU until it knows the type of PDU, such as its header contents and syntax.

These identifiers are depicted in Figure 9–5. They are known by various names and vary in how they are used. Some of these encapsulation

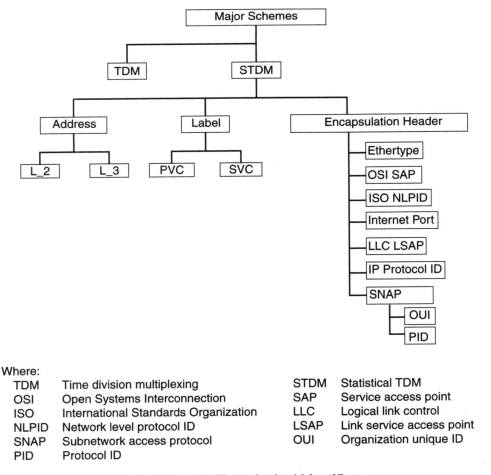

Where:

TDM	Time division multiplexing	STDM	Statistical TDM
OSI	Open Systems Interconnection	SAP	Service access point
ISO	International Standards Organization	LLC	Logical link control
NLPID	Network level protocol ID	LSAP	Link service access point
SNAP	Subnetwork access protocol	OUI	Organization unique ID
PID	Protocol ID		

Figure 9–5   The principal identifiers

identifiers perform the same functions, and indeed are redundant. The reason that overlapping identifiers exist is that they have been developed by different standards groups, and have evolved and changed over time. Detailed descriptions are beyond the scope of this book.[5]

Figure 9–6 shows how a tag switching router (TSR) or a label switching router (LSR) processes an incoming IP datagram.[6] The incoming IP packet, encapsulated in a Frame Relay frame or an ATM cell, is stored in a queue to await processing. Error checks are performed next (the ATM FEC or the Frame Relay FCS operations). If these checks reveal no errors, the label is examined. If it is determined that the label is local, the Frame Relay or ATM header is removed (decapsulated), and the IP address is processed. Next, the IP protocol ID field (the IP encapsulation field, discussed earlier) in the header is used to pass the data field to the next module, such as TCP, UDP, ICMP, etc.

If the label is not local, the user packet is transported directly to a next node in the ATM or a Frame Relay network. The Frame Relay or ATM label is correlated to a tag or label that is stored in a table in the LSR. The cell or frame is sent to the outgoing interface for transport to the next node, where the label is examined to determine the actions to take on the packet.

The process is straightforward. The ATM cell or Frame Relay header is processed, and the packet is processed only if the packet has reached the final destination. If the packet has indeed reached the final destination, the encapsulation header is processed to determine the nature of the user's packet (for example, an IP datagram, an SNA message, etc.). Based on the values in the encapsulation header, the packet is passed to the proper module in the LSR, or passed to a local machine (such as a router, server, or host) for further processing.

The overall concepts of layer 3 to layer 2 mapping are found in other techniques, such as tag switching, Multiprotocol Over ATM (MPOS), and Multiprotocol Label Switching (MPLS). All of these systems perform some type of L_3 to L_2 mapping; they simply go about it in different ways.

---

[5]For more details, I refer you to *ATM Volume III: Internetworking with ATM,* by Uyless Black, Prentice-Hall, 1998.

[6]TSR and LSR are different terms that describe the same kinds of operations. Some vendors use the term TSR and others user the term LSR. I will use the term LSR in this text, unless the specific explanations warrant the user of TSR.

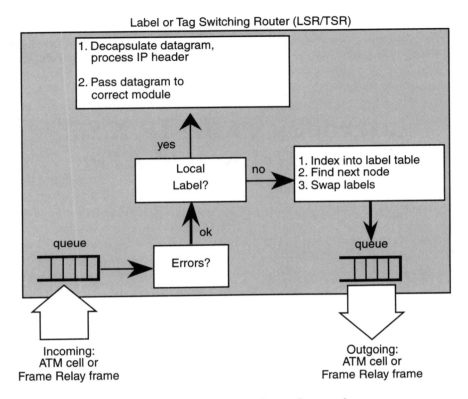

Figure 9–6   Layer 3 to layer 2 mapping

SUMMARY

Effective QOS depends to a great extent on the ability of the QOS domain to forward the customer's traffic quickly through the domain. This operation uses labels or addresses at layer 2 or 3 to make forwarding decisions. Although these forwarding concepts are simple; the almost bewildering array of terms (and actual implementations) associated with these operations contribute to their complexity.

10

Internetworking IP, X.25, Frame Relay, and ATM

T his chapter examines the internetworking of IP, X.25, Frame Relay, and ATM networks. We first look at the reasons for internetworking, and explain two forms of internetworking: network interworking and service interworking.[1] The bulk of the chapter is devoted to Frame Relay and ATM internetworking, and how QOS features are mapped between these networks.

ATM VS. IP

There is considerable interest in the industry regarding the potential use of ATM or IP to support multiservice operations. In some quarters, the issues revolve around IPv6 versus ATM, since IPv6 is designed to support different types of traffic. The task force that developed the IPv6 specification believes that IPv6 can compete with ATM with the use of three fields in the IP header: (a) the priority field, (b) the flow label field, and (c) the routing extension header.

However, IPv6 is not being deployed as of this writing. IPv4 remains the IP version in use today. As we have learned in this book, many net-

---

[1]Internetworking and interworking are used in the same context in this chapter.

works now run IP over Frame Relay, ATM, or X.25. Since Frame Relay has the lion's share of the market in wide area network switching technologies, and ATM is growing, it is a good idea to examine how Frame Relay and ATM can be internetworked with each other.

INTERNETWORKING FRAME RELAY AND ATM

Why should an organization wish to internetwork Frame Relay and ATM networks? Before we analyze Frame Relay and ATM internetworking, let us answer this question.

The intent of Frame Relay and ATM internetworking is to allow the continued use of a widely used technology, Frame Relay, and at the same time, provide a platform to migrate to ATM. This approach assumes that Frame Relay is viewed as a transient technology—one that serves the enterprise for a while, and is then replaced by a more effective technology, in this case, ATM. One could argue this premise, but that is not the subject of this discussion.

Since ATM is still an emerging technology, and its place in the telecommunications marketplace is yet to be determined, the final scenario for the internetworking of Frame Relay and ATM is not known. Nonetheless, the widespread use of Frame Relay and the emergence of ATM leads to situations where these two networks must be able to exchange traffic. If one user is attached to a Frame Relay network for example, and another is attached to an ATM network, then it makes sense to have a means for these two users to be able to communicate with each other—thus the reason for internetworking Frame Relay and ATM.

NETWORK INTERWORKING AND SERVICE INTERWORKING

Figure 10–1 depicts two concepts that are used in this chapter: network interworking and service interworking. To emphasize, interworking is used in the same context as internetworking, and the machine that performs these operations is called an interworking unit, an internetworking unit, or simply a gateway.

Network interworking entails the support of Frame Relay systems through an ATM network, typically called a backbone, as shown in Figure 10–1(a). As we shall see in more detail later, network interworking is an operation in which the ATM service user performs Frame Relay functions by executing the FR-SSCS (FR-service specific convergence sub-

(a) Network Interworking—Frame Relay operates on each side of ATM "backbone"

(b) Service Interworking—ATM backbone sits between Frame Relay and ATM

Where:
   IWF   Interworking function (also known as a gateway or internetworking unit)

Figure 10–1   Key definitions

layer) functions of AAL5. These operations are performed by the user machin'e, known as the broadband customer premises equipment (B-CPE). The B-CPE must have knowledge of remote Frame Relay system.

Service interworking, shown in Figure 10–1(b), entails the support of a Frame Relay system with an ATM system, through an ATM backbone. Service interworking is similar to network interworking, but the ATM service user has no knowledge of the remote Frame Relay system. The Frame Relay service user performs no ATM services and the ATM service user performs no Frame Relay services. All interworking operations between the user are performed by the interworking function (IWF).

COMPARISON OF FRAME RELAY AND ATM

While I assume that you are now familiar with Frame Relay and ATM operations, it is a good idea to pause briefly and compare some of the major attributes of these two technologies. Table 10–1 makes such a comparison. It consists of three columns: the first column is labeled Attribute, which describes the characteristics (attributes) of the technology in a short phrase; the next two columns, labeled Frame Relay and ATM, describe how these technologies use or do not use the attribute. The table

Table 10–1   Major Attributes of Frame Relay and ATM

Attribute	Frame Relay	ATM
Application support?	Asynchronous data (with voice gaining in use [but not designed for voice])	Asynchronous, synchronous voice, video, data
Connection mode?	Connection-oriented	Connection-oriented
Congestion management?	Yes, congestion notification, traffic tagging (DE bit), and possibly traffic discard	Yes, congestion notification, traffic tagging (CLP bit), and possibly traffic discard
Method of identifying traffic?	Virtual circuit id: The DLCI	Virtual circuit id: The VPI/VCI
PVCs?	Yes	Yes
SVCs?	Yes	Yes
Congestion notification?	FECN and BECN bits	CN bits in the PTI field
Traffic tagging?	The DE bit	The CLP bit
LAN or WAN based?	WAN based	Either
PDU size?	Variable "frame"	Fixed-length "cell"
Sequence numbers?	No, but sequencing preserved	No, but sequencing preserved
QOS?	Yes, but limited	Yes, extensive
ACKs/ACKs/Resends?	No	No
Encapsulation?	Yes	Yes

Where:
BECN	Backward explicit congestion notification
DLCI	Data link connection identifier
CLP	Cell loss priority
CN	Congestion notification
DE	Discard eligibility
FECN	Forward explicit congestion notification
LAN	Local area network
PDU	Protocol data unit
PTI	Payload type identifier
PVC	Permanent virtual circuit
QOS	Quality of service
SVC	Switched virtual call
VCI	Virtual channel identifier
VPI	Virtual path identifier
WAN	Wide area network

is self-explanatory, but the I will take you through several thoughts related to the column and row entries (if you have read the previous chapters, this table should merely be a review).

As these comparisons suggest, Frame Relay and ATM have many similar operating characteristics. But their differences are significant enough to require several protocol conversion operations at the IWU that operates between them.

Figure 10–2 illustrates the headers for Frame Relay and ATM. They are more alike than different. Each contains a virtual circuit ID which is called the DLCI in Frame Relay and the VPI/VCI in ATM. Both contain bits to allow the traffic to be tagged; for Frame Relay this is called the discard eligibility (DE) bit and for ATM it is called the cell loss priority (CLP).

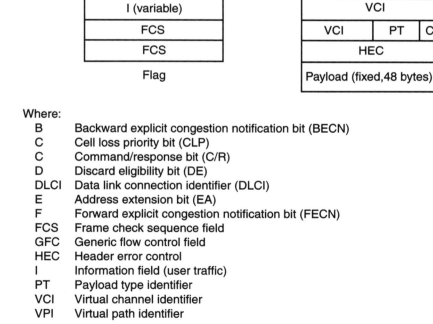

Where:

B	Backward explicit congestion notification bit (BECN)
C	Cell loss priority bit (CLP)
C	Command/response bit (C/R)
D	Discard eligibility bit (DE)
DLCI	Data link connection identifier (DLCI)
E	Address extension bit (EA)
F	Forward explicit congestion notification bit (FECN)
FCS	Frame check sequence field
GFC	Generic flow control field
HEC	Header error control
I	Information field (user traffic)
PT	Payload type identifier
VCI	Virtual channel identifier
VPI	Virtual path identifier

Figure 10–2   Frame Relay and ATM headers

Both technologies provide for congestion notification. For Frame Relay, this feature is provided in the forward explicit congestion notification (FECN) and the backward explicit congestion notification (BECN) bits. For ATM, this feature is provided in the bits residing in the payload type identifier (PTI) which is known generically as explicit congestion notification (ECN).

The figure provides other information that is pertinent to this discussion. Notice that the Frame Relay protocol control information is surrounded by special bits called flags. The flags are used to delineate the beginning and ending of traffic; and the frame check sequence field (FCS) is used to error check at the receiver to determine if any of the information between the flags was damaged while in transit.

In contrast, ATM does not contain flag-type fields and its error checking is performed with the fifth byte of the header called the header error correction (HEC) field. This field error corrects any 1-bit error in the header and will error check most others. But it operates differently from the Frame Relay FCS field in that it does forward error correction on a 1-bit error in the header. Keep in mind the Frame Relay FCS only does error detection on all bits between the flags.

AAL 5 OPERATIONS FOR FRAME RELAY SUPPORT

Figure 10–3 shows the operations on the AAL 5 on the Frame Relay frame. AAL 5 performs its conventional segmentation and reassembly functions by delineating the traffic into 48-byte data units with the addition of an 8-byte trailer as part of the last data unit. The error detection operation is provided by the AAL5 CRC-32 calculation over the FR-SSCS PDU.

MAPPING QOS BETWEEN ATM AND FRAME RELAY

This part of the chapter explains how the ATM and Frame Relay QOS features are mapped from one network to another as the user traffic is transported across these networks. To help you in following this analysis, I have reproduced the relevant entry in Table 10–1 and inserted it at the top of each figure (when a figure is used of course).

Congestion Management

The IWF equipment must support two modes of operation for discard eligibility (DE) and cell loss priority (CLP) bit mapping. Be aware

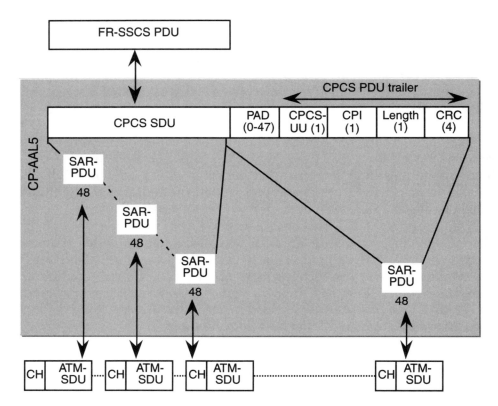

Note: Error detection is provided over the complete FR-SSCS PDU for the AAL5 CRC
      operation

Where:
  ATM   Asynchronous transfer mode
  CH   Cell header
  CP-AAL5   Common part ATM adaptation layer type 5
  CPCS SDU   Common part convergence sublayer service data unit
  CPCS-UU   CPCS user to user
  CPI   Common part indicator
  CRC   Cyclic redundancy check
  FR-SSCS   Frame Relay service specific convergence sublayer
  SAR PDU   Segmentation and reassembly protocol data unit

Figure 10–3   FR-CPCS operations

that these modes operate in the Frame Relay to B-ISDN direction. See
Figure 10–4.

For mode 1, the DE bit in the Frame Relay frame header must be
copied without alteration into the DE bit which is coded in the FR-SSCS
header. Next, this bit must be mapped into the CLP bit in the header of

Attribute	Frame Relay	ATM
Congestion management?	Yes, congestion notification, traffic tagging (DE bit), and possibly traffic discard	Yes, congestion notification, traffic tagging (CLP bit), and possibly traffic discard

Where:
CLP   Cell loss priority
DE   Discard eligibility
Approach:

FR-to-ATM (Mode 1)

DE (from Q.922 Core)	DE (mapped to FR-SSCS)	CLP (mapped to ATM layer)
0	0	0
1	1	1

Note 1

FR-to-ATM (Mode 2)

DE (from Q.922 Core)	DE (mapped to FR-SSCS)	CLP (mapped to ATM layer)
0	0	Y
1	1	Y

Note 2

ATM-to-FR (Mode 1)

CLP (from ATM layer)	DE (from FR-SSCS)	DE (to Q.922 Core)
0	0	0
1	X	1
X	1	1

Note 3

ATM-to-FR (Mode 2)

CLP (from ATM layer)	DE (from FR-SSCS)	DE (to Q.922 Core)
X	0	0
X	1	1

Note 1: For all cells genergated from the segmentation process of that frame.

Note 2: Y can be 0 or 1.

Note 3: For one or more cells of the frame, X indicates that the value does not matter (0 or 1).

Figure 10–4 Implications regarding congestion management

each ATM cell that is generated as a result of segmenting each specific Frame Relay frame.

For mode 2, the DE bit in the Frame Relay frame header must be copied without alteration into the DE bit in the FR-SSCS header and the ATM CLP bit shall be set to a constant value of 0 or 1. This value is decided when the connection is set up and must be used for all cells generated from the segmentation process for every frame. It must remain unchanged until such time that an ATM connection has its characteristics changed.

To support DE and CLP mapping in the ATM-to-Frame Relay mapping, the network provider can choose between two modes of operations. For mode 1, if one or more ATM cells pertaining to a segmented frame have its CLP bit set to 1 or if the DE bit of the FR-SSCS PDU is set to 1, then the IWF must set the DE bit to 1 of the Frame Relay frame. For mode 2, the FR-SSCS PDU DE bit is copied without alteration into the Q.922 DE bit. This operation is independent of any CLP indications received by the ATM layer.

Mapping Frame Relay and ATM Connection Identifiers

Figure 10–5 illustrates the mapping of Frame Relay and ATM connection identifiers. The frames are identified at the Frame Relay interface through the 10-bit DLCI, which is an identifier with local

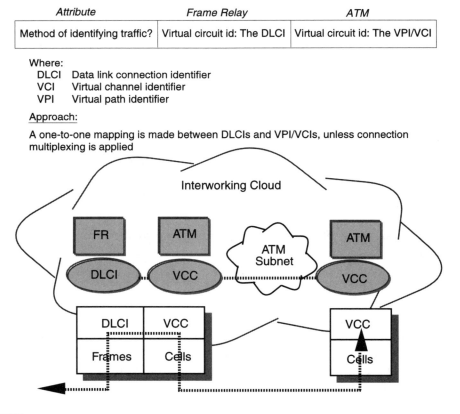

Attribute	Frame Relay	ATM
Method of identifying traffic?	Virtual circuit id: The DLCI	Virtual circuit id: The VPI/VCI

Where:
DLCI   Data link connection identifier
VCI   Virtual channel identifier
VPI   Virtual path identifier

Approach:

A one-to-one mapping is made between DLCIs and VPI/VCIs, unless connection multiplexing is applied

Where:
VCC   Virtual channel connections

Figure 10–5   Implications regarding method of identifying traffic

significance only. The DLCI permits multiple logical connections to many destinations over a single access channel. Frames belonging to each logical connection are identified by distinct DLCI values and are correlated with an ATM VCC.

It may be desirable to map multiple Frame Relay connections to a single ATM connection. For the networking interworking specification, the FR-SSCS must support connection multiplexing on either a one-to-one basis (a single FR connection is mapped to a single ATM connection) or many-to-one basis (multiple FR connections are mapped to a single ATM connection). In both cases, a correlation must be made between the Frame Relay DLCI and the ATM VPI/VCI. These operations are also described in ITU-T I.555. Let us now examine the two modes of connection multiplexing.

For the case of one-to-one multiplexing, the multiplexing is performed at the ATM layer using ATM VPIs/VCIs. The Frame Relay DLCIs can range from 16–991 and the values must be agreed upon between the ATM end systems (that is to say, IWFs or ATM end users). Otherwise, a default value of 1022 will be used for the operation. These rules apply for 2-octet Frame Relay header. If 3- or 4-octet headers are used, the DLCI value must be agreed upon between the two ATM end systems and the Frame Relay/ATM standards do not specify a default value.

For the case of the many-to-one multiplexing, the Frame Relay connections are multiplexed into a single ATM virtual channel connection (VCC) and identification of the Frame Relay traffic is achieved by using multiple DLCIs. The many-to-one operation is restricted to Frame Relay connections that terminate on the same ATM-based system.

The Frame Relay specification has no rules on the DLCI values that are to be used. Therefore, they must be agreed upon between the two ATM end systems.

Correlation of SVC Operations

Both Frame Relay and ATM use signaling protocols that are based on the layer 3 ISDN Q.931 as shown in Figure 10–6. Whereas Q.931 is concerned with setting up, managing, and tearing down B channels (64 kbit/s slots on a channel), Frame Relay and ATM are concerned with setting up, managing, and tearing down virtual circuits.

The Frame Relay signaling specification, published in ANSI T1.617 and ITU-T Q.933, is used to set up switched virtual calls (SVCs) and explains the procedures for the user-to-network signaling to support Frame Relay calls. The procedures covered include both B channel and D channel frame-mode connection operations. The signaling specifications establish the procedures for the interactions between the user and the network for ISDN support of Frame Relay. The specifications define procedures for S, T, and U reference points and the B, H, and D channels.

As just stated, the ATM signaling operations at the UNI are also based on the ISDN layer 3, Q.931, modified and published as Q.2931. The operations deal with call and connection control procedures. The focus of Q.2931 is placed on how connections are set up on demand between users and the ATM network.

Figure 10–7 shows the message flow for an SVC at a Frame Relay or ATM UNI. The operations of SVCs for Frame Relay and ATM are similar. But the SVC messages differ, and mapping/translation operations must be implemented at the IWU to accommodate these differences. In addition, the SVC timers and states also differ, and the IWU designer must be aware of these differences.

Mapping the Congestion Notification Bits

The rules for mapping the congestion notification bits vary slightly between service interworking and network interworking. Figure 10–8 shows the rules for service interworking:

In the Frame Relay to ATM direction, two modes of operation can be selected for mapping forward congestion indication. In mode 1, the FECN

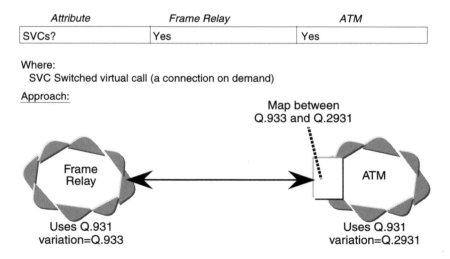

Attribute	Frame Relay	ATM
SVCs?	Yes	Yes

Where:
  SVC Switched virtual call (a connection on demand)

Approach:

Figure 10–6   Implications regarding SVCs

Attribute	Frame Relay	ATM
SVCs?	Yes	Yes

Where:
  SVC Switched virtual call (a connection on demand)
Messages and flows are quite similar (general view):

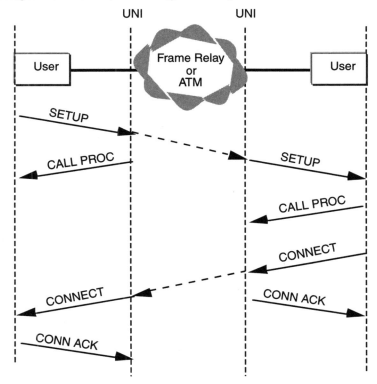

Figure 10–7   Continuation of implications regarding SVCs

bit in the Frame Relay frame header is mapped to the ATM explicit forward congestion indication (EFCI) field of every cell generated from the SAR operation. In mode 2, the FECN field of the Frame Relay frame header is not mapped to the ATM EFCI field. The EFCI field is set to a constant value of "congestion not experienced." In the ATM-to-Frame Relay direction, the ATM EFCI field (congestion or not congestion) is set to the FECN bit of the Frame Relay frame header.

Congestion Indication Backward [BECN has no equivalent function in AAL5 or ATM, unless ATM resource management (RM) cells are used]: (a) In the Frame Relay-to-ATM direction, the BECN bit is ignored, and (b) in the ATM-to-Frame Relay direction, the BECN bit is always set to 0.

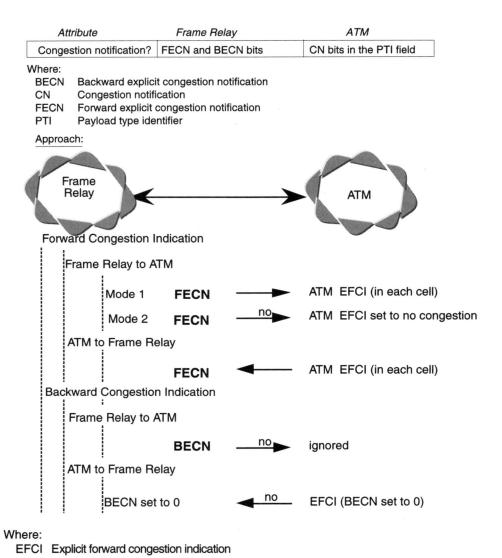

Attribute	Frame Relay	ATM
Congestion notification?	FECN and BECN bits	CN bits in the PTI field

Where:
BECN   Backward explicit congestion notification
CN   Congestion notification
FECN   Forward explicit congestion notification
PTI   Payload type identifier

Approach:

Forward Congestion Indication

Frame Relay to ATM

Mode 1   **FECN** ⟶ ATM EFCI (in each cell)

Mode 2   **FECN** —no⟶ ATM EFCI set to no congestion

ATM to Frame Relay

FECN ⟵ ATM EFCI (in each cell)

Backward Congestion Indication

Frame Relay to ATM

BECN —no⟶ ignored

ATM to Frame Relay

BECN set to 0 ⟵—no EFCI (BECN set to 0)

Where:
EFCI Explicit forward congestion indication

Figure 10–8   Implications regarding congestion notification

Discarding Frames or Cells

The operations described for DE and CLP mapping are organized in the Frame Relay-to-ATM direction and the ATM-to-Frame Relay direction. In both directions, two modes of operation are supported, see Figure 10–9.

Attribute	Frame Relay	ATM
Traffic tagging?	The DE bit	The CLP bit

Where:
  CLP   Cell loss priority
  DE   Discard eligibility
Approach:

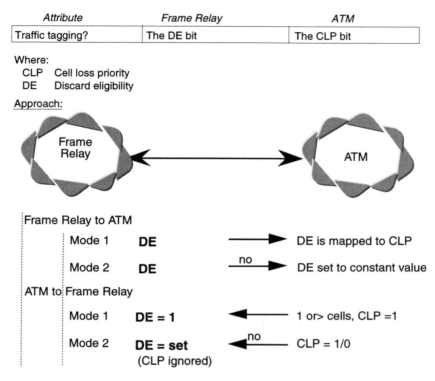

Figure 10–9   Implications regarding traffic tagging

For the Frame Relay-to-ATM direction, mode 1 must be supported with mode 2 provisioned as an option. If both modes are supported in the IWF equipment, they must be configurable on a specific virtual connection basis.

In the mode 1 operation, the Frame Relay DE bit is mapped to the ATM CLP bit in every cell generated by the segmentation process. In the mode 2 operation, the DE bit of the frame header is set to a constant value. The value is configured on a PVC basis at subscription time.

For the ATM-to-Frame Relay direction, two modes of operations also are permitted with mode 1 required and mode 2 optional. Once again, if both modes are available, each must be configurable per virtual connection.

In the mode 1 operation, if at least one cell belonging to a frame has its CLP bit set, the IWF must set the DE bit of the resulting Frame Relay frame. In the mode 2 operation, the DE bit of the frame is set to a constant value. The value is configured on a PVC basis at subscription time.

Segmentation and Reassembly (SAR) Functions

Figure 10–10 provides an example of the Frame Relay/ATM and AAL5 operations. The interface between the Frame Relay entity and the AAL entity occurs through the Frame Relay core SAP (service access point) that is defined in the Frame Relay specifications. Therefore, the IWF must accommodate to the Frame Relay service definitions at this SAP. Ideally, the Frame Relay entity has no awareness of the AAL and ATM operations.

In accordance with the Frame Relay specifications, the service primitives contain up to five parameters: core user data, discard eligibility (DE), congestion encountered (CE) backward, congestion encountered (CE) forward, and connection endpoint identifier (CEI).

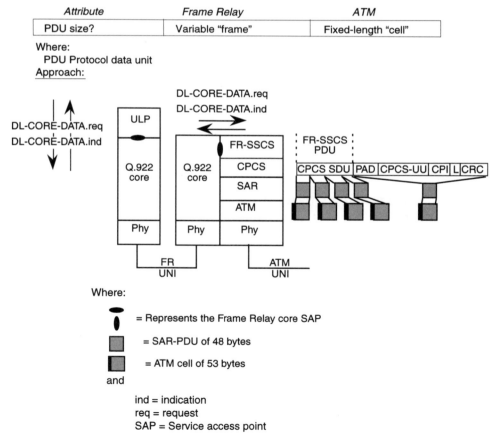

Figure 10–10   Implications regarding PDU size

The *core user data* parameter is used to convey data between the end users in the Frame Relay service, and represented by FR-SSCS PDU. The DE parameter is sent from the core service user to the service provider (FR-SSCS), and is mapped into the ATM CLP bit, subject to the rules explained earlier.

The two congestion parameters supply information about congestion that is encountered in the network. The *congestion encountered forward* parameter is used to indicate that congestion has occurred in transferring data to the receiving user. The *congestion backward parameter* indicates that the network has experienced congestion in transferring these units from the sending user.

The *connection endpoint identifier (CEI)* parameter is used to further identify a connection endpoint. For example, this parameter would allow a DLCI to be used by more than one user and each user would be identified with a connection endpoint identifier value.

The AAL type 5 PDU is used to support Frame Relay and ATM interworking. As before, the CPI field is not yet defined. The CPCS-UU field is passed transparently by the ATM network. The length field is check for oversized or undersized PDUs. CRC violations are noted, and a reassembly timer can be invoked at the terminating endpoint.

Sequencing Operations

Frame Relay and ATM do not use sequence numbers in their headers, so the issue of correlating sequence numbers between a frame and the cell is not as issue.

One other point regarding sequencing: Frame Relay and ATM require that the sequencing of the frames and cells for each connection be preserved through the networks. If a user submits traffic in a particular order to the networks, it must leave the network in the same order. This process is illustrated in Figure 10–11

Mapping QOS between Frame Relay and ATM

Table 10–2 shows the traffic management operations for Frame Relay-ATM service interworking are established in Q.933 Annex A, T1.617 Annex D and vendor-specific operations. This section focuses on the service interworking operations implemented by Nortel in its Frame Relay and ATM products.[2] Traffic management across the FR-ATM IWF focuses on two areas:

---

[2]I thank Nortel Networks for their information on this aspect of ATM internetworking. Further information is available in Nortel Network's various user and programming guides on Nortel's ATM family.

Attribute	Frame Relay	ATM
Sequence numbers?	No, but sequencing preserved	No, but sequencing preserved

Approach:

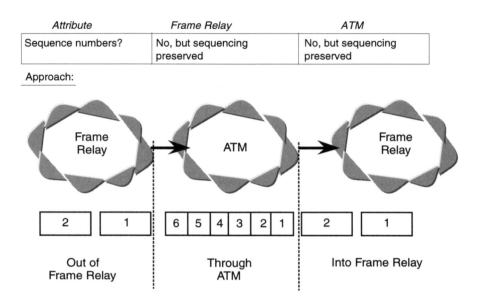

Figure 10–11   Implications regarding sequencing of traffic

1. QOS class mapping between Frame Relay and ATM, to determine emission priority and discard priority
2. Traffic management

To provide maximum versatility, and recognizing that the selection of the mapping between the Frame Relay and ATM classes of service depends on network traffic types and engineering considerations, no restrictions are imposed on the selection of the available QOS classes. The network provider can tailor this mapping to best match network capacity.

The table in this figure shows a typical mapping between the Frame Relay and ATM QOS classes. Voice applications are assigned to the highest Frame Relay emission priority and the ATM variable bit rate (VBR) class. This table also differentiates between three types of data. This differentiation allows the best match of application demands to network performance.

The discard priority of the connection also depends on the settings of the Frame Relay DE and ATM CLP bits. Based on the assumption that the DE-CLP mapping option is enabled, this table shows the effect that these bits have on the connection discard priority that results from applying FR-ATM IWF for each direction.

Table 10–2 Implications regarding QOS

Attribute	Frame Relay	ATM
QOS?	Yes, but limited	Yes, extensive

Where:
  QOS Quality of service
<u>Approach</u>:

FR-ATM Typical Mapping between FR and ATM QOS Classes

Traffic type	FR emission priority	FR discard priority	ATM QOS class	ATM QOS name
Packetized Voice	Class 0	Class 1	Class 2	VBR
Data	Class 1	Class 2	Class 2/3	VBR/CO
Data	Class 2	Class 2	Class 3	CO/CNLS
Data	Class 3	Class 3	Class 0	UBR

Note: Frame Relay discard priority Class 3 is not directly provisionable. Traffic can be forced to DE=1 by provisioning CIR=0

Where:
  CO   Connection-oriented
  CLNS   Connectionless layer network service
  VBR   Variable bit rate
  UBR   Unspecified bit rate

Discard Priority Mapping

ATM CLP	Provisioned Frame Relay Discard Priority	Resulting FR Discard Priority	Frame Relay DE
0	Class 1	Class 1	0
0	Class 2	Class 2	0
1	Don't care	Class 3	1

Frame Relay DE	ATM Discard Priority (see Note)	Resulting ATM Discard Priority	ATM CLP
0	Class 1	Class 1	0
0	Class 2	Class 2	0
0	Class 3	Class 3	1
1	Don't care	Class 3	1

Note: Provisioned by selecting ATM QOS.

ACKs and NAKs

Frame Relay and ATM do not support the ACKing (positive acknowledgment), NAKing (negative acknowledgment), or resending of traffic at the Frame Relay core layer, and the ATM layer. Therefore, this feature (or the lack of the feature) is not an issue in their internetworking operations.

Encapsulation Rules

Recall that the term encapsulation refers to an operation in which a transport network, such as an Ethernet, ATM, or Frame Relay, carries packets from other protocols through the transport network. The other protocols could be IP, Appletalk, SNA, DECnet , etc. that operate at the upper layers of the OSI-layered model, typically at layer 3 and above. The transport network performs lower layer bearer services, typically at layers 1 and 2, and perhaps layer 3 of the model.

Figure 10–12 shows the location of the encapsulations headers in the Frame Relay and ATM protocol data units. Frame Relay carries the header in front of the payload, and just behind the Frame Relay header. In contrast, ATM carries the header as part of the CS-PDU header.

Figure 10–13 shows the formatting and identification conventions for the interworking of Frame Relay frames with the AAL5 CPCS PDUs. The frame and the PDU use the ongoing standards for these operations. They are:

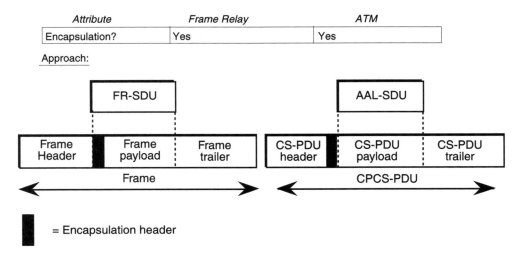

Figure 10–12   Implications regarding encapsulation

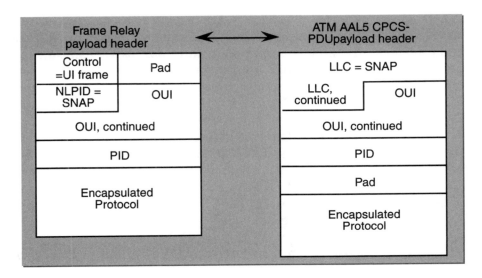

Where:
   LLC   Logical link control
   NLPID   Network level protocol id
   OUI   Organizationally unique id
   Pad   Align to a 2-octet boundary (optional)
   PID   Protocol ID
   SNAP   Subnetwork access protocol
   UI   Unnumbered acknowledgment frame

Figure 10–13   Formatting and identification conventions

Control	The control field, as established in High Level Data Link Control (HDLC) standards
NLPID	The network level protocol ID, as established in the ISO/IEC TR 9577 standard
OUI	The organizationally unique ID, as established in RFCs 826, 1042, and several other RFCs
LLC	The logical link protocol, as established in the IEEE 802.x standards

IP AND FR/ATM

Since Frame Relay and ATM are connection-oriented technologies and use labels (DLCIs and VPIs/VCIs) to identify traffic, a router must be able to translate a connectionless IP address to a label, and vice versa.

While this operation is not complex, it does require the careful construction of mapping tables at the routers. The Frame Relay and ATM standards do not describe how this mapping and address translation takes place. Typically, each router has a table that correlates IP addresses to labels and vice versa.

In the example shown in Figure 10–14, the destination addresses in the IP headers are mapped to labels at the source router (router 1). The labels are then used to relay the traffic to the destination router (router 2). Recall from earlier chapters that the labels change as the traffic traverses intermediate nodes from the source to the destination.

The issue of mapping IP QOS to Frame Relay or QOS is really a nonissue. In most implementations, the IP datagram is simply encapsulated into the payload of Frame Relay and ATM, and the IP traffic is tunneled across the Frame Relay or ATM network to the end user.

It is certainly possible to correlate the IP TOS field to a label of a given priority, and increasingly, vendors and service providers are using IP addresses, along with TCP or UDP port numbers, to decide how to

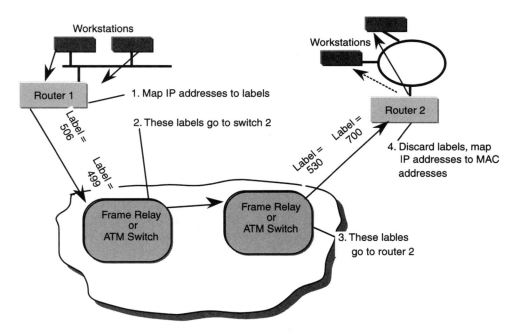

Figure 10–14   Mapping IP addresses to DLCIs or VPIs/VCIs (i.e., labels)

treat the IP traffic. In some implementations, the IP addresses and port numbers are mapped to a specific Frame Relay or ATM virtual circuit.

SUMMARY

Frame Relay and ATM interworking is an important operation today, because of the many Frame Relay and ATM networks that have been deployed. The standards in place now enable the merging of these technologies in a graceful manner. The mapping operations are extensive but straightforward. The operations of IP over ATM and Frame Relay are quite common now, and entail a straightforward tunneling (encapsulation) operation.

Appendix A

RTP, RTCP, RSVP, and Multicasting

This appendix examines four operations and associated protocols used to support QOS operations in public and private internets. The discussion begins with multicasting and the Internet Group Management Protocol (IGMP), with examples of multicasting tunnels. Next, the Real Time Protocol is explained, showing mixing and translation operations. The feedback procedure, implemented with the Real Time Control Protocol (RTCP) in then examined, followed by the Internet IntServ protocol, the Resource Reservation Protocol (RSVP).

MULTICASTING

The IP multicast system is a one-to-many operation. The sender of the multicast traffic need only create one copy of the packet. This packet is sent to a multicast server (for example a router), which is then responsible for creating as many copies as needed to send to the router's outgoing ports to reach the receiving nodes. This approach saves bandwidth at the sender since only one copy of the PDU is sent from the user. It also saves bandwidth at the receiver if multiple multicast recipients are attached to the same shared bus network. IP multicasting is used in audio

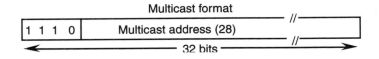

Where:
  Range is 224.0.0.0 - 239.255.255.255

Figure A–1   P multicast address

conferencing and video conferencing environments and is also seeing use for remote distance learning, meetings, and interactive chalk talks.

The format for the IP multicast address is shown in Figure A–1. This address is also known as a class D address and the first four digits of the address are set to 1110. The remaining 28 bits are set aside for the multicast address. The IP address can take the values ranging from 224.0.0.0 to 239.255.255.255.

UNICASTING

Figure A–2 shows a conventional unicasting operation where host A is sending traffic to hosts B, C, and D. Since this example does not support multicasting, host A creates a packet for each of the three destina-

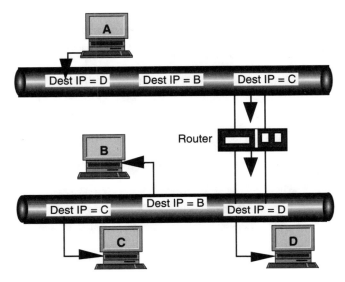

Figure A–2   Unicasting concepts

tion hosts. These hosts are located on the same local area network, such as an Ethernet, and Ethernet LANs use a shared bus. Hosts B, C, and D received all the packets on this bus. If a packet goes to B, then C and D also receive it. These three packets are identical copies of each other which, of course, translates into wasted bandwidth on both the LAN segments shown in the figure, as well on the link between the LANs.

THE MULTICASTING ALTERNATIVE

Figure A–3 shows how multicasting saves bandwidth. Host A is required to create only one copy of the packet and place the proper multicasting address in the destination address field of the multicast header. The packet is routed to the router (which of course must be configured with the multicasting software). The routing table at the router reveals that the multicast packet is destined for the egress port to the LAN that connects multicast hosts B, C, and D. Consequently, instead of generating three packets as in the previous example, only one packet is generated.

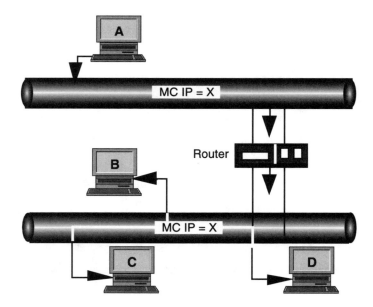

Where: X = multicasting address

Figure A–3   Multicasting concepts

MULTICASTING EXAMPLES

The multicast traffic runs inside the data field of the IP datagram and relies on the conventional IP header for delivery of the traffic through an internet. This concept is called multicast tunnels in the sense that the multicast traffic is tunneled through an Internet by riding inside the IP datagram.

Figure A–4 shows that multicasting traffic is destined to the hosts residing on the networks attached to routers B and C. The traffic emanates from a host attached to router A. The figure shows that the multicast IP address is 224.0.0.99. The figure also shows the unicast IP addresses of the sending host (172.16.1.3) and router B (172.16.1.1), and router C (172.16.1.2). The unicast addresses are used to forward the multicast packets through the multicast tunnel; thus, two headers are used for this operation.

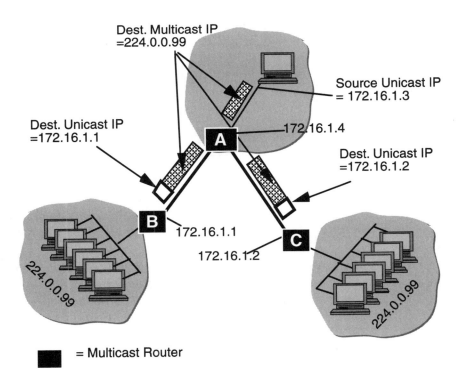

Figure A–4   Multicast tunnels

IGMP

The IGMP permits a machine to advertise a multicast address to another machine. This advertisement is called an IGMP query. In Figure A–5(a), router A is sending the IGMP query to a host. The addresses of the router and host are the same as in the previous example.

The IGMP report operation allows the host to inform the router as to whether it wishes to join the multicast group. In Figure A–5(b), the message is returned from host 172.16.1.3 and sent to router 172.16.1.4.

THE REAL TIME PROTOCOL (RTP)

Terms and Definitions

Before we examine RTP and RTCP, we need to define several terms and concepts. They deal with:

RTP session: The association among a set of participants communicating through RTP and each other. For each participant, the session is defined by a particular pair of destination transport addresses (one network address plus a port pair for RTP and RTCP). The destination transport address pair may be common for all participants, as in the case of IP multicast; or it may be different for each, as in the case of individual unicast network addresses and ports. In a multimedia session, each medium is carried in a separate RTP session with its own RTCP packets. The multiple RTP sessions are distinguished by different port number pairs and/or different multicast addresses.

Synchronization source (SSRC): The source of a stream of RTP packets, the SSRC identifier is carried in the RTP header. All packets from a synchronization source form part of the same timing and sequence number space, so a receiver groups packets by synchronization source for playback.

Contributing source (CSRC): A source of a stream of RTP packets that has contributed to the combined stream produced by an RTP mixer. The mixer inserts a list of the SSRC identifiers of the sources that contributed to the generation of a particular packet into the RTP header of that packet.

Mixer: An intermediate system that receives RTP packets from one or more sources, possibly changes the data format, combines the packets

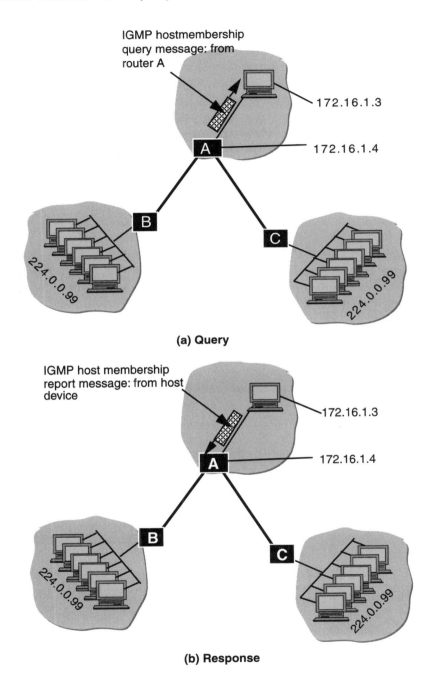

IGMP hostmembership
query message: from
router A

172.16.1.3

A

172.16.1.4

B

224.0.0.99

C

224.0.0.99

(a) Query

IGMP host membership
report message: from host
device

172.16.1.3

A

172.16.1.4

B

224.0.0.99

C

224.0.0.99

(b) Response

Figure A–5 IGMP host membership query and response

in some manner, and them forwards a new RTP packet. Since the timing among multiple input sources may not be synchronized, the mixer will make timing adjustments among the streams and generate its own timing for the combined stream. All data packets originating from a mixer will be identified as having the mixer as their synchronization source.

Translator: An intermediate system that forwards RTP packets with their synchronization source identifier intact. Examples of translators include devices that convert encoding without mixing, replicators from multicast to unicast, and application-level filters in firewalls.

Monitor: An application that receives RTCP packets sent by participants in an RTP session and estimates the current quality of service for distribution monitoring and fault diagnosis.

The next two figures show two major features of RTP in how it supports diverse traffic from senders to receivers. In Figure A–6, the RTP system is acting as a translator. The RTP translator translates (encodes) from one payload syntax to a different syntax. This figure shows how the RTP translator operates. The user devices on the left side of the figure are set up to use a 512 kbit/s video stream for their video application. The user device on the right side of the figure uses a 384 kbit/s video stream. As another possibility, the transit network may not be able to support the 512 kbit/s rate. So, whether from the user station on the right or the network in the middle, the users cannot communicate with each other.

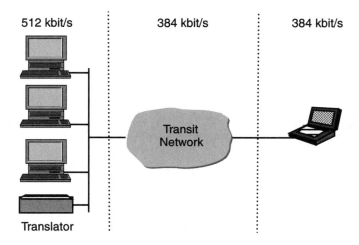

Figure A–6   Translator functions

The RTP translator allows these user stations to interact with each other. The job of the translator is to accept the traffic of the stations on the left side of the figure, translate (encode) that traffic into a format that is (a) in consonance with the bandwidth limitations of the transit network, and/or (b) in consonance with the bandwidth limitations of the user station on the right side of the figure. The user's RTP packet shows that the user is the synchronization service.

Figure A–7 shows an RTP server performing a mixer operation. Mixers combine multiple sources into one stream. Typically, mixers participate in audio operations and they do not decrease the quality of the signal to the recipients. They simply combine the signals into a consistent format. As I stated earlier, the RTP mixer operation is particularly suited to audio conferences. As a general rule, it does not work well with video conferencing because it is quite difficult to combine multiple video sources into one syntax.

RTP mixers do not translate each source payload into a different format. The original format is maintained, and the various source payloads are combined into one stream. The mixer is used for audio conferences, but not for video sessions, since mixing video streams is not yet a commercial reality. On the other hand, if the audio streams are uncomplicated pulse code modulation (PCM) traffic, it is possible to arithmetically sum the values of each source payload and combine them into a single stream.

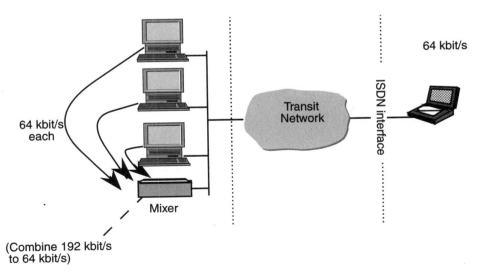

Figure A–7   Mixer functions

REAL TIME CONTROL PROTOCOL

The Real Time Control Protocol (RTCP) is responsible for the management of the real-time session between sending and receiving applications. The protocol is designed to allow senders to inform receivers about the RTP traffic that they should have received from the sender and it also allows the receiver of the traffic to generate reports back to the sender. This idea has been found to be quite useful in IP multicasting because it is used to troubleshoot faults in packet distribution.

Figure A–8 shows the relationships of the RTP and RTCP message flows. The RTP traffic flows from the sender to their receivers, and the RTCP message flows in both directions.

The sender and receiver reports can generate a considerable amount of bandwidth use and RTCP contains provisions to define the frequency with which theses reports can be sent. The concept is to keep the overall traffic flow for a session constant regardless of how many users are participating in the session. Since these reports are being multicast to all parties in the conference call, each application can keep track of the number of reports being disseminated and increase or decrease its reporting interval accordingly. In addition, RTCP provides procedures for

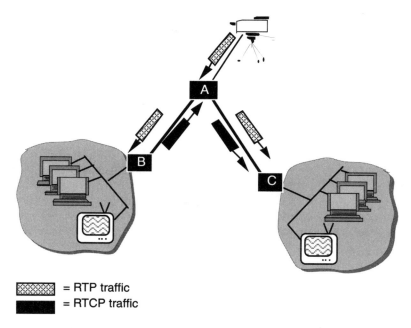

= RTP traffic
= RTCP traffic

Figure A–8   RTP and RTCP traffic flows

the calculations of the reporting intervals to vary between the users in a session in order to prevent a heavy peak load with each user sending a message at the same time.

Each source of the RTCP packet sends source descriptions which provide information about the nature of the application sending the traffic. Within these messages are contained source description items that define attributes such as email addresses, geographic locations, phone numbers, mailbox names, etc. Participants in a conference call (video or audio) may leave the conference at any time they choose by sending a log-off message which is known as a by. And then finally, RTCP messages can be coded specific to each application. RTCP really does not care about the contents of these messages, the RTCP operation conveys them transparently between applications.

THE RESOURCE RESERVATION PROTOCOL (RSVP)

We have learned that RTP and RTCP are companion protocols that allow applications to control real time, unicast, or multicast conferences for video or audio applications. We also learned that these protocols, while supporting unicast operations, also support multicasting. They allow systems to provide translation or mixing functions, converting different payload syntaxes and changing high-bit rate streams to low-bit rate streams, if necessary. They also provide extensive feedback between the users in an audio-video conference to ascertain the quality of the signals that are receiving and to inform each other about their ongoing activities.

The Resource Reservation Protocol (RSVP), as its name implies, defines a reservation procedure for real-time multimedia sessions. RSVP is unique from some other systems that have been implemented in other technologies such as ATM and Frame Relay and X.25 because it is the recipient of the traffic that places the reservation. In contrast, other technologies allow the sender of the traffic to establish the requirements. The rationale for this approach is that it is the recipient of the traffic that has the best knowledge of its capacity and limitations. For example, a video server may be sending traffic out to its recipients at a very high bit rate, perhaps 100 Mbit/s for high-quality video. However, the various recipients (clients) may vary in their ability to receive this high-quality transmission. Consequently, they may send their reservation resource request to the server defining different types of throughput requirements. As an example, a device attached to an ATM network running an OC-3 line card might be unable to support the full 100 Mbit/s bandwidth transmission. Conversely, a personal computer attached to an Ethernet may only be able to support 10 Mbit/s of bandwidth. Therefore, these two devices can send to the server the reservation request noting what their capacity is (their bandwidth availability).

The RSVP Flow

The RSVP uses the concept of a flow for its reserved traffic. Flows are somewhat similar to connection-oriented virtual circuits found in Frame Relay and ATM. They identify the traffic streams from the sending application to the receivers. This concept works well with IPv6 by using the IPv6 flow label field. It (in conjunction with the source address) will uniquely identify each flow. The idea of flow and flow label is to delineate between different kinds of traffic and to treat this traffic differently in the network depending on its timing and synchronization requirements. Indeed, the flow labels would most likely be used to place traffic in different queues at the intervening switches between the servers and the clients.

The Path Message

RSVP does not provide routing operations but utilizes IPv4 or IPv6 as the forwarding mechanism in the same fashion as the Internet Control Message Protocol (ICMP) and the Internet Group Message Protocol (IGMP). RSVP operates with unicast or multicast procedures and inter-

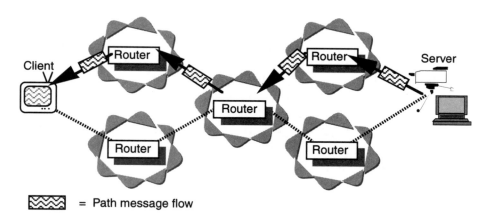

= Path message flow

Figure A–9   RSVP path messages

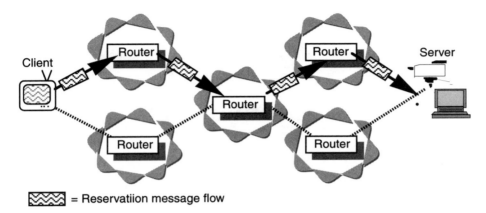

= Reservatiion message flow

Figure A–10   RSVP reservation messages

works with current and planned multicast protocols. Like IP, it relies on routing tables to determine routes for its messages. It utilizes IGMP to first join a multicast group and then executes procedures to reserve resources for the multicast group. RSVP requires the receivers of the traffic to request QOS for the flow. The receiver host application must determine the QOS profile that is then passed to RSVP. As shown in Figure A–9, after the analysis of the request, RSVP is used to send request messages to all the nodes that participate in the data flow. As this figure shows, the path message is used by a server (the flow sender) to set up a path for the session.

Reservation Messages

Figure A–10 shows that the reservation messages are sent by the receivers of the flow, and they allow sender and intermediate machines (such as routers) to learn the receivers requirements.

SUMMARY

IP multicasting is a common internet operation, and has been used for several years. RTP, RTCP, and RSVP are "companion" protocols, although they need not be used together. RSVP reserves bandwidth for the session. RTP transports the session traffic, and RTCP provides feedback about the connection's quality.

Abbreviations

AAL   ATM Adaptation Layer
ABR   available bit rate
ACR   allowed cell rate
AF   assured forwarding
ASIC   application specific integrated circuits
ATM   Asynchronous Transfer Mode
BA   Behavior Aggregate classifier
Bc   committed burst rate
BCN   backward congestion notification
B-CPE   broadband customer premises equipment
Be   excess burst rate
BECN   backward explicit congestion notification
B-ISDN   broadband ISDN
BRI   basic rate interface
BT   burst tolerance
C/R   command/response bit
CAC   connection admission control
CBR   constant bit rate
CCR   current cell rate

CDV   cell delay variation
CE   congestion encountered
CEI   connection endpoint identifier
CH   cell header
CI   congestion indication
CID   Channel ID
CIR   committed information rate
CLP   cell loss priority
CN   congestion notification
COPS   Common Open Policy Service
CP-AAL5   common part ATM adaptation layer type 5
CPCS SDU   common part convergence sublayer service data unit
CPCS-UU   common part convergence user to user
CPI   common part ID
CRC   cyclic redundancy check
CSRC   contributing source
CSU   channel service unit
CU   currently unused
DCE   destination packet network node

DE   discard eligibility
DES D   destination end station D
DES   destination end system
DesRP   destination Reference Point
DiffServ   Differentiated Services
DIR   direction
DLCI   data link connection identifier
DS   DiffServ
DSU   data service units
EA   address extension
ECN   explicit congestion notification
EETD   end-to-end transit delay
EF   expedited forwarding
EFCI   explicit forward congestion indication
EqiRP   Egress Queue Input Reference Point
EqoRP   Egress Queue Output Reference Point
ER   explicit rate
ERR   round robin algorithm
EXP/LU   experimental or local use
FCN   forward congestion notification
FCS   frame check sequence
FDM   frequency-division multiplexing
FDMA   frequncy-division multiple access
FEC   forward error correction
FEC   Functional Equivalence Class
FECN   forward explicit congestion notification
FR-SSCS   frame relay service specific convergence sublayer
FSDU   fram relay service data units
GFI   general format identifier
GCRA   generic cell rate algorithm
GS   guaranteed service
HDLC   high level data link control
HDTV   high-definition television
HEC   Header error control
I   increment
ICI   inter-exchange carrier interface

ICMP   Internet Control Message Protocol
ICR   initial cell rate
IETF   Internet Engineering Task Force
IGMP   Internet Group Message Protocol
IngRP   Ingress Reference Point
INH   internal network header
INSI   intra-network switching interface
IntServ   integrated services
IP   Internet Protocol
ISO   International Standards Organization
ISP   Internet Service Provider
ISSI   inter-switching system interface
IT   information type
IWF   interworking function
IXC   interchange carrier
L   limit
LAN   Local Area Network
LAPB   Link Access Procedure, Balanced
LAPD   link access procedure for the D channel
LCFN   logical channel group number
LCN   logical channel number
LCT   last conformance time
LDAP   Lightweight Directory Access Protocol
LDP   Label Distribution Protocol
LEC   Local Exchange Carrier
LGCN   logical channel group number
LI   length field
LI   length indicator
LLC   logical link control
LP   loss priority
LSAP   link service access point
LSI   large scale integration
LSP   label switch path
LSR   label switching router
MAC   media access channel

MBS   maximum burst size
MCR   minimum cell rate
MF   multifield classifier
MID   message ID
MPLS   Multiprotocol Label Switching
MPOA   multiprotocol over ATM
MSR   minimum cell rate
NA   not applicable
NE   network elements
NHRP   next hop resolution protocol
NI   no increase
NLPID   network level protocol ID
NLPIS   network level protocol ID
NNI   network to network interface
NSAP   network service access point
OSF   offset field
OSI   Open Systems Interconnection
OUI   organization unique ID
P   parity
Pad   align to a 2-octet boundary
PAD   Padding bytes
PBH   per hop behavior
PCM   pulse code modulation
PCR   peak cell rate
PDU   protocol data unit
PDV   packet delay variation
PH   packet header
PID   Protocol ID
PPP   Point-to-Point Protocol
PT   processing time
PTI   payload type identifier
PTT   Postal, Telephone, and Telegraph Ministry
PVC   permanent virtual circuit
QLR RR   queue length-weighted round robin algorithm
QOS   Quality of Service
RD   receive delay
RDF   rate decrease factor
REJ   reject
RIF   rate increase factor
RLWE   receive lower window edge
RM   resource management

RNR   receive not ready
RPC   Remote Procedure Call
RR   receive ready
RSVP   Resource Reservation Protocol
RTCP   Real Time Control Protocol
RTP   Real Time Protocol
RTT   round trip time
RUWE   receive upper window edge
Rx   receive
S   start field
SAP   service access point
SAR PDU   segmentation and reassembly protocol data unit
SAR   segmentation and reassembly
SCR   sustainable cell rate
SD   send delay
SDLC   synchronous data link control
SES   source end station
SES A   source end station A
SLA   Service level agreement
SMDS   Switched Multi-Megabit Data Service
SN   Sequence Number
SNAP   subnetwork access protocol
SNI   subscriber network interface
SNMP   Simple Network Management Protocol
SNP   sequence number protection
SR   service representation
SrcRP   Source Reference Point
SSRC   synchronization source
STDM   statistical time-division multiplexing
SVC   switched virtual circuit
SW   switching
Ta(k)   time arrival of a cell
TAT   theoretical arrival time
TB   token bucket
TCA   Traffic Conditioning Agreement
TCB   traffic conditioning block
TCP   Transmission Control Protocol
TCS   traffic conditioning specification
TDM   time-division multiplexing
TFTP   Trivial File Transfer Protocol

TLWE   transmit lower window edge
TOS   type of service
TpRP   Traffic Policing Reference Point
TSR   tag switching router
TSI   time slot interchange
TTL   time-to-live
TUWE   transmit upper window edge
Tx   transmit
UBR   unspecified bit rate
UDP   User Datagram Protocol
UI   Unnumbered information
ULP   upper layer protocol
UNI   User-To-Network
UPC   usage parmeter control

UUI   User-to-user indication
VBR   Variable Bit Rate
VBR-nrt   variable bit rate nonreal time
VBR-rt   variable bit rate real time
VC   virtual circuit
VCC   virtual channel connections
VCI   virtual channel identifier
VoATM   voice over ATM
VoFR   voice over Frame Relay
VP   virtual path
VPI   virtual path identifier
WAN   Wide Area Network
X   value of leaky bucket counter
X'   auxiliary variable

Index

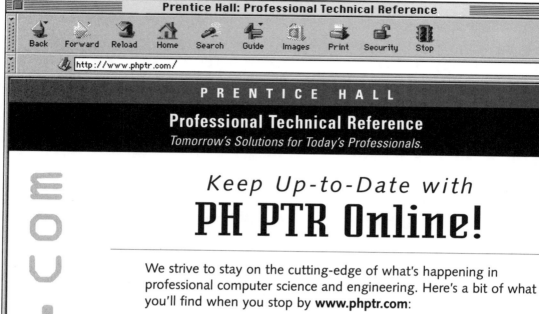